PRINCETON SERIES ON THE MIDDLE EAST

Bernard Lewis and András Hámori, Editors

THE AFRICAN DIASPORA IN THE MEDITERRANEAN LANDS OF ISLAM

The African Diaspora in the Mediterranean Lands of Islam

John Hunwick and Eve Trout Powell

Markus Wiener Publishers
Princeton

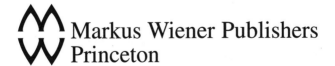

For information write to: Markus Wiener Publishers
231 Nassau Street, Princeton, NJ 08542

Hunwick, John O.
The African diaspora in the Mediterranean lands of Islam/
by John Hunwick and Eve Trout Powell.
(Princeton Series on the Middle East)
Includes bibliographical references.
ISBN 1-55876-274-4 (hc: alk. paper)
ISBN 1-55876-275-2 (pb: alk. paper)
1. Slavery and Islam—Mediterranean Region.
2. Slavery—Mediterranean Region—History.
3. Slavery—Religious aspects—Islam. 4. African diaspora.
5. Mediterranean Region—Race relations.
I. Powell, Eve Troutt. II. Title
HT1317.H86 2001
306.3'62'0917671—dc21
2001057466

Markus Wiener Publishers books are printed in the United States of America on acid-free paper, and meet the guidelines for permanence and durability of the committee on production guidelines for book longevity of the council on library resources.

◆ Contents ◆

◆ Illustrations ◆

◆ Preface ◆

The initial impulse to write this book came from Bernard Lewis, who was kind enough to send me a collection of source materials he had assembled, and encouraged me to put together a reader on Africans in slavery in the Muslim world. I then worked at broadening the documentary base over several years until in 1992 I had sufficient material to use as the basis of an undergraduate course at Northwestern University. Bernard Lewis was also kind enough to put me in touch with publisher Markus Wiener, who decided that a publishable book could be made out of such material. Finally, I had the good fortune to become acquainted with Eve Troutt Powell of the University of Georgia, and impressed by both her knowledge of the subject and her critical sensitivity, I quickly invited her to collaborate with me in the project, with the result that is now before readers.

It is my hope that this volume will serve to introduce the topic to a wider audience of persons who study and teach aspects of the enslavement and global diaspora of Africans, as well as students of Islamic history, so that the broader question of slavery in Muslim societies may be more actively addressed. The volume contains a series of original texts, some from Islamic writers, and some from non-Muslim external sources. Although some contextualization is given, our hope is that the texts will stimulate critical discussion, and hence we have not undertaken any critical evaluation of the texts. We hope the book may be used as a teaching instrument, and foster in-depth discussions of the validity and significance of these original sources. It is left to the reader to draw conclusions, and to raise issues of the nature of slavery in the Islamic world, and compare it with the practice of slavery involving Africans elsewhere in the world.

Innumerable friends and colleagues have unwittingly contributed to this volume as they listened to, and critiqued, presentations of some of the material. My daughter Yvette was good enough to read through many of the translations and let me know when they did not read smoothly or sensibly. I also wish to thank my colleagues Nasreen Qadir and Muhammad Eissa for checking respectively some of my translations from French and Arabic.

As will be apparent to the reader, most of the accounts of slavery refer to the past three centuries, although there have been Africans in slavery in Muslim lands for more than a thousand years. There are two reasons for this: first, the material during this period is much richer, despite the fact that much of it reflects outsiders' impressions of the Muslim world, and such pieces should, of course, be read with much critical care and caution. Secondly, confining the view of slavery to the eighteenth to the twentieth centuries, gives the approach to slavery greater chronological coherence. This was the age of the most intense enslavement and transportation of Africans into the Islamic Mediterranean world—the geographical focus of the volume (including the Arabian penninsula)—the age of the Ottoman empire, the age of the abolition of slavery, and of European encroachment on the world of Islam. Nevertheless, some earlier texts are included if their views or concepts continued to have relevance to Muslims' thinking about slavery until the nineteenth century, such as the Qurʾān and Ḥadīth, and the *sharīʿa* texts. Echoes of medieval views of black Africans in some cases are also evident in writings as late as the nineteenth century

Note: All translations are by John Hunwick, unless otherwise stated. Punctuation, spelling, and paragraphing of sources in English are retained as in the original text.

J.O. Hunwick

◆ Introduction ◆

THE SAME BUT DIFFERENT: AFRICANS IN SLAVERY IN THE MEDITERRANEAN MUSLIM WORLD

by

John Hunwick

It is probably true to say that for every gallon of ink that has been spilt on the trans-Atlantic slave trade and its consequences, only one very small drop has been spilt on the study of the forced migration of black Africans into the Mediterranean world of Islam and the broader question of slavery within Muslim societies. In the preface to his book *Race and Slavery in the Middle East*, Bernard Lewis spoke of "the remarkable dearth of scholarly work on the subject," and he went on to say:

> The bibliography of studies on slavery in the Greek and Roman worlds, or in the Americas, runs to thousands of items. Even for medieval Western Europe, where slavery was of relatively minor importance, European scholars have produced a significant literature of research and exposition. For the central Islamic lands, despite the subject's importance in virtually every area and period, a list of serious scholarly monographs on slavery—in law, in doctrine, or in practice—could be printed on a single page. The documentation for a study on Islamic slavery is almost endless; its exploration has barely begun.[1]

There are many reasons for this. In the first place, until quite recently Arab scholars were reluctant to probe this aspect of their past. Politically, in terms of Arab relations with sub-Saharan Africa, the less said the better, and it was always more useful to depict the enslavement of black Africans as a uniquely European sin. Those who ventured into the subject were inclined to do so apologetically, emphasizing the "mildness" of slavery in the Muslim world. At a 1983 conference on "The Arabs and Africa" the Algerian scholar Abdel Kader Zabadia brought both approaches together in a single comment: "The issue of slavery should be addressed, and emphasis [placed] on the Arabs' humane and familial treatment of their slaves compared with other slave-owning people. The contrast, especially regarding transatlantic slavery is so striking, that it should be emphasised in this context."[2] His comment was made in the course of discussion of a paper by the Sudanese scholar Yusuf Fadl Hasan on "The historical roots of Afro-Arab relations." Professor Hasan had been bold enough to state: "Slavery is slavery and cannot be beautified by cosmetics. It left extreme bitterness in the central parts of the [African] continent against the Arab minority which lived on the coast. Because this issue disturbs Afro-Arab relations it should be studied courageously and objectively."[3]

These two remarks bring into sharp focus the problem that faces us in discussing slavery and the African diaspora in the context of Muslim societies. Yes: slavery is slavery and cannot be beautified by cosmetics. The forceful seizure of human beings and their total subjection to the will of other human beings, and the humiliation and degradation involved in this process, cannot be portrayed in positive terms. Yet the comparison (rather than "contrast") with other systems of slavery, and particularly slavery in the New World, is not only inevitable, but is essential for a global understanding of the African diaspora. The question of "the Arabs' humane and familial treatment of their slaves" is another matter—one which indeed challenges us to explore the social and economic realities of enslaved (and also freed) Africans in the greater Islamic world. We must be careful in our studies not to import assumptions based on other systems of slavery, whether transatlantic or otherwise, just as we must not be led astray by theories about the nature of Islamic societies. Instead, we must explore with great care the realities of different Muslim societies, taking account both of the commonalities among them which proceed from Islamic law and ethics, and of the differences born of underlying cultures—Arab, Berber, Turkish, Persian, etc.—as well as the differences born of economic and political conditions, and often of very local, and even individual, circumstances.

There are signs that this field of study is at last beginning to receive some of the attention it deserves in the Arab world, especially in North Africa, where historians have started to recognize the need to study slavery and the history of black communities in their midst as a significant element in the understanding of their national cultures and histories. In 1987 the Tunisian historian Abdel Jalil Temimi, in advocating such studies, remarked: "There are far too few studies dealing with the social position of the black minority in Tunisia and the roles allotted to them, to allow us to say that we have a *tradition* of writing in this field, since the history of African minorities in Arab countries has not been given attention, unlike the history of other minorities, Muslim, Christian and Jewish that have been the subject of colloquia, studies and conferences." More recently a Moroccan scholar Mohammed Ennaji published in French a book on "concubines, servants and soldiers" examining the social roles played by slaves in his country in the nineteenth century.[4] In July 2000 a conference was held in Morocco, organized by Mohammed Ennaji, on "Liberté, identité, intégration et servitude."

A second reason for the lack of studies on Africans in slavery in the Mediterranean Islamic world is the lack of a constituency within such societies that would press for an investigation of its past history and present condition. As a French observer of Algeria wrote in 1988: "No movement capable of giving structure to the black minority has ever arisen in contemporary North Africa. Under such circumstances its neglect and devaluation can only be perpetuated. The African-ness of the Algerian, which is attested by history, is something he is largely unconscious of; thus there can be no question of his admitting to it. He will only take an interest in it when the black world becomes essential for him. Then Algeria will belong not only geographically or even politically to Africa, but also culturally."[5]

This raises the interesting question as to why there is a lack of "black consciousness" in Algeria, and indeed, more widely in the Mediterranean lands of Islam. On the one hand this could mean that former slaves have become so successfully integrated into these Arabo-Berber Muslim societies that they have no cultural need to explore their remote past or to question their present social status, and in one sense this may be true. There is reluctance to acknowledge a past in slavery, not only for reasons of personal pride, but because in the Muslim world a past in slavery indubitably points to a past in "unbelief" (*kufr*), i.e. at one's ancestors having been at some earlier stage "pagans," which is a particularly heavy burden to bear. Being part of the community of Islam is an important—even *the* most important—platform of identity.

On the other hand, the lack of what may be called a "black voice" in the Mediterranean lands may also be due to the relatively small number of clearly identifiable descendants of slaves and to their depressed social status and lack of education. The only scholarly monograph specifically dealing with a black community in North Africa concerns an isolated agricultural community in southern Tunisia, which has the telling title "Societies to be remembered. Societies to be forgotten."[6] In general the greatest concentrations of black North Africans tend to be in interior towns and oases, not in the great cities and centers of political and economic life. This kind of answer of course immediately raises a host of questions, to many of which we do not yet have even the beginnings of answers. How many slaves crossed the Sahara into North Africa? How many, in particular, were brought across in the 19th century? What percentage of these were women who became concubines and whose offspring were thus free and "Arab" or "Arabo-Berber"? What were the mortality rates for black slaves compared with free Arabo-Berber populations? What kinds of occupations did slaves undertake and what skills may they have acquired that prepared them for economic viability as free persons? What role did Islamic law play in ensuring that freedom meant social equality? What role may racism have played in denying them such equality? Future research, it is to be hoped, will address such questions.

Finally, one reason for the comparative lack of study of the question of Africans in slavery in Muslim societies has been the lack of interest in the matter in the American and European academy. The principal reason for this seems to be that such studies invite the researcher to cross the established boundaries between African Studies and Middle Eastern Studies. The compartmentalization of Africa into zones that are treated as "Middle East" and "Africa" is a legacy of Orientalism and colonialism. North Africa, including Egypt, is usually seen as forming part of the Middle East, though Middle East experts are not generally keen to venture farther west than the confines of Egypt. Northwestern Africa—the Maghreb—is generally regarded as peripheral to Middle Eastern studies and extraneous to African studies. Even the Sahara has been generally viewed as something of a no-go area (especially among anglophone scholars), while the Sudan and Mauritania (which are impossible to label as either "sub-Saharan" or "Middle Eastern") remain in limbo. Northwestern Africa (from Morocco to Libya), despite the area's close and enduring relationship with West Africa, has been excluded from the concerns of most Africanists. Although both the *Cambridge History of Africa* and the Unesco *General History of Africa* made valiant attempts to integrate the whole of northern Africa into continental history, the most recent major encyclopedia of Africa, for example (that edited by John Middleton), is pointedly an *Encyclopedia of Africa South of the Sahara*.[7] The old construction of the African continent remains in place, and it is a bold graduate student who would attempt to deconstruct it by working on the history of black Africans in the Maghreb, not least because s/he may have a hard time finding an interested (not to say knowledgeable) supervisor, but also because s/he may have an even harder time finding a job.

I would argue, on the other hand, that the study of black Africans in the Islamic Mediterranean world (including the northern Ottoman shores of that sea and embracing the Arabian penninsula and both sides of the Gulf) both in slavery and in post-slavery constitutes a field that rightly belongs to *both* the relevant area studies—

African studies and Middle Eastern/Islamic studies—and deserves to be embraced by scholars of both areas. Even more importantly it belongs to the fields of global history, comparative slavery, and African diaspora studies, and in this capacity it is a topic that ought to attract the attention of an even broader range of scholars. Some leaders in the field of slavery studies have already implicitly acknowledged this, for instance David Brion Davis in his *Slavery and Human Progress*,[8] but the effect of such recognition is only just beginning to have an impact, and much more needs to be done to integrate slavery in Islamic society into studies of world slavery and the African diaspora. An encouraging initiative in this respect has been the recent move by Michael Gomez to create an Association for the Study of the World-Wide African Diaspora (ASWAD), aimed at stimulating interest in the question of Africans in slavery both in the Americas and in the Mediterranean and Asian worlds.

One of the factors that has held back many aspiring Africanist scholars from working in this field is their lack of the special knowledge of the culture of Islam and of the language skills necessary to pursue research; but let me assure them that their efforts to acquire such special cultural and linguistic skills would be amply rewarded in terms of the new research domains they would thereby open up.

Let me now return to the primary question behind this introduction: namely, how do we approach the question of slavery in Muslim societies, bearing in mind that in relation to slavery in other societies it is both "the same" yet "different" (or perhaps one should say "different but the same"). Let us start by looking at the history of the institution in the Islamic world and at Islamic theory about slavery. While we must not, of course, confuse theory with practice, we must acknowledge that as far as literate slave owners were concerned the theory of slavery, and also the literature dealing with racial images, must have played some role in their actual practice of the institution. Since slave owners were mainly if not entirely from the middle or upper classes economically, it is likely that a high percentage of slave owners were, in fact, literate and had imbibed, to a greater or lesser extent, Islamic attitudes towards slaves and slavery, and may also have been influenced in their attitudes towards issues of race by what Arab authors had written, as, of course, they were by attitudes to both issues in oral culture—an interesting area for contemporary inquiry.[9]

It may seem superfluous to say that Islam did not invent slavery, but it is useful to bear in mind that the practice of slavery was a fundamental social assumption of Arab society at the rise of Islam and of the various Mediterranean societies in which Islamic culture developed and assumed its overarching characteristics in the medieval period. Thus until attempts at abolition in the second half of the nineteenth century, largely under pressure from Europe, Muslim societies of the greater Mediterranean Basin considered slavery as part of the natural order of things—indeed part of the God-given order of things—and not as something to be interrogated or challenged. In pre-Islamic Arab society slaves had in the main been captives of war, and, under the Islamic dispensation, war was in theory only to be fought against non-Muslims—a *jihād*; hence captives to be enslaved would, by definition, be "unbelievers." This rapidly became an established rule of law: i.e. that it was legitimate to enslave only the unbelievers, and indeed it became common to justify enslavement of such persons as a punishment for their failure to accept the religion of Islam. This was not, in fact, the way in which slaves were generally acquired in practice, but on the basis of a "don't ask, don't tell" policy, slaves could be purchased from Muslims in the borderlands of Islam on the tacit assumption that they were originally captives taken in a *jihād*.

Slavery thus became, in effect, a religious issue, and was incorporated into the religious discourse of Islam. In so doing it also became a matter of law, since in Islam law (*sharīᶜa*) is an outgrowth of divine word and Prophetic practice. This had both its positive and its negative aspects. On the positive side, the law recognized the slave as something more than a mere chattel. Indeed, inasmuch as the law in many cases allotted to slaves only half the punishment of a free person and provided for only half the privileges (e.g. for a male to be married concurrently to a maximum of two women, rather than the four allowable to free males), it could be argued that a slave was granted partial humanity or was even half free. The law also provided for numerous avenues through which a slave could gain his/her freedom. On the negative side, since slavery was written into the *sharīᶜa*, it was considered a divinely sanctioned practice that mere human beings could not abrogate or interfere with. In fact, abolishing slavery effectively took away from the believers certain paths for redemption. Freeing a slave could constitute atonement for the commission of certain forbidden acts, and when manumission was carried out as an act of piety it was a path to Paradise.

From the historian's point of view, the fact that slavery was a significant issue in law is extremely useful. It means that issues of slavery, ownership and freedom became the subject of legal records — *qāḍī*'s court proceedings, inheritance documents, purchase and manumission documents, legal opinions (*fatwā*s), state registers (as in the case of the seventeenth century Moroccan slave army, the ᶜAbīd al-Bukhārī), of correspondence, and even of polemical tracts.[10] Such documents enable us not only to study the mechanics of slavery, but help us better to understand the underlying culture of slavery in the Muslim world. A document of manumission drawn up in Timbuktu in 1176/1762–3 provides a neat illustration of some of these issues:

> *Jāmiᶜ son of Shaykh Marzūq who died and went to the mercy of his Lord acknowledged and testified before me [prior to his death] that he had freed his old slave woman called Fama Surku for the sake of God, and desiring reward from God in the abode of the Hereafter for [freeing] her—may God accept her [freedom] on his behalf in goodly fashion and make her a proxy for him, [thereby freeing him] limb for limb from the fire of Hell. She becomes one of the free Muslims, men and women. [Shaykh Marzūq's] children have no access to her except through clientship pursuant to manumission.*[11]

We would draw attention here to the theology of the document. It is clearly implied by the wording that the man freeing the slave did so when he was close to death, hoping, as the document says, that this "pious act" would spare him from the torments of Hell, each limb of the freed woman corresponding to a limb of his to be saved from the fire. Thus the woman by being redeemed from slavery unwittingly became a redeemer of her master. How powerful was this redemptive factor in freeing slaves, one may ask? The document also indicates that the person freed was an old woman, leading us perhaps to assume that her days of usefulness as a slave were already over, so perhaps her manumission was no great sacrifice. Is there a moral-legal literature on this, as there is, for example, on sacrificial animals which must be sacrificed in their prime without blemish in order to qualify for divine reward?

This is not an isolated document; hundreds more such documents exist in Timbuktu alone. We need to be able to examine hundreds, or perhaps thousands, of such documents to see how common it was to free slaves for "pious" purposes; what the ratio of men to women freed was; how many were released in their prime as opposed to old age; or how many years men or women served in slavery (some sources hint that slaves would be freed after seven years, by which time their labor had repaid their purchase price; others would argue that the economic benefit of slavery only begins at such a point, and that purchasing a slave represents a long-term investment in labor).

If manumission was a tacit assumption of Islamic slavery, it was (whether for pietistic or other reasons) a two-edged sword. Since there were—with rare exceptions—no consciously self-reproducing slave communities in the Mediterranean world, the removal of persons from the existing pool of slaves meant others had to be brought in to take their place. Thus the demand for an ongoing process of slave capture at source in sub-Saharan Africa was increased. Of course there were other factors playing into this vicious circle of slave replacement, including, in particular, death from unfamiliar diseases, and the absorption of women slaves into the dominant community through concubinage, with resulting freedom for their offspring. But the whole question of supply and demand needs to be addressed carefully, especially since, unlike the New World, there were no huge new demands for slave labor (much of such labor being broadly domestic) that might necessitate a continuing trade. This in turn raises the question of why there was a trade in the first place.

Whatever the answers to this question might be, we know that the Mediterranean Muslim world over time drew its supply of slaves from many sources. "Unbelievers," and hence slaves, could, of course, be of any color or ethnicity. The law was color-blind. Thus, not only were Africans taken into slavery, but Europeans—"Slavs" in the early period, and Europeans at large in the age of corsairs—Turkic peoples from Central Asia, Indians, Georgians and Armenians from Caucasia, Greeks, etc.

In the early literature there is a certain stereotyping of slaves from different origins. Central Asian Turkic peoples were considered very amenable to military duties; males from the Indian subcontinent were thought trustworthy and good with money, though their women were said to pine away in captivity; women of the Caucasus were highly prized as concubines and often eventually wives; Ethiopian women were likewise prized, especially in Arabia, and Nubian women in Egypt; East African men (Zanj) were considered good laborers and their womenfolk good for menial household tasks or as wet-nurses. Black Africa, however, was the earliest source for slaves and the last great reservoir to dry up; already in the 640s slaves were part of the "non-aggression pact" between the Arab conquerors of Egypt and Nubian rulers to their south, while as late as 1910 slaves were still being shipped out of Benghazi,[12] supplied, it would seem, via an eastern Saharan route from Wadai (in Chad).[13] Although the Ottoman Empire remained a source of demand for slaves of Caucasian or south-east European origin into the nineteenth century, these were mainly men destined for military service and often high rank, and women destined for the harems of beys and pashas (as either concubines or wives), and hence slavery was a nominal condition; they were termed *mamlūk* (possessed one). Not so for slaves of African origin. By the seventeenth century blackness of skin/African origin was virtually synonymous in the Arab world with both the notion and the word "slave"; they were *ᶜabīd*. Even to this day the word for Africans in many dialects of Arabic remains just that—*ᶜabīd* —"slaves."[14]

While we may not be able to identify any ideology of racism or any institutionalization of discrimination against black Africans, can we say that Muslim Mediterranean society was devoid of racism? The question is a complex one. Certainly we can find within Arabic scholarly and creative literature passages that we would now define as being racist in sentiment, though it must be said that some of the stereotypes of blacks in the geographical/ethnographic literature merely echo material that originated in ancient Greek writing.[15] The geographical construction of the world that the Arabs inherited from the Greeks saw the middle region of the world, embracing the lands of the Mediterranean, as being the most "moderate" in all respects. The farther away one lived from this region the more savage was the lifestyle. Extreme cold in the north and extreme heat in the south produced individuals who were distorted mentally and physically. (Nigerians and Norwegians would have been thought of as equally savage!) But it was only with those human beings from the south—from black Africa—that the inhabitants of the Mediterranean had much contact, and most of that was with enslaved Africans, predisposing them to look at such persons as inferior and less civilized than themselves. Why otherwise would they be slaves? The circular argument holds: the enslaved person is an inferior person; if people are inferior, they are ripe for enslavement.

On the other hand, there is another literature that speaks of the virtues of black Africans: books with titles like "The Boast of the Blacks over the Whites" [*Fakhr al-Sūdān ᶜalā 'l-bīḍān* of al-Jāḥiẓ], or "Lightening the Darkness, concerning the virtue of the Blacks and Ethiopians" [*Tanwīr al-ghabash fī faḍl al-sūdān wa'l-ḥabash* of Ibn al-Jawzī] or "Blacks and their superiority over Whites" [*Kitāb al-sudān wa-faḍluhum ᶜalā 'l-bīḍān* of Ibn al-Marzubān],[16] as well as a separate literature on the virtues of Ethiopians—a people who were considerd to have some superiority by virtue of their having sheltered early migrant Muslims in the Prophet's day, and whose ruler at the time was believed to have embraced Islam. One can, of course, argue that the very existence of books in defense of blacks is a reflection of prejudice against them. True enough, but on the other hand there is lack of a consistent literature that theorizes the inferiority of black people. Islam did not have its Gobineau. The so-called "Hamitic myth," in which Ham is cursed by his father Noah and hence his descendants are made black and destined to be slaves of Ḥam's lighter-skinned brothers, does appear in a number of early Arabic writings, but by the fourteenth century it was firmly refuted by Ibn Khaldūn, in favor of a theory of the effect of climate on skin color.[17] It is also noteworthy that even if on one level black Africans were considered inferior human beings, black African women were often thought fit to be concubines (and sometimes wives), and to be the mothers of "Arab" children, even of Arab rulers.

Nevertheless the question of whether black Africans were (and deserved to be) "natural slaves" was an ongoing matter of debate in northwestern Africa. At the end of the 19th century a Moroccan scholar [al-Nāṣirī] could still rail against "the indiscriminate enslavement of the people of the Sūdān,[18] and the importation of droves of them every year to be sold in the market places in town and country where men trade in them as one would trade in beasts —nay worse than that. [And comment that] People have become so inured to that, generation after generation, that many common folk believe that the reason for being enslaved according to the Holy Law is merely that a man should be black in color and come from those regions."[19]

That view may well have been more widespread. In about 1906 Hanns Vischer chatted with a Libyan shaykh who protested against attempts to stop the slave trade, saying: "You stop slave traffic and treat the negroes like free men. Allah has created them slaves, as He has made their skins black, and you can change the one as little as you can change the other."[20]

Of course, in the end (during the French protectorate in Morocco, and the Italian occupation of Libya) all such persons eventually became free, but one must ask to what extent the association of blackness with slavery died out with emancipation. It is worth recalling that in the western Sahara and along the Saharan borders of North Africa there is a continuing issue of the inferior status of *ḥarāṭīn*, dark-skinned persons—probably "aboriginal" populations joined by ex-slaves—who live in a state of clientship with members of the dominant "white" (*biḍān*) population.

Perhaps one of the most notable distinguishing features of slavery in the Mediterranean Muslim world was that slaves were rarely used as a means of production, in sharp contrast to the New World. While slaves were used to cultivate oasis gardens, dig wells, tend date palms, mine salt, and dive for pearls, there were no large tracts of uncultivated land awaiting the hand of a large labor force. There were no fertile frontiers to be opened up; the division and ownership of land in the southern Mediterranean, the Levant and the Arabian penninsula had been established in antiquity, and the pattern of land use was one of agricultural smallholding, nomadism or semi-nomadism. Slaves were therefore required mainly as domestic servants—pre-modern "labor-saving devices," child-minders, and gentlemen's gentlemen; females as concubines, and castrated males as keepers of the harems of the rich. They were also valued as manifestations of social status in societies where high status was deemed to find its reflection in large numbers of dependents. Wealth in people was often deemed more important than wealth in property.

Another distinguishing feature of slavery in the Mediterranean Muslim world was the use of slaves as soldiers, initially as bodyguards whose loyalty was guaranteed by their lack of local kinship ties, but also in some cases as internal security forces who could be trusted to put down rebellions for similar reasons, and who may even have felt good about being able to take their revenge on a segment of the society that had held them as slaves. Such soldiers acquired their own sense of communal solidarity and pride and to a large extent thereby escaped the stigma of slavery—the case of the Sudanese slave soldiers who fought on behalf of the French in Mexico in the 1860s being a particularly clear one.[21] While slaves fighting for their masters is not unique to the Muslim world, the scale and persistence of the custom does single it out. One has to ask why, apparently, these armed slaves seem never to have taken advantage of their privilege to turn against their masters and fight for their freedom. Indeed, the theme of slave revolts, runaways and maroon communities is not a significant one in the history of Islamic slavery (give or take the famous "Zanj revolt" of ninth century Iraq, which is a much more complex issue). Or is it that the state of our research is such that we have not yet researched this issue, or perhaps even posed the question?

This leads to a further and final issue: the qualitative nature of the African slave experience in the lands of Islam. To what extent were slaves in North Africa and the Middle East allowed to "settle down," to form communities, to enjoy at least some of the benefits of citizenship? To what extent did the general ethic of Islam and the incorporation of slaves within the community of Islam facilitate such settlement and discourage revolt? Is such a suggestion merely a refurbishing of the patriarchal "happy slave" myth we are familiar with from transatlantic pro-slavery discourse? The evidence so far marshalled is, not surprisingly, contradictory. But let us at least look at the role which religion may have played in the process. Earlier I mentioned that the theoretical cause for enslavement was being an "unbeliever." The good slave owner, however, was expected to indoctrinate his slaves in the beliefs and practices of Islam. In fact, by the time black African slaves came on the market in North Africa, Egypt or the Arabian penninsula, they had usually been "seasoned," a process which included a technical conversion to Islam (sealed for men by circumcision) and learning of the rudiments of Arabic. A "pagan," speaking no Arabic, would be unsaleable.

In North Africa, and apparently also in Turkey, however, slaves, at least in the first generation, retained many of their ancestral beliefs and were able to perform religious practices associated with them. As in Brazil, Cuba, Haiti, and elsewhere in the western hemisphere, so in the Mediterranean diaspora, African religious practices provided mechanisms through which enslaved Africans could cope with the psychological crisis brought about by enslavement, transportation, and transplantation into an alien cultural environment. These practices brought from the homelands were transformed in many ways as slaves accommodated themselves to their new cultural milieu, displaying differing degrees of islamization and naturalization.

The most widespread religious practice among African slaves (and freed persons) in the Mediterranean was the spirit possession and healing cult generally known by the Hausa term *bori*. Similar cults exist in other Sahelian cultures, including *zār* and *ṭumbura* in the Nile valley, *holey* among the Songhay, and similar cults among the Fulbe and Bambara. In these cults a wide (and changing) pantheon of spirits is invoked through the performance of differing melodies and rhythms and the burning of incense; chickens, sheep or goats are sacrificed so that the spirit may drink the blood. The spirits both cause illness and cure it. If a person is diagnosed as having a disease caused by one of the spirits, s/he is initiated into the *bori* cult, and the spirit is summoned to "mount" the sick person. Sacrifices are then performed to satisfy the spirit, and henceforth the newly initiated person should make at least annual sacrifices for that spirit. Under the influence of Islam these spirits were often identified with the benevolent/malevolent class of spirits known as *jinn*. In North Africa and the Sudan a further Islamic refinement of the process might involve invoking the Prophet or the great saint ᶜAbd al-Qādir al-Jilani, as in the Stambali cult of Tunis, or the *tumbura* cult of the Sudan.[22] In North Africa these spirit cults were sometimes fused with ancient Berber spirit cults to produce new syntheses, such as the "Seven Springs" cult in Algiers.

Such possession cults not only provided slaves and their descendants with avenues for expressing themselves religiously, but also constituted the building blocks of social organization, and their very existence indicates that slaves were able in certain times and places to enjoy a measure of autonomy both as individuals and as communities. In Algeria at the beginning of this century communities of former slaves still organized themselves around religious cult houses that were based on areas of origin: Bornu, Katsina,

Zazzau, Bambara, Songhai and Tombo (Dogon).[23] Elements of many of these cults have continued to survive among descendants of slaves who tend to be endogamous and lead communal lives isolated from the dominant communities.

To close let us return to the title of the essay: "the same but different." The implication is two-fold, and is designed to alert us to two possible pitfalls. The first implication is that although slavery is slavery and the Mediterranean diaspora has many parallels with the transatlantic diaspora, it also has many quite different features and is embedded in a wholly different cultural nexus. While we may benefit from the borrowing of methodologies and learn from the questions that have beeen asked, we must at the same time remain alert to the differences and avoid culturally loaded assumptions and facile comparisons. The second implication is that although slavery is slavery in the Islamic world and we should expect to find parallels between region and region, we should also be alert to very considerable differences in the culture of slavery and race consciousness within the different societies that have been permeated by Islamic culture and by slavery, both synchronically and diachronically. Although in the end we may indeed be able to talk of certain features of "Islamic" slavery (at least as regards the law), we may be sure that in-depth studies will provide us with a rich diversity of histories of slavery and experiences of freedom.

◆ Introduction ◆

THE SILENCE OF THE SLAVES

by

Eve M. Troutt Powell

As my colleague John Hunwick has pointed out, the silence surrounding the experience and history of African slaves in the Islamic Mediterranean has been enforced by many factors: the politics of modern relationships between North and sub-Saharan Africa; the lack of a constituency who feel it helpful to press for investigations into the lives of their slave ancestors and the lack of concern within either the American or European academy. As he notes in his introduction to this volume, the unwillingness of specialists in either Middle Eastern or African Studies to cross the boundaries of area studies and investigate the connections between these geographical regions has also helped to weave the net of invisibility around those taken as slaves from Africa to work in the households or armies of the Islamic Mediterranean.

To this important list I would add two other reasons as well, motives with which, as a specialist in Middle Eastern Studies, I am more familiar. As documents in this anthology show, there were certainly constructions of racial differentiation in the Arab world that trace back to the early medieval period, which imbued black Africans with certain unalterable characteristics that rendered them "suitable" to enslavement. But there were also white slaves, from as far back as the early medieval period as well, who performed different duties and were valued for different reasons. By the time that the trade in African slaves and abolition had become an international issue of human rights, in the Ottoman Empire of the late nineteenth century for example, many slave owners of the upper classes were themselves directly descended from, or married to, slaves from the Caucasus mountains or the Balkans. Questions raised by European abolitionists about the nature of slavery in Islam often affected their listeners in Ottoman society as unwelcome intrusions into the intimate realm of marriage and the family itself (and their families in particular) and many reacted to these seeming investigations as such. As Ehud Toledano has also pointed out, many Ottoman statesmen could not or would not acknowledge a difference between African and Circassian slavery and instead "gentrified" the domestic work of African slaves whose positions did not offer the same opportunities for honor and status.[1]

Toledano also mentions a tendency among European abolitionists in the nineteenth century to "lump" all kinds of slavery together—plantation slavery as known in the West Indies and the southern United States with the domestic or military slavery of the Islamic Ottoman Empire.[2] Many who shared this tendency to dismiss the nuances of slavery also dismissed, or disparaged, Islam in general, which made their attacks on slavery sound like diatribes against the Islamic religion on the whole. This was certainly how Aḥmad Shafīq Pasha heard Cardinal Lavigerie's sermon in Paris in 1890; after all, Lavigerie was the famous founder of the White Fathers religious order and a firm believer in the colonization of Algeria as a means of stamping out Islamic practices.[3]

The sensitivity displayed by so many in the Ottoman Empire in the late nineteenth century to foreigners' critiques and investigations did not disappear with the Empire after World War I, but only changed in form, particularly as the Arab-Israeli conflict became a more volatile issue. It has been difficult for many scholars in the Arab world to address these issues of slavery when so many see the questioners coming from the United States or Israel, where the image of the Arab Muslim as a bloodthirsty, fanatical zealot does nothing to deepen awareness of the plight of the Palestinians under Israeli occupation. In such cases, the scholar's investigation also appears as a means of distorting the image of the Arab in particular, and Muslims in general, adding to stereotypes of Arabs that many (myself included) feel continue to be promulgated in the press, popular literature, and films, year after year. These caricatures of Arabs and Arab culture have picked up where the older stereotypes of Orientalism left off, and in such an environment, the airing of the issue of slavery seems to bare too much before so hostile an audience.

With these critical issues in mind, it still remains important that the slaves themselves be both seen and heard and not relegated to the background of political and cultural affairs. Why? Because the history and the experience of African slaves also continues to bear weight on twenty-first century political and cultural affairs, and should not be considered secondary to the plights of others in the Middle East or Africa. From Mauritania to the Sudan to the Gulf states, the legacy of slavery still lives; in fact, many cases of slavery continue to be documented in these areas to this day.[4] For example, civil war in the Sudan has reportedly brought a return of slave raids, again from the North to the South, reintroducing a long and sad part of Nile Valley history to its residents. Clearly, neglecting the issue of African slavery in Islamic countries has done nothing to help prevent the return of such conditions, nor has it stamped out the stigma of a heritage of slavery on the descendants of slaves (or slave masters).

The Meanings of Slaves and Slavery

> Slavery, in fact, had many faces; its diversity constantly surprises us.[5]

So, as historians hoping to "hear" and "see" into the lives of African slaves within the Mediterranean diaspora, we turn to records and documents of the eighteenth and nineteenth centuries. The overwhelming majority of these were written by foreign observers: European merchants, adventurers, explorers, advisors to local rulers. By the middle of the nineteenth century, a lot of accounts of the slave trade in the Islamic Mediterranean were also written by emissaries from the Anti-Slavery Society in London, or missionaries of the White Fathers order. These messengers portrayed themselves as deeply sympathetic to the plight of the enslaved African.

But as well-meaning as they may have seemed, it is also important to examine the motives and perspectives of those observers, foreign to the Islamic Mediterranean, who were often as hostile to Muslims and Arabs as they were pitying of the African slaves, and who successfully turned the issue of the African slave trade into an international controversy in the mid- to late nineteenth century. What traditions came to their minds when observing Muslims? How did they see Africans, either before or after slavery had been abolished in their own countries? How did they define slavery in Europe?

It is also important to ask whom these authors envisioned as their audience. The literature of travel and adventure to exotic regions like Africa and the Middle East had become very popular by the early nineteenth century. Being a trustworthy eyewitness to events in places most European readers could only imagine, the narrator had to be able to translate his experiences into metaphors and comparisons that his readers would understand. Such first-hand accounts quickly became canons of information about the areas that each author had explored, and such canonization has endured until today. For instance, Gustav Nachtigal, a medical doctor, traveled to North Africa in 1862, and became deeply involved in political events of Tunis. His experience in things North African now established, he was asked by a representative of King William of Germany to take gifts to Shaykh ᶜUmar, the Sultan of Bornu, in 1868. Nachtigal was thrilled to be able to "see more of the mysterious continent to the north coast of which fate had led me, and which, though it had played such a prominent role in history and lies so near to Europe, has remained for us a sphinx-like riddle..."[6] His journeys were published in German upon his return to Europe in four volumes, between 1879 and 1889, and they remain critical sources to this day, as his translators insist, particularly his journey to Tibesti (now in central Chad): "No one had ever before entered that mysterious district and on his return given a full account of it; and no European was to enter it again for more than forty years after Nachtigal. Everything that he has to say, therefore, of the civilization and history of Tibesti is of special value."[7] In even more admiring terms, they go on to say that "his journey to Tibesti was one of the most courageous episodes in the exploration of Africa..."

I do not write this to disparage Nachtigal's fascinating account of his journeys, or to deny him the powerful curiosity that is attributed to him and other explorers, like Snouck Hurgronje, a Dutch student of Islam who traveled to Mecca between 1884 and 1885 and published his accounts in 1888–89. At the time of their travels, these men embarked on what seemed to be terribly dangerous expeditions. But it must be kept in mind that these men were men of a certain time, and that Africans and Arabs looked a certain way to each. Hurgronje particularly enjoyed recounting juicy tidbits about the Arabs he met, e.g.: "the very widely spread paederasty is a conspicuous result of that West Arabian Babel-culture which is so abhorred of the Central Arabians. One of the most famous Qur'an reciters in Mekka was so addicted to this vice that everyone was careful to keep his young sons far away from his house."[8] And Nachtigal confessed the challenge of representing on paper the Tubu people because "their physiognomy was quite different from the type which in a vague way one is accustomed to describe as Negro."[9]

Their constructions of race also affected their understanding of slavery. How did each look at European enslavement of Africans? Western examples of slavery were always embedded in Hurgronje's mind, and at times he berated his reader for the same preconceptions, as he did when describing certain methods of corporal punishment:

> Such scenes are not pleasant, and they are nor (*sic*) rare either in Jeddah or Mekka. Would the European then be right in taking his strengthened Uncle Tom impressions home with him as the truth about slavery? By no means: more experience would have shown him that the Arab punishes his own son just as severely if he has committed some fault. The traveller has witnessed no scene of slave life, but an example of the Arab "pedagogy," which is the same for slaves and offspring and is entirely out of agreement with modern ideas.[10]

It is fascinating that Hurgronje posits such a scene not as an example of "slave life," but as an illustration of Oriental despotism —this is the way of the Arabs. There is also a timelessness attributed to Mekka, a place where nothing modern is able to occur. But to me, the most visible person in the scene of punishment is not the slave, or the Arab master, but Hurgronje himself, without whose perceptions we, the reader, would learn nothing. This occurs again a page later, when he relates the "many stories which I have heard from African slaves (they are glad to speak to good friends about their past)"[11] that make it clear to Hurgronje that "the thousands of negroes and Abyssinians who have been carried off into Moslim lands and there remember their earlier life consider themselves as made men by slavery: all are contented and none wishes to return to his native land."[12] With such a statement, Hurgonje dissolves any idea that the "negroes and Abyssinians" came from any real location possessing its own culture. Such depictions, as Mary Louise Pratt has stated, "portray the African peoples not as undergoing historical changes in their lifeways, but as having no lifeways at all, as cultureless beings . . . ."[13] Many of the documents in this collection reveal a similar tendency, to find a place on the map for enslaved Africans only after they have been removed from their geographic homelands, making them shadow people in the homes, fields and families of their Muslim masters. Such a shadowy existence in history is surely as sad as a silent one. I hope that the reader of this compilation of documents will also look closely at these accounts and wonder who is more visible, the slaves, their masters, or the narrator-explorer himself.

Fictionalizing Slaves: Another Way of "Seeing" Slavery

As Hurgronje and other Europeans of the mid- to late nineteenth century often claim, the idea of abolition was not indigenous to the regions of the Islamic Mediterranean. To European administrators of colonized Middle Eastern regions, this was an important justification for intervention and another instance where Islamic concepts of justice were found lacking. Lord Cromer, the Consul-General of Egypt from 1882 to 1906, discussed this point often in his two-volume work *Modern Egypt,* notably here when he writes:

> On the whole, save that the stigma of slavery is attached to them—a consideration which is all-important from the European, but relatively unimportant from the Eastern point of view,—it may be doubted whether in the majority of cases the lot of slaves in Egypt is, in its material aspects, harder than, or even as hard as that of many domestic servants in Europe.[14]

Cromer wrote this in 1908, soon after his return to England from Egypt, convinced that Egyptians themselves were both unwilling and unable to understand where the crime of slavery lay. But there were Egyptians who saw the problems of slavery, although often in very different terms from those framing Cromer's perspective. One of the most sensitive challenges to slavery was written by ᶜAbd Allāh al-Nadīm, orator, journalist and nationalist politician, considered an outlaw by Cromer. Al-Nadīm had in fact been exiled by Cromer in 1882 after the defeat of the ᶜUrābī rebellion and had begun, on his return ten years later, a new newspaper called *al-Ustādh* ("The Teacher"). In this newspaper, he created a dialogue, in Egyptian colloquial Arabic, between two recently freed Sudanese slaves, Saᶜīd and Bakhīta, in which the two try to figure out what to do with the rest of their lives.

The dialogue begins when Saᶜīd meets Bakhīta and asks her where she is now working. She answers that she has no work, and that she wishes they were still slaves, still being cared for and fed by their masters. Saᶜīd reminds her that they were also regularly beaten by these same masters and Bakhīta concedes that she finds pleasure in freedom, but still she laments; "We came from our country like beasts *(zayy al-bahāyim)* and it was our masters who taught us about Islam *(al-kalām wa'l-ḥadīth)* and taught us about cleanliness, food, drink, how to dress and how to speak properly since we spoke in a way that no one could understand." Continuing to praise the kindness of her masters, Bakhīta recounts how she was like a daughter to her mistress: "If my master tried to beat me, she would argue and yell at him. We always held hands, even when we were eating our meals."[15]

Saᶜid, however, remembers physical torments and the terrible journey with the slave dealers more vividly than he does any kindnesses from his former masters. But Bakhīta makes one point on which they both agree, that it is confusing and difficult to parcel themselves out to different households, to work for one household one month and another the next. Slavery is not better than freedom, she admits, but the uncertainty of independent living is too hard to tolerate. Saᶜid agrees that the precarious employment situation of former slaves is very dire, and he tells Bakhīta that he thinks the government should take responsibility for them and give to every manumitted slave a plot of land from royal estates and the necessary machinery and tools. After all, he says, they used us to cultivate a lot of land, year after year, in addition to the government having conscripted so many soldiers out of the Sudan. Saᶜid says he's even heard that the Ottoman sultan offered such a gesture to the Sudanese, from whose agricultural bounty the empire is profiting.[16]

This was a daring and singular suggestion on al-Nadīm's part, asking the Egyptian government to take responsibility for the futures of the men and women formerly enslaved by Egyptians. He also recognized, in this dialogue, how difficult it was for freed slaves to find an independent place for themselves in society, particularly women. Much to Saᶜīd's annoyance, Bakhīta cannot stop referring to her previous "masters" even as her friend tries to get her to see them as simply *the* wealthy class (*al-jamāᶜa al-aghniyāʾ*) who could help create of their former slaves a new entrepreneurial collective;[17] Saᶜīd envisions the freed slaves as storekeepers and as contractors with their own teams of workers. Saᶜīd imagines Sudanese working in a wide range of fields, not only as the servants many had been for so long. Bakhīta balks at the impossibility of Saᶜīd's dreams.[18]

His interesting dialogue reveals al-Nadīm's awareness that slavery, rather than making slaves a part of their Egyptian families, had the terrible power to render them too immature or unprepared for the creation of their own families, or for the chance to be adult men and women. His method demonstrates an ironic way to address the silence of the slaves, since al-Nadīm intended this dialogue, like many of his others, to be read aloud in the coffeehouses of Alexandria and Cairo. Written in the dialect of Egyptian colloquial Arabic, the dialogue could therefore easily be acted out by al-Nadīm's readers, who, through the very act of reading the lines of Sa^{c}īd and Bakhīta, would become mouthpieces for the concerns of African slaves. Yet these slaves would remain fictional characters, given very little physical characterization, and their embodiment would depend on the imaginations of those "reading" them out loud. In other words, they would emerge only as symbols, dependent on the ways in which Egyptians of the 1890s envisioned Sudanese slaves to look, and sounding just like Egyptians. Al-Nadīm's approach, although unique, did not put an end to the silence of the slaves; this was more an act of ventriloquism.

Hearing Slaves Through Prayer

I would like to include one final example in the search for slaves' voices, one that began in the Sudan, spread to Egypt and was recently amplified by the Vatican. This is the voice of Sister Josephine Bakhīta, born in 1869, enslaved in 1877, a novice of the Catholic Church in 1893. This unusual woman left behind a narrative, one which is now influencing the daily lives of contemporary southern Sudanese communities in exile in Egypt.

Her story bore important cultural and religious significance for late nineteenth–early twentieth century Catholic churches and missions in Egypt and the Sudan, and continues to do so in present-day churches. As a former slave, her experiences represented a type of suffering that has been increasingly honored by the Catholic Church in the late twentieth century, and this honor culminated in her official canonization in the fall of 2000. But Sister Josephine

Bakhīta has also come to represent a certain type of perseverance in the modern world, or at least the world as experienced by displaced Southern Sudanese women.

Several masters bought and sold her before she passed into the hands of an agent of the Italian consul to the Sudan. When this agent decided to return to Italy, Bakhīta insisted on accompanying him. Italy did not immediately free her from the experience of slavery, however, and she was sold once again in Genoa to a young family. Her new owners entrusted her with the care of their daughter, and when the little girl was sent to a convent school, Bakhīta went with her. Bakhīta never left the convent. When the family who then owned her tried to get her to return with them to Africa, Bakhīta refused. Church authorities quickly launched a protest against her status as a slave and had her freed. She was accepted as a novice in 1893 in Venice.

In more ways than one, Bakhīta gave her life to the Church. She became a nun in 1896 and as she grew more active in the church, Catholic authorities began the charting and processing of Bakhīta's narrative. At the request of "her religious superiors" she told her story to another nun in 1910, and her narrative was published as a manuscript in 1919. In 1929 a series of interviews with Bakhīta was serialized in VITA, the monthly publication of the Canossian missions, and was soon published as a separate volume. Since then her story has circulated widely among Italian and other missionaries in the Sudan. So vibrantly has her memory resonated with the Church that it continues to be translated and reprinted until today.

Her life's itinerary, from the village in the Sudan to the caravan to different masters to Italy, is what signified her to the Church.

The transition from slave girl to nun was difficult for Bakhīta; it is rendered miraculous on the pages of the pamphlet that celebrate her life. That is indeed Bakhīta's only miracle: she bore no stigmata, nor performed any other miraculous feat other than living through two such disparate identities. The cultural and racial chasm which this woman crossed never leaves the consciousness of her editors, as their enframing text makes clear. Physically, Bakhīta is enshrined in a picture of her as a nun, which decorates all of the pamphlets and prayer folders about her.

After her investiture in the Church, Bakhīta never herself returned to the Sudan. But through missionary work and publications, she was returned as a symbol, and the audience most hungry for news of Bakhīta has been the Christian Sudanese community living in exile from their homes. Introduced to this woman through the church, Bakhīta's community, those most affected by these pamphlets, have transformed Bakhīta into a relative, an ancestor whose escape from the Sudan prophesied their own.

This community of southern Sudanese Catholics was created in the years immediately following Bakhīta's enslavement, when the Sudan underwent many dramatic social and political changes. The Muslims who had conquered Khartoum in 1884 lost political control of the north to the British in 1898; Islam, however, remained firmly entrenched. The British authorities tried to divorce the southern regions of the Sudan from the culture of the North, a culture they both respected and feared for its fostering the enslavement of the non-monotheistic southerners. The south became ripe for missionaries, and the spread of the Catholic Church was profound.

This cultural and religious split did a terrible disservice to the Sudanese; it made Christians and Muslims distrustful of the other, particularly when the question of national identity arose after the Sudan became independent in 1956. Christians in the South were alienated both linguistically and religiously from northerners, and although there were deep political divisions within the Muslim community, the southerners' historic connection to the British did little to inspire faith in their commitment to the idea of Sudanese unity. Added to this was the shadow of slavery, and the hard fact that the south for decades had been raided and ruined by northern traders.

The Sudan erupted in civil war several years after independence. This war was ended in the 1970s, but erupted again in the early 1980s. It rages on to this day, and although the north is wrestling with great changes in government, areas of the south have been depopulated by bombings, famine and the trek northward to escape. Many of the southern Sudanese have emigrated to Egypt. In 1992, the Egyptian official newspaper *al-Ahrām* noted that there were over a million Sudanese in Cairo alone. *Al-Ahrām* did not differentiate among northern or Southern Sudanese, but thousands of these refugees are southerners. Unlike northerners, many do not blend so easily into Egyptian daily life, and have sought asylum with Catholic churches and missions in Cairo and Alexandria.

It was in one of these churches that in 1992 I found a community of southern Sudanese celebrating a festival for St. Bakhīta. Her picture was everywhere, and posters and T-shirts commemorating her trek through the desert, towards eventual freedom, were being sold, the proceeds intended to benefit these refugees. As it became clear, with all of their refractory contextualizing of Bakhīta's text, the nuns who wrote the pamphlet also allowed Bakhīta to be recontextualized by the Sudanese. By displaying her warm, yet strangely distant smile on countless prayer books and on the cover of all the pamphlets and describing the typicalness of her features, Bakhīta was made the universal Sudanese woman and given qualities she could share with other Sudanese, regardless of ethnic origin.

But many Catholic refugees have created meanings for Bakhīta which are independent from those created by the Church, or expand on her identity in almost completely new ways. It is interesting that, as the nuns' text makes clear, Bakhīta never did belong to the South of the Sudan; her place of origin, Dār Fūr, is in the West. But even without the actual chain of descent being present, refugees from the south, particularly women, have claimed her as theirs, in her importance as a symbol of their own alienation from home, of their own move northwards and the kinds of work many feel forced to do. Exile in Egypt has brought financial circumstances that have made it necessary for many Sudanese women to find work, often domestic work, in the homes of Egyptians and expatriates. This is work they find humiliating, and the limited Egyptian economy offers little but jobs that many of their husbands refuse to perform, leaving the men unemployed and bitter. As Mary John Malou, secretary of the Blessed Josephine Bakhīta Women's Association, described, exile is reshaping the very structure of family life for many southern Sudanese, making home life very difficult. Many women have come to identify their own hard work and emotional turmoil with the labor Bakhīta was forced to perform as a young slave, or, as Ms. Malou put it, "What Bakhīta went though is what many of us are now going through."[19]

Bakhīta has also come to symbolize motherhood and the unique power many Sudanese believe mothers have within the family. Her image is used to celebrate the ability to maintain a home even in the most trying of circumstances, circumstances which many in the Bakhīta Women's Association liken to a new kind of slavery. In two important ways, then, this woman who was forcibly removed from her family is being reclaimed by later generations, who use her story to find honor, and not stigma, in slavery.

Conclusion

It remains very difficult to find the original, independent voices of African slaves in the Islamic Mediterranean world. The example of St. Josephine Bakhīta offers one way in which slave narratives published by Catholic missions can help, but like the black shadows described by travelers like Nachtigal, Hurgronje and others, like the figurative slaves of ᶜAbd Allāh al-Nadīm's imagination and like the romanticized victims of Oriental despotism so often published in the journals of the Anti-Slavery Society, very few give us the real, autobiographical narratives we still hope for. But as John Hunwick wrote earlier, the search has only recently begun in earnest. Through police records, archives, *sharīᶜa* court records, the memoirs of slave-owners, family histories—to name just a few sources—the experiences of slaves in the Islamic lands of the Mediterranean will be remembered, and eventually heard.

◆ I ◆

Basic Texts on Slavery

(1) THE QURʾĀN ON SLAVES

The Qurʾān nowhere advocates or justifies slavery. But the text clearly takes it for granted that slavery is a fact of life, and while it does not clearly advocate the abolition of slavery, many of the Qurʾānic texts speak to the various ways in which slaves can be set free: the act of freeing is left to the conscience or Godfearingness of the owner. Text no. 2 in Section II below argues that it was divine wisdom not to seek an abrupt abolition of slavery, but rather to encourage the ending of slavery by making the freeing of a slave an act of piety.

The common Arabic word for "male slave" is ʿabd, *and for "female slave"* ama, *but in the Qurʾān the word ʿabd is also used to signify "servant of God" (with the plural* ʿibād *rather than* ʿabīd*). While Qurʾānic vocabulary does use these terms, it also uses more frequently euphemisms such as "those whom your right hands possess," or "necks" (*riqāb*), both terms emphasizing submission. The verses given below are the only ones in which any of these terms occur. Verse 4 of sūra 47 makes no reference to slaves, but is included because it provides options for dealing with those captured in war. Sūra 33:50 below makes it clear that a divinely permissable way of obtaining female slaves—at least for the Prophet—is through capture in battle. This was to become the primary legal basis for obtaining slaves, both male and female, though in practice it was never the only way for an individual to obtain a slave.*

In the passages below, the first figure refers to the number of the sūra, and the second to the verse. The translations are by John Hunwick from a text of the Qurʾān published in Egypt at the Royal Press (al-Maṭbaʿa al-amīriyya) *in 1371/1951–52.*

2:177: Righteousness does not consist in turning your faces toward the East and the West; but righteousness is he who believes in God and the Last Day and the angels and the Scripture and the Prophets; and gives his wealth for the love of Him, to kinsfolk and orphans and the needy and the wayfarer and to beggars, and for [freeing] slaves . . .

2:178: O you who believe! Retaliation is prescribed for you in the matter of those slain: the freeman for the freeman, and the slave for the slave, and the female for the female . . .

2:221: Do not marry polytheistic women until they believe. A believing slave woman is better than a polytheist, even though she please you. Do not marry polytheistic males until they believe. A believing male slave is better than a polytheist, though he please you . . .

4:25: And those of you who are unable to marry chaste, believing women, [let them marry] from the believing maids whom your right hands possess . . .

4:36: And worship God, and do not ascribe any partner to Him. And [show] kindness to parents, and kinsfolk, and orphans, and the needy, and to the neighbor who is of your kin, and also to the neighbor who is not, and the to fellow-traveller, and to the wayfarer and to those whom your right hands possess . . .

4:92: A believer should not kill a believer unless accidentally. Whoever kills a believer accidentally must set free a believing slave, and pay blood money to the [slain man's] family, unless they [decide to] give it away as charity. If [the victim] belongs to a people who are your enemies, and he is a believer, then [the penalty is] to set free a believing slave. If he belongs to a people between whom and yourselves there is a pact, then [the penalty is] the payment of blood-money to the slain man's family and the freeing of a slave . . .

5:89: God will not take you to task for [breaking] casual oaths, but He will take you to task for [breaking] oaths solemnly sworn. The expiation for such is the feeding of ten needy persons with the normal kind of food with which you feed your own folk, or providing them with clothes, or liberating a slave . . .

9:60: Alms are only for the poor and the needy, and for those who collect them, and those whose hearts are to be reconciled, and [to free] slaves, and for debtors, and in the cause of God, and for the wayfarer . . .

16:71: And God has granted some of you more means than others. Those who have been granted more are not about to hand over their means to those whom their right hands possess, so that they may be equal with them in this respect. Would they then reject the bounty of God?

23:1–6: The believers shall prosper who are humble in their worship, and who turn aside from idle play, and who practise charity, and who observe chastity except with their wives or those whom their right hands possess; such are not to be blamed.

24:32–33: Marry such of you as are solitary and the pious among your male and female slaves. If they are poor, God shall enrich them from His bounty. God is of ample means, Aware. And let those who do not find [the means for] marrying remain chaste until God enriches them from His bounty. And whomever among those whom your right hands possess desires a document [of manumission], write it for them if you know of any good in them, and give them some of the wealth that God gave you. And do not compel your slave-girls to [engage in] prostitution so that you may seek worldly benefit, if they wish to remain chaste. And if any of you should force them [into prostitution], then after they have been forced, God will be Forgiving and Merciful [toward them].

24:58: O you who believe! Let those whom your right hands possess and those of you who have not reached puberty, ask leave of you at three times [before entering your presence]: before the dawn worship, and when you have divested yourself of your garments during the heat of noon, and after the evening worship. Three times of privacy for you . . .

33:50: O Prophet! We have made lawful to you your wives to whom you have paid their marriage portions, and those that your right hand possesses among those whom God allotted to you [as spoils of war] . . .

33:52: [O Prophet!] It is not lawful for you to take [other] women hereafter, nor for you to change them for other wives, even if their beauty pleases you, except for those whom thy right hand possesses . . .

47:4: When you meet those who disbelieve, then [it is a] smiting of necks, and then when you have got the better of them, fasten the bonds, and thereafter [it is] either graciousness [in freeing them] or ransom, until war lays down its burdens . . .

58:3: Those who put away their wives [by saying they are to them as their mother's back] and afterwards would go back on what they said, [for them the penalty is] freeing a slave before they touch one another again.

70:28–30: Those who observe chastity, except with their wives or those whom their right hands possess; such are not to be blamed.

90:11–16: What will convey to you what the steep path is? [It is] to free a slave. Or to feed on the day of privation, an orphan closely related, or one who is indigent and in misery.

(2) THE ḤADĪTH

The next most authoritative source of law and conduct after the Qurʾān is the *Ḥadīth*, the reputed sayings of the Prophet Muḥammad. The following are translations by John Hunwick from the Arabic text of *al-Jāmiʿ al-ṣaḥīḥ* of al-Bukhārī, generally considered to be the most authentic collection of the Prophet's sayings. The text used is that published by Kazi Publications (Chicago, 1977) (accompanied by an English translation by Muhammad Muhsin Khan).

Ḥadīth no. 693. Abū Hurayra said: "The Prophet said: 'Any man who frees a Muslim slave, God will spare from Hell for every limb of the slave a limb [of the liberator].' "

Ḥadīth no. 694. Abū Dharr said: "I asked the Prophet—may God bless him and grant him peace: 'What is the preferred act?' He said: 'Belief in God and *jihād* in His path.' I said: 'Which is the preferred slave [to set free]?' He said: 'The most highly priced, and the one most precious to its owners.' "

Ḥadīth no. 696. Asmaᵓ daughter of Abū Bakr said: "We used to be told to free slaves during a lunar eclipse."

Ḥadīth no. 697. Sālim narrated, on the authority of his father—may God be pleased with him: "He [the Prophet] said: 'Whoever frees [his share of] a slave owned by two persons shall be charged [for the other half] if he is well off; then [the slave] shall be [completely] freed.' "

Ḥadīth no. 702. Ibn ᶜUmar—may God be pleased with him—used to give a legal opinion regarding a male or female slave jointly owned, saying that, if one of the owners frees his share of the slave, "It is incumbent upon him to free all of the slave, if the one granting freedom has the money; a fair price should be charged against his funds, and the partners in ownership should be paid their shares, and the freed slave should be let go."

Ḥadīth no. 712. Shuᶜba told us that ᶜAbd Allāh b. Dīnār heard Ibn ᶜUmar say: "The Prophet—may God bless him and grant him peace—forbade the sale or giving away of clientage."

Ḥadīth no. 717. Ibn ᶜAwn said that Nāfiᶜ wrote to him saying that the Prophet—may God bless him and grant him peace—raided the Banū al-Muṣṭaliq at a time when they were off guard and their herds were being watered. He slaughtered their warriors and captured their offspring. That day he obtained Juwayriya.[1]

Ḥadīth no. 720. Abū Mūsā said: "The Messenger of God—may God bless him and grant him peace—said: 'Whoever owns a slave girl and educates her, and is good to her, and frees her and marries her, shall have a double reward [from God].' "

Ḥadīth no. 721. The Prophet—may God bless him and grant him peace—said: "Your brothers are your slaves. God placed them under your control. Whoever has his brother under his control should feed them and clothe them out of what he himself eats and wears, and should not impose upon them labor that overcomes them. Should he do so, then he should help them."

Ḥadīth no. 722. Abū Mūsā al-Ashᶜarī reported that the Prophet—may God bless him and grant him peace—said: "If a slave is faithful to his owner and worships his Lord truly, he will receive his reward [from God] twice over."

Ḥadīth no. 728. The Prophet—may God bless him and grant him peace—said: "None of you should say: 'Feed your lord,' [or] 'Wash your lord,' [or] 'Give your lord a drink.' Let him rather say 'my master' or 'my guardian.' Let no one say 'my slave' or 'my slave-girl,' but rather 'my boy' or 'my girl,' or 'my lad.' "

* * * *

Not much was ever written before modern times to justify slavery, or to deal with ethical issues relating to it. Perhaps the most notable exception is the Persian medieval theologian, philosopher, and mystic, Abū Ḥāmid al-Ghazālī (d. 1111), who is one of the most respected medieval writers on Islamic ethics.

(3) THE RIGHTS OF SLAVES

Source: Extracts of Abū Ḥāmid al-Ghazālī, "Ḥuqūq al-mamlūk," in *Iḥyāʾ ʿulūm al-dīn* (Beirut: Dār al-Maʿrifa, n.d.), ii, 219–21.

One of the last injunctions of the Prophet—may God bless him and grant him peace—was his saying: "Fear God concerning those whom your right hands possess. Feed them with what you eat, and clothe them with what you wear, and do not assign them work that is beyond their capacity. Those whom you like, retain; and those whom you dislike, sell. Do not cause suffering to God's creation. He gave you them to possess, and had He so wished, he would have given you to them to possess." He also said—may God bless him and grant him peace: "The slave has a right to his fair share of food and clothing; do not assign him a task beyond his capacity." He also said—peace be upon him: "The following shall not enter Paradise: the imposter, the arrogant, the traitor, and he who treats the slaves he owns badly." ʿAbd Allāh son of ʿUmar—may God be pleased with them both—said: "A man came to the Messenger of God—may God bless him and grant him peace—and said, 'O Messenger of God, how many times should we pardon a slave (*khādim*)?' The Messenger of God was silent, then he said, 'Seventy times every day.' " ʿUmar—may God be pleased with him—used to visit slave owners on Saturdays, and if he found a slave (*ʿabd*) engaged in work beyond his capacity he would release him from it.

Ibn al-Munkadir said: "One of the Companions of the Prophet—may God Most High bless him and grant him peace—was beating a slave of his, and the slave began to say, 'I beseech you by God. I beg you for God's sake,' but he did not pardon him. The Messenger of God—may God Most High bless him and grant him peace—heard the the cry of the slave and went to him. When the Companion saw the Messenger of God, he stopped what he was doing. The Messenger of God said to him, 'When he begged you for God's sake you did not pardon him, but when you saw me, you stopped.' The Companion said, 'He is free for the sake of God, O Messenger of God.' The Prophet said, 'Had you not freed him, the Fire of Hell would have scorched your face.' "

The Messenger of God—may God Most High bless him and grant him peace—said: "If a slave is loyal to his master and is diligent in his worship of God, he will be rewarded doubly." When Abū Rāfi[c] was freed he wept, saying, "I had the potential of two rewards and one of them has been lost." The Messenger of God also said: "He who owns a slave girl and protects her [chastity] and acts kindly towards her, then frees her and marries her, shall have two rewards." He also said: "Each one of you is a shepherd and each is responsible for his flock."

In sum: the rights of one possessed are that he should share in the owner's food and clothing and should not be assigned work above his capacity. The owner should not look at him/her with arrogance or disdain, and should pardon his mistakes. When he is angry with him, he should reflect on his own shortcomings, or the sins of disobedience he has committed, his infringement of God's rights and his failure to obey Him fully, despite the fact that God's power over him is greater than his power over his slave.

◆ II ◆

Some Muslim Views on Slavery

Prior to the nineteenth century, there is no evidence of condemnation of slavery by Muslim writers, nor any attempt to justify the institution. Enslavement was considered retribution for the rejection of the Islamic faith, since the sole legal method of obtaining a slave (at least in theory) was through the defeat of non-Muslims in a jihād *that had as its aim to "make the word of God supreme and to bring men to His religion which he chose for His servants" (see below, pp. 51–52). In the nineteenth and twentieth centuries some Muslim writers felt a need to rationalize the acceptance of slavery in Islamic thinking, in response to European condemnation of slavery and criticism of Islam.*

* * * *

(1) IN DEFENSE OF ISLAM AND SLAVERY

Source: Aḥmad Shafīq Bek, *al-Riqq fī'l-Islām* [translated from the original French, *L'esclavage au point de vue musulman* (Cairo, 1891) by Aḥmad Zakī (Cairo, 1309/1892)], 93–94. Aḥmad Shafīq's original book was written as a response to an address by Cardinal Lavigerie in Paris in 1888, in which he attacked Islam and laid the blame for the horrors of the African slave trade at its doors.

From the noble Qur'ānic verses and the Prophetic *ḥadīth,* and the statements of the imams and the testimonies of history which we have enumerated in the previous sections, it is clear without doubt or dispute that the Islamic religion narrowed the confines of slavery and worked to eradicate it at source, since it laid down conditions and imposed restrictions that had to be observed in order for enslavement to take place, just as it clarified the paths and explained clearly the means by which deliverance from its clutches might be achieved. If it happened that, despite all these expedients, destiny caused a man to fall into slavery, then we have seen that the Islamic *sharīʿa* did not abandon him or leave him to his own devices, but extended over him the wing of protection and the banner of safekeeping, and considered him worthy of compassion and deserving of mercy because of the weakness and misery it saw in the slave.

Hence the *sharīᶜa* set forth injunctions that make it obligatory for masters to treat their slaves as they treat themselves and to strive to make them happy, to give them ease of mind, to teach them, to train them and educate them, and not to belittle them or put them down, to marry them off, both males and females, so as to hasten their release from the noose of slavery and to conduct them to the pathways of freedom.

I refer here to manumission—a topic I have hitherto only mentioned summarily in terms of its general principles and its most important guidelines—which is, if truth be told, one of the greatest sources of pride in Islam. Our Muḥammadan *sharīᶜa* strove to destroy the supports of slavery and to demolish its manifestations. The question was how to do so. Would it have been appropriate to take an initiative to outlaw a practice which had been part and parcel of the customs of the whole world since the beginning of human society and had been practised throughout the ages? That would no doubt have brought in its wake a huge revolution in the organization of human society and a great upheaval in the souls of peoples and nations. Hence Islam achieved this end by another path in the face of which difficulties dissolved and obstacles faded away, instead of agitating men's minds and provoking their thoughts and feelings by abolishing slavery once and for all. So Muslims were invited to draw close to God by freeing downtrodden slaves in many circumstances and various situations.

(2) A TUNISIAN PHILOSOPHY OF SLAVERY

Source: Extract of Muḥammad Bayram al-Khāmis (1840–1889), *al-Taḥqīq fī masʾalat al-riqq*, in al-Munṣif b. ᶜAbd al-Jalīl & Kamāl ᶜImrān, *Muḥammad Bayram al-Khāmis: bibliyūghrāfiyya taḥlīliyya maᶜ thalāth rasāʾil nādira* (Carthage: Bayt al-Ḥikma, 1989), as reproduced in Munṣif al-Jazzār & ᶜAbd al-Laṭīf ᶜUbayd, *Wathāʾiq ḥawl al-riqq wa-ilghāʾihi min al-bilād al-Tūnisiyya* (Tunis: Maᶜhad Būrqība, 1997), 45–46.

Know that God Most High said in His Mighty Book: "I only created jinns and men so that they might worship Me," etc.[2] Worship is acting in conformity with God's commands and prohibitions in regard to everything He created in this abode. Hence all action and inaction on the part of the slave [of God][3] should be in accordance with what he is given permission to do by Him who created him and who created those things in which the slave has discretion, such as will bring about salvation for him in this world and the next. Man is only what he is in this regard on account of the power of reason he possesses, as the experts in the principles of law (*al-uṣūliyyūn*) declared in their discussion of legal responsibility (*taklīf*).

Saᶜd al-Dīn said in the *Talwīḥ*[4]: "Chapter Four. On the one who is subject to a legal ruling. He is the person who has legal responsibility, who is judged in accordance with his deed and his fitness [to be judged], his fitness depending on his rationality, since the child and the madman have no legal responsibility," etc. For rationality gives rise in a human being to a quality called, in the language of the jurisprudents, "fitness," that is to say moral responsibility (*dhimma*), through which one becomes liable for both reward and punishment (*qābil li-mā lahu wa-mā ᶜalayhi*). This quality is universal in all types of human being and all individuals. Thus they are on a par as regards being considered "legally responsible," and also as regards the application of its various aspects to them. However there are some non-inherent impediments which hinder one from being so considered and prevent some aspects of legal responsibility from being applicable. The scholars of the principles of law set forth the basis for fitness, and the impediments to it as well as the logic behind them and the details of them. Among those who did so were Ṣadr al-Sharīᶜa in the *Tawḍīḥ*, and al-Saᶜd in the *Talwīḥ* in their relevant sections.[5] Among the impediments they enumerated were factors of youth, madness, sickness, and feeble-mindedness.[6] They also listed slavery among such impediments.[7] It thus becomes clear from what has gone before that the inherent status (*aṣl*) of human beings is freedom.

It remains now to demonstrate that slavery is contingent, and the reasons for it being so. As regards its being contingent, this is because the experts in the principles of law declared it to be so, and because of the statement of the *Talwīḥ* about that in the enumeration of the impediments to fitness for legal responsibility as follows: "One of them is slavery, which semantically means 'weakness/tenderness/delicacy (*al-ḍuᶜf*),' as in the phrase 'tenderness of heart,' or 'a soft garment delicately woven.' In the law it means legal incapacitation, meaning that the Lawgiver[8] did not make the slave fit to undertake many things that the free man is in a position to do, such as giving witness, being a judge, holding state office, and so forth."

As for the reason for its being contingent, the basis is that when a man who has attained maturity declines to accept legal responsibility [imposed upon him] by the Lawgiver, and persists in this, then he conjoins himself with animals and inanimate objects devoid of reason, that quality upon which depends the understanding of arguments for the unity of God and belief in miracles through the effort that is expended in close examination of the claims and proofs of faith. If a man fits this description, then he deserves to be subject to laws applicable to what he resembles. Hence the Lawgiver permitted that in his case he be given a legal status other than a human being, on account of his being an owned object, rather than one who owns. But he should not have the status of an animal or an inanimate object in all respects and from every point of view, but only in so far as he is denied the outward signs of wholeness and the various levels of privilege.[9]

As regards the general basis for respecting human beings, the slave is not excluded from it, so that he can be fit to return to his original condition of freedom, through being manumitted. There are many statements of the scholars in the same vein as what we have mentioned, including that of the *Talwīḥ*: "It is primarily a right of God Most High, meaning that it was established as a punishment for unbelief, for since unbelievers have disdained worship of God Most High and made themselves as one with animals in failing to examine and reflect upon the message of divine unity, God Most High has punished them by making them slaves of His slaves, living in degradation with the status of animals.[10] Hence, one who is already a Muslim cannot be enslaved."

(3) ISLAM'S STAND ON SLAVERY: A TEXTBOOK APPROACH

Source: Muḥammad Jumᶜa ᶜAbd Allāh, *al-Kawākib al-durriyya fī'l-fiqh al-Mālikiyya*, vol. 4 (Cairo: Maktabat al-Kulliyyāt al-Azhariyya, 3rd edn., 1400/1980), 175–76. The work is a set text for students of the Secondary Certificate in al-Azhar institutes.

Islam is the eternal world religion which came into existence for the happiness of humankind, and to guide it to what is best for it in this world and the next. It is not possible for any system of law, whether religious or civil, to produce that which was produced by the scripture of Islam, the Noble Qur°ān, since it is a revelation from the Knowing One, the Wise One. Nothing is hidden from Him, and His ordinances are not inspired by that which is not in accord with the interests of humanity as a whole. He desires ease for His servants and does not desire hardship for them. The Qur°ān came to lead people out from the darkness of idolatry, injustice, violence in the land, and humiliation and enslavement of the other, to the light of truth, justice, righteousness, self-esteem and nobility.

So as to establish in human society the law of equality of rights and obligations, and to put an end to differences of sex and color amongst all peoples of humankind [the Qur°ān] brought the following message: "Surely this community of yours is a single community, and I am your Lord, so be wary of me."[11] It also says: "O people! We created you as males and females and made you into peoples and kin groups that you might know one another. Surely, the most noble of you in God's sight is the most righteous. God is Knowing, Informed."[12] The noble Messenger—may God bless him and grant him peace, confirmed that, saying: "'God does not look to your bodies, or to your appearances, but looks to your hearts,' and he pointed to his chest with his fingers." This was related by Muslim on the authority of Abū Hurayra.

Islam and its scripture came with this, and found numerous ills and insurmountable obstacles in human society preventing it from civilized progress. And it cured those ills with its healing balm and removed the obstacles with its cleansing current. God spoke truly [when He said]: "We reveal of the Qur'ān that wherein is healing and mercy for the believers, while it only causes the wicked to be greater losers."[13]

One of the obstacles in the way of the happiness and progress of human society was the problem of slavery—a problem whose roots extended into the depths of history and which had reached its zenith by the dawn of Islam—and [Islam] cured it, but not by way of a single advance, as it had done with other problems, lest this should produce a counterreaction that would shake the pillars of society and tear apart its structures. Rather it followed the path of gradualism in solving it, as is its practice in tackling deep-rooted problems it faces such as unlawful gain and alcohol, since abolition of slavery at a single stroke, given its widespread practice, would have been impossible in the human social order from two points of view: the interests of the masters, and the interests of the slaves. When the United States freed its slaves some of them roamed the land seeking a means of living without finding something that would improve their lives, or that they were able to do. So they would return to their masters seeking to be accepted into their service as before. That also happened in the Egyptian Sudan. The British rulers tried to find means of subsistence for them through some work they could undertake independently and which would support them adequately, but they were unable to do so. Hence they were forced to allow them to return to the service of their former slavery on condition that it was not permitted for their employers to sell them or trade them.

This is a palpable and observable proof that the abolition of slavery—which was widespread among humankind and involved such a large number of persons—through a religious system of law by means of which human beings have worshipped God Most High from day one, would not have constituted wisdom, nor would it have been in the interest of human beings who could carry it out.

The system of law in Islam is a practical one having no mitigation in it. What it ordained in regard to dealing with slavery was the highest order of wisdom, combining the general good with mercy. It taught the slave, refined him and perfected him, and raised his status and made him equal with his master. It provided a livelihood for him and then freed him.

In order to reach this goal Islam followed a threefold path: (1) reducing the avenues to enslavement and closing them off; (2) caring for the slave and perfecting him; (3) opening wide the gates to freedom for the slave.

◆ III ◆

Slavery and the Law

Rules dealing with slaves evolved during the developmental period of Islamic law in the first four centuries of Islam. The law deals with the acquisition of slaves only as an aspect of the fate of captives of "holy war" (jihād).

The principal works of Islamic jurisprudence (fiqh) *were composed in the first seven centuries of Islam, and remained authoritative down to the time when Muslim nation-states began to formulate their own individual codes of law in the twentieth century. The passages below are all from medieval manuals of jurisprudence according to the Mālikī school, the predominant approach to law in North and West Africa, and the Nile Valley south of Egypt. Although the authors are medieval, their works were regarded as authoritative in Muslim juridical circles through the nineteenth century.*

* * * *

(1) RULES OF *JIHĀD*

Source: the *Mukhtaṣar* of Khalīl b. Isḥāq al-Jundī, a fourteenth-century Egyptian Mālikī law compilation, regarded as most authoritative in North and West Africa, and the Sudan. It is a summary of the corpus of mainstream (and some minority) interpretations of law according to Mālikī scholars. The texts consulted are: the Paris edition of the *Mukhtaṣar* (1900), 77; the commentary of al-Kharashī (Cairo, 1316/1898–99), iii, 121; G-H. Bousquet, *Abrégé de la loi musulmane selon le rite de l'imâm Mâlek* (Alger, 1956), section 101. Enslavement of prisoners in a *jihād* is only one of five options—and by no means the worst.

The imam [i.e. the Muslim ruler conducting the *jihād*] should look into the fate of adult male prisoners, and take whichever of the following options he considers most beneficial: to put them to death, to release them without penalty, to ask ransom for them, to demand capitation tax (*jizya*), or to enslave them.

(2) THE LEGALITY OF OWNING SLAVES

Source: Questions of Sa^c^id b. Ibrāhīm al-Jirārī of Tuwāt, addressed to Aḥmad

Bābā of Timbuktu in the late 16th or early 17th century, as part of an inquiry about which Black Africans it was lawful to own as slaves. See John Hunwick and Fatima Harrak, *Miʿrāj al-ṣuʿūd: Aḥmad Bābā's Replies on Slavery* (Rabat: Institut des Etudes Africaines, Université Mohammed V, 2000), 13.

It is known that, according to the *sharīʿa*, the reason why it is allowed to own [others] is [their] unbelief. Thus, whoever purchases an unbeliever is allowed to own him, but not in the contrary case. Conversion to Islam subsequent to the existence of the aforementioned condition has no effect on continued ownership. Were those lands which we mentioned, and other similar lands of the Muslims of the Sūdān, conquered and [their people] enslaved in a state of unbelief, while their conversion occurred subsequently—hence there is no harm [in owning them]—or not?

(3) SLAVE CRIMES

Source: Muḥammad b. Aḥmad al-Gharnāṭī al-Kalbī, known as Ibn Juzayy (d. 1340), *Qawānīn al-aḥkām al-sharʿīyya wa-masāʾil al-furūʿ al-fiqhiyya* (Beirut, 1974), 381–82. Ibn Juzayy was an Andalusian jurist whose *Qawānīn al-aḥkām* was highly regarded in Muslim Africa right down to the nineteenth century. It summarizes Mālikī juridical principles and rulings, with comparisons with those of other law schools.

The crimes of slaves can be divided into three categories: (1) crimes against other slaves, (2) crimes against free persons, and (3) crimes against property. As for crimes against slaves, there are no exceptions whether they be deliberate or accidental. If it is an accidental offense then the owner of the offending slave has the option either to hand over the slave in compensation for his offense to the owner of the slave against whom the offense was committed, or to redeem him against the value of the slave against whom a homicide was committed, or against the extent to which bodily harm diminished the slave's value in the case of injury. If the wound did not diminish the injured slave's value then the offender has no liability.

If the offense is deliberate then the owner of the slain or injured slave has two options: (1) to seek retaliation, or (2) to take the slave who caused the injury, unless his master redeems him for the price of the slain slave, or the amount by which the value of the injured slave was diminished. Abū Ḥanīfa said that there can be no retaliation between slaves for anything short of the taking of a life. Al-Ḥasan al-Baṣrī[14] said there was no retaliation as between slaves, whether for the taking of lives or anything less.

As for slaves' crimes against free persons, if the crime is accidental homicide, then the owner of the killer has the option either to hand the slave over or to redeem him against the blood-money. If it was deliberate, then the ruling concerning it has already been given in the chapter on homicide. If the crime against free persons involves less than homicide, then it makes no difference if bodily harm was intentional or accidental, since the slave cannot have his blood spilt in retaliation by a free man on account of an injury. The owner of the slave inflicting the injury has two choices: (1) to hand over the slave, or (2) to redeem him against the blood money due for the injury.

As regards slaves' offenses against property, it makes no difference whether the property belongs to a free person or to a slave, for it is accountable to the person of the slave who committed the offense. His master has the option to hand him over against the value of the property he damaged or destroyed, or to redeem him for that. It makes no difference whether what was damaged or destroyed is equivalent to the price of the slave, or whether it is greater or smaller.[15]

All this concerns property over which the slave has not been given trust. What he has been given trust over, whether goods on loan, or on hire, or on deposit, or where approval to act in their regard has been given, is all accountable to the slave's moral responsibility, not to his person.[16]

(4) THE SLAVE AUTHORIZED TO TRADE

Source: Muḥammad b. Aḥmad al-Gharnāṭī al-Kalbī, known as Ibn Juzayy (d.

1340), *Qawānīn al-aḥkām al-sharᶜīyya wa-masā'il al-furūᶜ al-fiqhiyya* (Beirut, 1974), 317–18.

There are three issues. The first concerns the slave's property. He owns his property, but his ownership is incomplete compared to that of a free man, since, according to the consensus of juristic opinion, the owner may take it away from him whenever he wishes. Al-Shāfiᶜī and Abū Ḥanīfa denied that the slave could own anything at all. According to the *madh'hab* [of Mālik] the slave is allowed to have a concubine and to engage in sexual intercourse with what his right hand possesses, with the permission of his owner, but not according to the two above-mentioned authorities.

The second issue. Slaves are of two types: the one who has been given permission to trade, and the one not so authorized. The unauthorized slave is not allowed any freedom of action, either in terms of making a deal, such as a sale; or in terms of an act of kindness, such as making a gift or a charitable donation, or granting manumission. His status is that of the legally incapacitated (*al-maḥjūr*); for him to conduct a sale requires the permission of his owner. The authorized slave is allowed freedom of action in all matters coming under the heading of commerce, such as making a deal, and in this respect he is like a plenipotentiary agent. There is a difference of opinion about whether a slave's owner can stop him from trading on account of a debt. His making a gift, or giving a charitable donation, or manumitting a slave is dependent upon his owner granting him authorization, or his not doing so. If the owner does not know that his slave manumitted someone until the deed is done, then the manumission is effective and is binding on the slave. The master cannot undo it.

The third issue. The authorized slave must pay from his own funds all debts he runs up. If he has insufficient means to pay them, they remain his personal obligation and the owner is not obliged to pay them on his behalf, nor can the slave be sold to pay them, contrary to what some people hold.[17]

Three subsidiary principles: (1) If one sells a slave who owns property, the property belongs to the seller unless the buyer stipulates to the contrary; (2) After authorizing his slave the owner must place restraints on him and inform the ruler of that, and draw people's attention to it; (3) The owner does not have to give permission to trade to a slave who is not trustworthy in regard to his debts, for fear he may deal in unlawful gain (*ribā*) or behave treacherously. The non-Muslim slave is more deserving of being denied the privilege.

(5) MANUMISSION

Source: Muḥammad b. Aḥmad al-Gharnāṭī al-Kalbī, known as Ibn Juzayy (d. 1340), *Qawānīn al-aḥkām al-sharʿīyya wa-masāʾil al-furūʿ al-fiqhiyya* (Beirut, 1974), 408–9.

There are seven types of manumission: (1) immediate manumission; (2) deferred manumission; (3) partial manumission; (4) manumission through a will; (5) by written agreement; (6) post-mortem manumission; and (7) through [a concubine] giving birth [to a child by her master]. There are six reasons for manumission, the first of which is voluntary manumission seeking divine reward, since this is one of the noblest of deeds. The remaining modalities are obligatory, and they are (1) manumission resulting from the swearing of oaths, i.e. acts of atonement [for having broken a vow]; (2) resulting from mutilation; (3) resulting from partial freeing; (4) resulting from family relationship.

(1) Mutilation. Whoever intentionally mutilates his slave in a visible fashion, e.g. if he cuts off his fingertips or the extremity of his ear or the tip of his nose, or if he cuts any part of his body, shall be punished and the slave freed without his authorization. Injury is only defined as mutilation if the slave thereby suffers gross disfigurement. If someone swears to give his slave a hundred lashes, the slave should rapidly be set free before the beating takes place, according to Aṣbagh,[18] but not according to Ibn al-Mājishūn,[19] though they were agreed that he should be freed if it were a case of more than a hundred lashes. There is no freeing on account of muti-

lation except through a judicial process. Ash'hab said that a slave becomes free automatically as a result of mutilation, but others disagreed.[20]

(2) Partial freeing. If anyone frees part of his slave, or a single limb, the rest of the slave is freed without his consent. As regards being the first [of several co-owners] to free a slave, or through judicial ruling, there are two reports: Abū Ḥanīfa and the Ẓāhiriyya held the view that what is freed of the slave is freed and the slave must be asked to work to free the remainder.[21] If a man frees a share of his in a slave, the remainder will be calculated monetarily and he will be made responsible for paying the co-owner's share, so the entire slave will be freed. Abū Ḥanīfa said the co-owner has three options: to free his share of the slave, to accept payment for the slave's value [from the other co-owner], or to ask the slave to work to free the remainder.

(3) As for manumission on account of blood relationship, this is occasioned by slaves' entering into ownership [of a blood relative]. According to the mass of mainstream jurists—though contrary to the view of the Ẓāhiriyya—male persons related by descent or ascent to a person into whose possession they pass through purchase or inheritance, or other means, are to be freed without the owner's authorization. According to the generally accepted [Mālikī] view, full brothers or half brothers, either maternal or paternal, come under the same rule, contrary to al-Shāfiᶜī. Ibn Wahb added the paternal uncle to the list.[22] Others say that it applies to any close blood relative, in agreement with the view of Abū Ḥanīfa.

(6) THE MOTHER OF HER MASTER'S CHILD

Source: Muḥammad b. Aḥmad al-Gharnāṭī al-Kalbī, known as Ibn Juzayy (d. 1340), *Qawānīn al-aḥkām al-sharᶜīyya wa-masāʾil al-furūᶜ al-fiqhiyya* (Beirut, 1974), 415–16.

Section 1. On becoming "mother of a child" (*umm walad*). If a man has sexual intercourse with his female slave and she becomes pregnant, she becomes for him "mother of a child," whether she gives birth to the child at full term, or as a premature foetus, or as "clot of blood" or just as blood, provided it is known that pregnancy occurred. Ash'hab held that a woman was not "mother of a child" simply through coagulated blood. Al-Shāfiᶜī[23] said that she would not be "mother of a child" until some element of the foetus was formed—an eye, a nail, or something similar. In the case of somebody who marries a slave woman, then purchases her when she is pregnant by him, there is a difference of opinion as to whether or not she becomes "mother of a child" through that pregnancy. A slave concubine of a slave does not become his "mother of a child" on account of a birth she gave whilst in a state of slavery. There is difference of opinion concerning the slave contracted to post-mortem freedom (*al-mudabbar*), the slave who has a written contract to purchase his freedom (*al-mukātab*), and the slave whose freedom has been deferred for a specified future date (*al-muᶜtaq ilā ajal*).

Section 2. On the regulations governing the "mother of a child." During her master's lifetime she is subject to regulations governing a slave woman, such as the prohibition on her inheriting, and as regards the fixed punishment (*ḥadd*) for adultery,[24] etc. The consensus is that her master may have sexual intercourse with her, but may only employ her in light work, and may not hire her out, contrary to the view of al-Shāfiᶜī. According to the mass (*jumhūr*) of jurists, he is not allowed to sell her, in conformity with the practice of [the caliphs] ᶜUmar and ᶜUthmān, whereas the Ẓāhiriyya allowed this in conformity with the practice of [caliphs] Abū Bakr and ᶜAlī.[25]

If a "mother of a child" commits a crime, she is not handed over [to the injured party] as would be the case with another slave woman, but the owner is to free her for the least possible penalty for the crime, or for the value of her person. If her master dies she is to be freed out of his estate, even if he leaves no property other than her. She then stands on an equal footing with free persons in regard to matters of inheritance, the prescribed punishment for adultery, punishment for crimes, etc.

Section 3. On paternity. Whoever acknowledges having had sexual intercourse with his slave woman is considered the father of any child she bears, even if he has practised *coïtus interruptus* with her, provided the child is born within a period of not less than six months and not more than the period of a pregnancy. This applies whether she bears the child during his lifetime or after his death, or after he has freed her, unless he claims that she underwent a period of waiting to ascertain absence of pregnancy, and that he did not thereafter have sexual intercourse with her. In such a case he is to be believed and the child is not to be considered his.

There is a difference of opinion as to whether he is to be believed as a result of swearing an oath, or without an oath, simply denying paternity without swearing that the woman has committed adultery (*liᶜān*). If she does not produce a child, but claims she gave birth to a child of his, she is not to be believed, and she will not be a "mother of a child" to him unless two women swear on her behalf that she gave birth to a child of his. If the master denies having had sexual intercourse with her and she brings two witnesses to testify against him, and produces a child, then rightly this constitutes his acknowledgement of having had sexual intercourse with her.

(7) POST-MORTEM MANUMISSION AND CLIENTSHIP

Source: The *Risāla* of Ibn Abī Zayd al-Qayrawānī (d. *c.* 996), with the commentary *Kifāyat al-ṭālib al-rabbānī* of Abū 'l-Ḥasan al-Mālikī and the supercommentary, *Ḥāshiya,* of ᶜAlī al-Ṣaᶜīdī al-ᶜAdawī (d. 1775) (Cairo: Muṣṭafā al-Bābī al-Ḥalabī, 1938), ii, 177–99 (summarized extracts).

It is fitting that he who has something to bequeath should draw up a will. There can be no bequest in favor of an heir. Bequests come out of the disposable one-third of the estate. Any bequests exceeding the one-third should be given back [to the designated heirs], unless they authorize otherwise. The specified manumission of a slave is to be dealt with before proceeding to bequests. [A declaration that] a slave is to be emancipated on the owner's death made when the owner was in good health takes precedence over a declaration made when he was [gravely] ill referring to manumission or other [dispositions regarding the slave, such as being given as a gift or a charitable donation]. It also takes precedence over the payment of outstanding alms-tax (*zakāt*) which a man decides to pay off from his estate. Such latter payments come out of the disposable third and take precedence over other bequests. A declaration of manumission on the owner's death made when the owner was in good health, however, takes precedence.

If the disposable one-third is insufficient [to cover all the bequests made], the legatees whose bequests have no precedence the one over the other, take proportionate shares. A man may annul a legacy, whether it involves manumission or any other matter.

The formula for declaring a slave free upon the master's death is: "You are *mudabbar*"[26] or "You are free after my demise." After this the master cannot sell him or give him away. The master may make use of the slave's services until he dies, at which point the slave is free. The master may confiscate his slave's possessions, so long as the slave is not [gravely] ill. The master may have sexual relations with his female slave, but he may not do so with one to whom manumission has been promised after a stated lapse of time, nor may he sell her. However, he may enjoy her labor and he has the right to confiscate her possessions, provided the time of her manumission is not close.

When a master dies the value of his *mudabbar* slave is considered part of the disposable one-third [of his estate], whereas the value of a slave to be emancipated after a fixed lapse of time is reckoned as a part of the total estate. The slave with whom a contract of manumission has been agreed remains a slave while he owes any portion [of the agreed price of his freedom]. A contract may be drawn up stipulating any sum of money agreed upon by the master and the slave, to be paid in installments, either few or many. If the slave becomes unable to pay, he becomes a simple slave again. What the master has taken from him [by way of installments] may lawfully be retained [by the master]. If a slave refuses [to acknowledge his insolvency] only the civil authority has the power to declare him insolvent [unilaterally] after first granting him a respite [during which he might become solvent].

The offspring of a woman [other than by her master] assume her status, whether she is a slave with whom a contract of manumission has been drawn up, a *mudabbar* slave, or one to be manumitted after a fixed lapse of time, or one who has been pledged. The child born to an *umm walad* (i.e. a slave woman who has already borne her master's child) fathered by someone other than her master shares his mother's rights and disabilities [if born after she became *umm walad*].

Patronage belongs to the one who manumits the slave, and it cannot be sold or given away. If a man frees the slave of another, clientage devolves upon the owner of the slave [not the one who emancipated him]. Clientage does not go to the man at whose hands a slave converts to Islam; it goes to the [community of] Muslims. If a woman emancipates a slave she becomes that slave's patron. She is also the patron of those attracted to this status, such as the child [of the freed slave] or [the slave's] slave. A woman does not inherit from a slave whom her father, her son, or her husband etc., freed. The inheritance of a slave [who is emancipated with the formula "You are like a camel] set free to roam" belongs to the community of Muslims. Patronage goes to the closest of the agnates of the dead man. If he leaves two sons they jointly inherit patronage of a client of their father. If one of these sons dies leaving two sons, the patronage goes back to the other brother rather than to the sons. If one of the two sons dies and leaves a male child, then the other dies leaving two children, the patronage is shared by these three equally.

• IV •

Perceptions of Africans in Some Arabic and Turkish Writings

Medieval Arab writers derived much of their initial understanding of Africa from translations of Greek works, notably the "Geography" of the 2nd-century Alexandrian Claudius Ptolemaeus. In this understanding the inhabited world was divided into seven latitudinal zones, the first being closest to the equator and the seventh near to the Arctic Circle. The middle zone, the fourth, corresponded to the Mediterranean lands, and was considered to be the ideal zone, whose inhabitants were the most civilized. The farther away one went from this zone, the more extreme the climate, and the more deviant from the Mediterranean "norm" the people became on account of the influence of the climate. Although this section initially focuses on medieval views of Africans, it is clear that some of these negative images of black people survived in some places into the nineteenth century.

* * * *

(1) THE SUN ALMOST BOILS THEIR BRAINS

Source: Shams al-Dīn Muḥammad b. Abī Ṭālib al-Dimashqī (d. 1327), *Nukhbat al-dahr fī ᶜajāᵓib al-barr wa ᵓl-baḥr,* ed. A. Mehren (Leipzig, 1923), 15–17, 273. This Syrian author was what may be called an "armchair geographer," who drew his information from earlier writers and from popular perceptions.

The equatorial region is inhabited by communities of Blacks who are to be numbered among the savages and beasts. Their complexions and hair are burnt and they are physically and morally deviant. Their brains almost boil from the sun's excessive heat. . . .

The human being who dwells there is a crude fellow, with a very black complexion, burnt hair, unruly, with stinking sweat, and an abnormal constitution, most closely resembling in his moral qualities a savage, or animals. He cannot dwell in the 2nd zone, let alone the 3rd and 4th, just as the people of the 1st zone live not in the 6th, nor those of the 6th in the 1st, or the equatorial region, because of the difference in the quality of the air and the heat of the sun. God knows best!

[p. 273] We shall now give an account of what has been said about the inhabitants of the seven zones in regard to their physique and their moral qualities, and the reasons for this. The 1st zone is from the equator, extending to what lies beyond it and behind it. It contains the following nations: the Zanj, the Sūdān, the Ḥabasha, the Nūba, etc. Their blackness is due to the sun . . . Since its heat is extreme and it rises over them and is directly over their heads twice in a year, and remains close to them, it gives them a burning heat, and their hair, pursuant to the natural processes, becomes jet-black, curly and peppercorn-like, closely resembling hair that has been brought close to a fire until it has become scorched. The most convincing proof that it is scorched is that it does not grow any longer. Their skins are hairless and smooth, since the sun cleans the filth from their bodies and draws it out. Their brains have little humidity for similar reasons and hence their intelligence is dim, their thoughts are not sustained, and their minds are inflexible, so that opposites, such as good faith and deceit, honesty and treachery, do not coexist among them. No divinely revealed laws have been found among them, nor has any divine messenger been sent among them, for they are incapable of handling opposites together, whereas divine laws consist of commanding and forbidding, and creating desire and fear. The moral characteristics found in their belief systems are close to the instincts found naturally in animals, which require no learning to bring them out of the realm of potentiality into that of reality, like the braveness to be found in a lion, and the cunning in a fox.

(2) NEGATIVE STEREOTYPES

Source: Yawānīs (al-Mukhtār b. al-Ḥasan b. ᶜAbdūn al-Baghdādī), generally known as Ibn Buṭlān, a Christian physician of Baghdad (11th cent.), *Risāla fī shirāʾ al-raqīq wa-taqlīb al-ᶜabīd*, ed. ᶜAbd al-Salām Muḥammad Hārūn in *Nawādir al-makhṭūṭāt*, vol. 4 (Cairo, 1954), 384. He gives stereotypical characterizations of the women of the various "races." Here he is discussing "Zanj" women, i.e. female slaves imported from East Africa.

The blacker they are, the uglier they are, the more pointed their teeth are, the less use they are and the more it is to be feared they will harm you. They are generally of bad character, and much given to running away. Their dispositions know no gloom. Dancing and rhythm are inborn in them and natural to them. Because of their inability to speak Arabic correctly, people turned to them for music (*zumr*)[27] and dancing. It is said that if a Zanjī fell down from heaven to earth he would surely do so to a beat. Their women have the most sparkling front teeth because of the abundance of their saliva produced by their bad digestions. They endure drudgery. A Zanjī who has been well fed can stand hard beating without feeling pain. No sexual pleasure is to be had from their women because of their smelly armpits and coarse bodies.

(3) RACE AND SLAVERY: THE HAMITIC MYTH

Source: Wahb b. Munabbih (d. 728), a south Arabian, of part Persian origin, who was considered an expert in Jewish legend. Translated from the text cited in Ibn Qutayba, *Kitāb al-Maᶜārif,* published in L.E. Kubbel & V.V. Matveev, *Arabskiye istochniki,* vol. 1 (Moscow-Leningrad, 1960), 21.

Ham, the son of Noah, was a white man, fair of face. God—Mighty and Exalted is He—changed his color and the color of his descendants because of the curse of his father. He went off and his offspring followed him and they settled on the sea shore. God increased and multiplied them, and they are the Blacks (*al-sūdān*). Their food was fish, so they sharpened their teeth until they left them like needles, since the fish used to stick in them. Some of his offspring settled in North Africa. Ham fathered Cush and Canaan and Fūṭ.[28] As for Fūṭ, he journeyed and settled in the lands of Hind and Sind,[29] and their people are of his offspring. As for Cush and Canaan, their descendants are various peoples of *sūdān*, and the Nuba, and the Zanj, and the Qurān,[30] and the Zaghāwa, the Ḥabasha, the Copts[31] and the Berbers.

* * * *

Ibn Khaldūn (d. 1406), perhaps the most original medieval Arab writer, sought to refute the genealogical arguments for blackness of skin which originate in the Hamitic myth and to replace them with a climate-based theory. The text below is translated by John Hunwick from Muqaddimat al-ᶜallāma Ibn Khaldūn, *Cairo: al-Maktaba al-Tijāriyya, n.d., 83–84.*

Some genealogists who had no knowledge of the true nature of beings imagined that the Blacks are the descendants of Ham, the son of Noah, and that they were characterized by black color as a result of a curse put upon him by his father (Noah), which manifested itself in Ham's color and the slavery that God inflicted upon his descendants. Concerning this they have transmitted an account arising from the legends of the story-tellers.

The curse of Noah upon his son is there in the Torah. No reference is made there to blackness. His curse was simply that Ham's descendants should be the slaves of his brothers' descendants.[32] To attribute the blackness of Negroes to Ham, shows disregard for the nature of heat and cold and the influence they exert upon the air and upon the creatures that come into being in it. That is to say that this color is common to the people of the 1st and 2nd zones through the mixing of their air with a heat doubled in the south, for the sun is directly over their heads twice a year at times close to one another. Thus the direct overheadness of the sun persists through most seasons, and because of this, light is abundant and extreme heat is constantly upon them, and their skins grow black because of the excessive heat. . . . The inhabitants of the southern two zones, the 1st and 2nd, go by the name of Ḥabasha and Zanj, though the name Ḥabasha refers specifically to those living opposite to Mecca and the Yemen, while Zanj refers to those facing the Indian Ocean. These names are not given to them because of their relationship to any black human being, whether Ham or otherwise.

* * * *

Despite Ibn Khaldūn's refutation of the Hamitic myth, the myth continued to have currency, as may be seen from a question put to Aḥmad Bābā of Timbuktu in the early 17th century. Although Aḥmad Bābā cites Ibn Khaldūn's refutation, his attitude towards Blacks is disparaging, or at best paternalistic.

Source: Aḥmad Bābā al-Tinbuktī (d. 1627), *Miᶜrāj al-ṣuᶜūd ilā nayl ḥukm majlūb al-sūd* ["The Ladder of Ascent towards grasping the Law concerning Transported Blacks"], replies written in 1615 in response to questions from Ibrāhīm al-Jirārī, an inquirer from the Saharan oasis of Tuwāt. Translation from John Hunwick and Fatima Harrak, *Miᶜrāj al-ṣuᶜūd: Aḥmad Bābā's Replies on Ethnicity and Slavery* (Rabat, 2000), 30–31. In the arguments made below, the term "unbelief" (and "unbelievers") is frequently used. "Unbelief" (*kufr*) simply means belonging to some faith other than Islam.

Question

What is the meaning of the *ḥadīth* mentioned by al-Suyūṭī in *Azhār al-ᶜurūsh fī akhbār al-ḥubūsh,*[33] when he said: "Ibn Masᶜūd[34] reported that Noah bathed and saw his son looking at him, and said to him, 'Are you watching me whilst I bathe? May God change your color!' And he became black, and he is the ancestor of the *sūdān.*[35] Ibn Jarīr [al-Ṭabarī][36] said: 'Noah prayed for Shem that his descendants should be prophets and messengers, and he cursed Ham, praying that his descendants should be slaves to Shem and Japheth.'" What is the meaning of Ham's descendants being slaves to the descendants of Shem and Japheth? If what is meant is the unbelievers among them, then [being slaves] is not confined to them, nor similarly is [ownership of slaves] confined to his two brothers Shem and Japheth, since the unbeliever is allowed to be owned whether he is black or white. What is the significance of restricting slavery through conquest to the Blacks (*al-sūdān*), despite the fact that others share with them the status that gives rise to that? Explain to us the aspect of wisdom [in this]—may yours be the reward.

Aḥmad Bābā's Reply

As regards the *ḥadīth* which you cited from Jalāl al-Dīn al-Suyūṭī's *Azhār al-ᶜurūsh fī akhbār al-ḥubūsh,* coming from the *ḥadīth* of al-Ḥākim,[37] on the authority of Ibn Masᶜūd, that Noah was bathing and saw his son looking at him and said to him, "Are you watching me bathe? May God change your color!" and he became black and is the ancestor of the *sūdān*—I came across it myself in his book entitled *Rafᶜ shaᵓn al-ḥubshān* ["Raising the status of the Ethiopians"], and the actual words are: "As for the blackness of their skins, Ibn al-Jawzī[38] said: 'It is evident that they were created as they are without any apparent reason.' However, we narrate [the following account]: 'The children of Noah divided up the earth and the children of Shem settled at the centre of the earth and they had amongst them both darkness of skin and whiteness. The sons of Japheth settled in a northerly and in an easterly direction, and they had amongst them both redness and blondness. The sons of Ham settled in the south and in the west, and their colors changed'. Ibn al-Jawzī said: 'As for what is related about Noah's nakedness being exposed and Ham not covering it and being cursed, this is something not proven and is not correct.'"[39]

Al-Jalāl al-Suyūṭī[40] said: "I say: This is supported by what Umm al-Faḍl informed me of through [my] study [with her, saying] Abū Isḥāq al-Thaᶜālibī told us [saying] Abū 'l-Ḥasan al-Dāwudī told us [saying] Abū Muḥammad al-Sarakhsī told us [saying] Abū Isḥāq al-Shāsī told us [saying] ᶜAbd Allāh b. Ḥumayd told us [saying] Hūd b. Khalīfa told us [saying] ᶜAwf b. Qasāma told us on the authority of Zuhayr who said: 'I heard al-Ashᶜarī[41] say: "The Messenger of God—may God bless him and grant him peace—said: 'Ādam was created from a handful [of earth] which [God] took from all parts of the world. Hence his offspring turned out according to the earth [they were made from]; some came out red, others white, others black, some were easy-going, others downcaste, some were evil and others good.' This is a sound *ḥadīth* published by al-Ḥākim in *al-Mustadrak,* and it is to be relied upon in [the matter of] the blackness of their colour, for it is a reversion to the clay from which they were created. As for what Ibn al-Jawzī denied, Ibn Jarīr [al-Ṭabarī] published it in his History.[42] He said: 'Salama told us on the authority of Ibn Isḥāq who said: "The people of the Torah claim that this only came about through a curse uttered by Noah against Ham. It happened that Noah slept and his nakedness was uncovered, and Ham saw it and did not cover it up. Shem and Japheth saw it and cast a cloth upon it and covered up his nakedness. When he awoke he realised what Ham had done and what Shem and Japheth had done and he made mention of it. Amongst what he said was: 'He,' that is Shem, 'is blessed and Ham shall be a slave to his two brothers.'" Ibn Jarīr continued: 'Others than Ibn Isḥāq said that Noah prayed that the prophets and messengers should come from Shem's progeny, and he prayed that kings should come from Japheth's descendants, and he cursed Ham saying that his color should be changed and his descendants should be slaves of the descendants of Shem and Japheth.'"'" End of quotation [from *Raf^c sha$^{\circ}$n al-ḥubshān*].

You asked: "What is the meaning of Ham's children being slaves to the children of Japheth and Shem? If he meant the unbelievers, then this is not a peculiarity of theirs.[43] On the contrary, it is so in regard to the children of his brothers Japheth and Shem, since unbelief allows their being possessed [as slaves], whether they are black or white." The Reply is that the legal position is like that. This is not a peculiarity of theirs. Indeed, any unbeliever among the children of Ham or anyone else may be possessed [as a slave] if he remains attached to his original unbelief. There is no difference between one race and another. Perhaps it was that his curse was effective on most of them, not all of them. In the Ḥadīth [we read]: "I prayed my Lord not to destroy my comunity by drought, and he granted me that" [etc.], down to where he said: "I called on my Lord not to let troubles occur amongst them, and he denied me that," etc.

As for the Ḥadīth: "Look after the *sūdān*, for among them are three of the lords of Paradise,"[44] there is a command in it to look after them, so that people would not dislike them on account of some of their objectionable characteristics, and their general lack of refinement. The Prophet only gave such a command—though God alone knows best—and encouraged people to observe it, because of the rapidity with which the *sūdān* are subdued and become obedient, and are driven in whichever direction they are led, and the speed with which they embrace Islam, so that there might well be among them lords like those elect Muslims or similarly others of their lords. Al-Jalāl al-Suyūṭī enumerated many of them in his book *Raf*ᶜ *sha*ʾ*n al-ḥubshān.*

As for the *ḥadīth*: "Your brothers are your slaves," it contains an admonition to be kind and compassionate to him among them who is owned, as well as others, and to treat him kindly and compassionately, since the mere fact of being owned generally breaks one's heart, because dominance and subordination are associated with this condition, especially when one is far from home. [As the poet said] "The stranger who is decked out in finery is [nevertheless] regarded with disdain."

For all men are the sons of Adam. Hence [the Prophet] said: "God caused you to own him, and had He so wished, He would have caused him to own you," or words to that effect, to make you aware of the fact that He made his favor to you complete through Islam, and that He afflicted the slave, or his forebears, with unbelief up to [the time when] he was captured. God knows best.

(4) BLACK EQUALS SLAVE

*The slaves that Moroccans were consistently familiar with over the centuries were black Africans, and the view became widespread that they were "natural" slaves. The Moroccan ruler Mūlāy Ismā*ᶜ*īl (1668–1727) argued that all blacks resident in Morocco were unfree, being merely runaway slaves who had attached themselves to new patrons. He claimed they made good soldiers because they were naturally subservient and long-suffering. In fact, his pressed recruitment of blacks was indicriminate, even including the* ḥarāṭīn *—free, or freed, black men originally from the northern Saharan oases who had migrated into Moroccan cities.*

Source: *Kunnāsha* of Sultan Mūlāy ᶜAbd al-Ḥafīẓ, entitled *Dāᵓ al-ᶜaṭb al-qadīm*, ms. 400-11z, Royal Library (al-Khizāna al-Ḥasaniyya), Rabat. This extract concerns the reign of Mūlāy Ismāᶜīl (1672–1727).

We found that free men in this age were unsuitable for military service on several counts, notably because they were overcome by inborn idleness, weakness, greed and sensual desires. . . . We therefore left them to earn their livelihood, to pursue their interests, and to pay taxes to the treasury. We turned to those slaves and purchased them from their owners after searching for them and investigating them in accordance with the law and the observed *sunna*s. We found that many of these slaves were runaways who had deserted their owners and escaped from their control. Every one of them bore the runaway mark and was known by it, either through his father or his paternal or maternal grandparents. . . . These runaways would attach themselves to other masters or to tribes, or become part of the entourage of shaykhs or big men commanding clan solidarity (*kabīr dh*[*ū*] *ᶜaṣabiyya*), and defraud their owners who had [the right] of [their] clientship and were the original owners. Thus they became dispersed throughout the lands and regions, especially during times of dearth and turmoil when the shadow of the caliphate receded from these western regions, until famines and the passing of years consumed many of those slaves. This, despite the fact that they are originally unbelieving blacks, imported from over there through purchase from those who neighbor them and raid them and campaign against them.

* * * *

The notion that black Africans were by nature slaves appears to have persisted in the popular view.

Source: A late 19th-century writer from West Africa, Muḥammad al-Sanūsī b. Ibrāhīm al-Jārimī, in his *Tanbīh ahl al-ṭughyān ᶜalā ḥurriyyat al-sūdān*, reported on Moroccan attitudes towards black Africans. His work is preserved at the Centre Ahmad Baba, Timbuktu, MS no. 1575.

When I traveled to the land of the Farther Maghrib [Morocco] . . . I found some of the uncouth Maghribīs claiming that all blacks without exception were slaves who did not deserve to be free, for how should they deserve that, being black of skin? On this matter they relate fantasies that have no foundation to them in law or the natural order. As for the law, nothing came down from the Lawgiver[45] that would explain why among all peoples they should be enslaved rather than others. With regard to nature, [such an argument is unacceptable] because the natural order rejects blacks being slaves without a compelling legal reason.

* * * *

Such racist views were, however, strongly condemned by a contemporary Moroccan, Aḥmad b. Khālid al-Nāṣirī, using arguments based in religious law.

(5) AN ATTACK ON RACIAL BIAS IN SLAVERY IN MOROCCO

Source: Aḥmad b. Khālid al-Nāṣirī, *Kitāb al-istiqṣāʾ li-akhbār duwal al-maghrib al-aqṣā* (Casablanca, 1955), V, 131–34. The *Kitāb al-istiqṣāʾ is* a chronicle of Moroccan history from early Islamic times until the late 19th century. The passage below follows an account of the Muslim kingdoms of West Africa, concluding with the Moroccan conquest of Songhay in 1591 and the exile to Morocco of Aḥmad Bābā and other Timbuktu scholars.

It will be clear to you from what we have related of the history of the Sūdān[46] how far the people of these lands had taken to Islam from ancient times. It will also be clear that they are among the best peoples in regard to Islam, the most religiously upright, the most avid for learning and the most devoted to men of learning. This state of affairs is to be found in most of their kingdoms bordering on the Maghrib, as you are aware.

Thus will be apparent to you the heinousness of the affliction that has beset the lands of the Maghrib since ancient times in regard to the indiscriminate enslavement of the people of the Sūdān and the importation of droves of them every year to be sold in the market places in town and country, where men trade in them as one would trade in beasts—nay worse than that. People have become so inured to that, generation after generation, that many common folk believe that the reason for being enslaved according to the Holy Law is merely that a man should be black in color and come from those regions. This, by God's life, is one of the foulest and gravest evils perpetrated upon God's religion, for the people of the Sūdān are Muslims having the same rights and responsibilities as ourselves.

Even if you assume that some of them are pagans or belong to a religion other than Islam, nevertheless the majority of them today as in former times are Muslims, and judgment is made according to the majority. Again, even if you suppose that Muslims are not a majority, and that Islam and unbelief claim equal membership there, who among us can tell whether those brought here are Muslims or unbelievers? For the basic assumption in regard to the human species is freedom and lack of any cause for being enslaved. Whoever maintains the opposite is denying the basic principle.

No confidence should be placed in what the slave-traders or dealers say, since it is established and well-known that all sellers lie about their goods when selling them and praise them lavishly for qualities they do not possess. Slave dealers are even more prone to do that. How could we believe them when we see that those who import them or deal in them are men of no morals, no manly qualities, and no religion, and when we know the [evil nature of the] times and see [the wickedness of] their people?

Nor should any reliance be put upon the protestations of a slave man or woman, as the jurists have ruled, since motives and circumstances differ in this regard. A seller may do them so much ill that they would not admit to anything that would affect their sale. Or a slave may have the objective of getting out of the hands of his master by any possible means, thus finding it easy to admit to slave status so that the sale may be promptly effected. Other motives may also exist.

Men of integrity and others have frequently made the point that the people of the [*bilād al-*] *Sūdān* today as in former times make war on one another and kidnap each other's children, enslaving them in places far removed from their tribal homes or inhabited places, and that in this they are like the nomadic Arabs of the Maghrib who raid one another and drive off or steal each other's flocks and herds out of lack of religious principles and the absence of anything that restrains them. How then can a man who has scruples about his religion permit himself to buy something of this nature? How, too, can he allow himself to take their women as concubines considering that this involves entering upon a sexual liaison of dubious legality?

Abū Ḥāmid al-Ghazālī, may God be pleased with him, said in the section "The Lawful and the Forbidden" of his *Iḥyāʾ ʿulūm al-din:* "Be aware that in regard to food brought to you as a gift, or that you wish to purchase or accept as a present, it is not up to you to institute inquiries about it and say that since it is something the lawfulness of which you cannot ascertain you will not take it without inquiring about it. Nor yet should you dispense with inquiry and merely accept all things whose forbidden nature you cannot determine. On the contrary, sometimes inquiry is obligatory, sometimes it is forbidden, sometimes recommended and sometimes objectionable. Therefore a distinction must be made [between the various cases]. The clear rule is that the existence of areas of doubt provides the presumption for inquiry." He went on to explain this at length—may God be pleased with him—and made it clear that if the seller is suspected of trying to promote the sale of his goods, then his word should not be relied on. If this is true about goods, then how much more is it true about the enslavement of human beings and mastery over women's genitalia, for both of which matters the Lawgiver had even greater concern, as is well known from the Holy Law and its sources.

Shaykh Aḥmad Bābā, in the treatise he set forth on this question entitled *Miʿrāj al-ṣuʿūd,*[47] produced an analysis with which he concluded the work, mentioning those tribes of the Sudan who were unbelievers, such as the Mossi, some of the Fulani and others. He stated that it was permissible to enslave anybody who came from those tribes. Ibn Khaldūn also said: "Beyond the Nīl[48] are a black people called Lamlam. They are unbelievers who brand their faces and their temples." He also said: "The people of Ghāna and Takrūr raid them, make them captive and sell them to merchants who carry them off to the Maghrib. These people make up the greater part of their slaves and beyond them to the south is no inhabited land of any consequence."

But this analysis which Shaykh Aḥmad Bābā made is only valid in so far as the people of the lands which border them are concerned and those who come across slaves brought from among them and others [beyond them]. As for the people of the Maghrib who are "beyond what is beyond" [in relation to such peoples] and between whom and the land of the Sudan is a wide waterless desert and a wilderness inhabited only by the wind, who can ascertain the facts for them? We have already said that no confidence should he placed upon what the slave-traders say, and who among us can tell whether those tribes still remain pagan? Moreover, people nowadays pay no heed at all to this, and whenever they see a slave put up for sale in the market they go ahead and buy him, ignoring all this. The only questions they put concern bodily defects, and in this matter it makes no difference whether the slave is black or white or any other color. Worse than that, in these days the evildoer and those who flout God, kidnap freeborn children in the tribes, villages and cities of the Maghrib and sell them openly in the markets without anyone showing resentment or being angered on behalf of the religion. Jews and Christians have begun to buy them and to enslave them with our full knowledge, and this is a punishment to us from God, were we but to reflect. God help us for the affliction which has overtaken us in the matter of our religion.

To sum up: since, as we have said, the basic human condition is freedom, and since it has been known from age to age that the people of the Sudan who border on us are mostly or wholly Muslims, and since men of integrity and others have frequently made the point that they make war on each other and kidnap each other's children and sell them unjustly, and we have seen with our own eyes that the slave merchants and dealers are men of no morals and no religion, we should have no hesitation in declaring that anyone who enters into a transaction of this forbidden nature is imperiling his salvation. As for [the argument] that the slave-traders have laid hand upon them, this is not a sufficient reason in Holy Law to allow one to enter into the purchase of slaves from them, since it is a weak indication [of validity] surrounded by pieces of factual evidence which give it the lie. Let a man therefore question his heart, for the Prophet, may God bless him and grant him peace, said: "Question your heart even if they [the jurists] give you a decision." For if one refers to one's heart over this dilemma one can scarcely hesitate over this burning question at all.

And now, leaving all that aside, we would say that even if there were no more than a strong doubt in this matter, coupled with the evilness of the times and the frivolity of its people in matters of religion, there would be in these three factors plus a care for preventive action, which is a principle of the Holy Law, especially in the view of Mālik, may God be pleased with him, sufficient to oblige one to cease having anything to do with an evil which is derogatory to honor and religion. We ask God to give success to him whom He has charged with the affairs of his servants in bringing to an end this wickedness.

For the reason in Holy Law which existed in the time of the Prophet and the pious forefathers for enslaving people does not exist today; that is being taken prisoner in a *jihād* which has as its object to make the word of God supreme and to bring men to His religion which he chose for His servants. This is our religion which was brought to us as law by our Prophet—may God bless him and grant him peace. What is in opposition to it is in opposition to the religion, and what is other than it is something not laid down by Holy Law, and success is in God's hand alone. "Lord, we have wronged ourselves, and if You do not pardon us and have mercy upon us we shall be among those who suffer [eternal] loss."[49]

* * * *

Not all Mediterranean Muslim views of Africans were as negative as some of those above. The following view by a 19th-century

Turkish woman of the elite class displays some sympathy and understanding, though the overall tone is paternalistic, and she admits to viewing black girls as exotic curios.

(6) A 19TH-CENTURY TURKISH WOMAN'S VIEW

Source: Leïla Hanoum, *Le Harem impériale au XIXᵉ siècle*, version française par son fils, Youssouf Razi (orig. published Constantinople, 1920–21, as a newspaper serial; first published in French in 1922, repr. n.p. [Brussels]: Editions Complexe, 1991), 85–86.

My readers will perhaps find that I have a peculiar taste, but I will not hide the fact that I like negresses very much. Their black skin, white teeth, fuzzy hair, their somewhat gauche manners please me and amuse me in the manner of an exotic curio. Moreover, I have compassion for these poor creatures disdained by everyone simply because their skin is black, these beings worthy of pity and sympathy by all because they have been violently snatched from their country and have been transplanted into a milieu so completely different from their own, in a country whose very climate is inhospitable to them.

People commonly say that the intelligence of forty negresses would not fill a fig seed. I claim that this allegation is simply a jest at variance with the truth, and I am going to give examples of several negresses I have known who are second to no other slaves in intelligence and moral aptitude.[50] I find it unjust to jokingly make accusations against other human beings who only differ from us in the color of their skins. Moreover, how can one demand proofs of intelligence of these unfortunate beings who, in their own country have grown up with some of the most limited mental horizons, with few ideas and little actual knowledge, and who, at Constantinople, are never allowed to see anything else but their kitchen stove? Would we ourselves dare to claim that, in our mature age, we could easily assimilate education and civilization if we, like the negresses, had spent our whole life up to now in the same narrow and limited horizons without any contact with the [wider] world?

The mental capacity of these unfortunate creatures has remained repressed and numbed beneath a thick envelope, and has had neither the leisure nor the means to develop. Those who reach Constantinople at a relatively advanced age seem to be narrow-minded and stupid; but those who arrive really young are very full of curiosity and have a desire to learn everything. They succeed in this, moreover, when they are well supervised and when one takes the trouble to pay attention to them.

◆ V ◆

Slave Capture

Although, from the point of view of Islamic law, the sole method of acquiring slaves at source was through capture as prisoners in a jihād, *most African slaves were obtained through non-religious wars, or by deliberate raiding, either by state organized expeditions or by private enterprise. Either way, it was a very cruel, and often murderous, activity, as the accounts below illustrate.*

* * * *

(1) OFFICIAL RAIDING, SUDAN 1838

Source: Extracts from an account by Ignatius Pallme, in R.R. Madden, *Egypt and Mohammed Ali, illustrative of the Condition of his Slaves and Subjects, &c. &c.* (London, 1841), 156–59. Pallme was an Austrian trader who went to Egypt as a merchant, and traveled into the Sudan in 1837. He accompanied an expedition sent by the Turkish governor of Kordofan to the Nuba mountains in 1838 to capture slaves for the army.

Towards the end of the year 1838, the Viceroy ordered the province of Cordofan to procure 5,000 slaves. At the end of the month of November of that year, the ordered corps consisting of 2,400 foot, 750 Mograbini,[51] 200 irregular horse, 300 riders on dromedaries, and 1200 country people, armed with shields and lances, with three cannon, commenced their march. As it was impossible to procure the whole number of camels in the short period that remained before their march, many being required to carry water, tents, &c., two of the infantry received but one camel between them. Provision and cattle, as well as the necessary provender for the horses, were provided only for a few days, expecting afterwards to obtain what was necessary by robbery and plunder.

A mountain that had suffered materially in former years from the troops of Mohammed Ali, as well as from the rapacious Bakkara,[52] and was almost dispeopled, being one of the first in the territories of free Nubia,[53] was first commanded to surrender. The Sheik readily descended into the camp and surrendered himself with all his subjects, consisting of 196 souls; he himself was set free and presented with a dress; but the Sheba[54] was fastened round the necks of the young men; and on the following day all the prisoners were transported to Lobeid.[55] The Sheik himself told me that about eighteen years ago, when the Turks went there for the first time, the population of his mountain amounted to more than 3000 souls; but on account of the annual tribute of slaves, which was always tenfold increased by the dissatisfied Turks, the number had been reduced to 196. These prisoners were treated humanely, and no suicide took place amongst them. They saw the impossibility of offering resistance, and became reconciled to their hard lot. Having found only a small store of provisions with the poor people of Dohna the bread of the troops soon failed, and they were obliged to advance. An attack was made upon the next mountain, but the soldiers were sadly disappointed in their expectations, when they found all empty. The inhabitants had been apprised of the arrival of the expedition, and had fled with all their goods and cattle; nothing but their empty huts remained, to which the soldiers in their anger set fire, and entirely destroyed everything they discovered.

They then proceeded to the third mountain. The inhabitants firmly resolved to defend their liberty at any price, and were willing rather to suffer death than deliver themselves into the hands of the Turks; they put forth all their strength, in order to make a desperate resistance. The village was stormed, but the negroes repulsed their enemy several times. After repeated attacks, however, it was at last taken; and then a horrible scene presented itself to the view of the spectator. Out of the 500 souls that inhabited the village, only 188 were found alive. All the huts were filled with the corpses of young and old, many of those who had not perished in the battle with their arms in their hands, killed themselves in order to escape slavery. The prisoners were all led away, the place ransacked, and the corpses left unburied, which presented a fearful scene of desolation upon the return of the few who had been fortunate enough to save themselves by flight.

(2) A SAHARAN RAID ON HAUSALAND

Source: Selected extracts from F.J.G. Mercadier, *L'Esclave de Timimoun* (Paris: Edition France-Empire, 1971; translated by permission), 13–19. Mercadier was commandant of Timimoun, the chief locality of the Saharan oasis of Gourara, from July 1944 to the end of 1947, a post he took up after serving as a *méhariste*, or camel corps commander, in the French Algerian Sahara. He says that he spoke Arabic and some Tamasheq. His book is derived from extensive discussions with Griga, a former slave, then in his late 90s, who worked in the oasis gardens of a certain Si Hamou ben Abdelkader, and died in 1945. Mercadier remarks that, despite Griga's advanced age, his memory was excellent, and Mercadier was often able to confirm some of what he was told from printed and archival sources. He calculated that Griga was born around 1847–48. At the time of his capture he is thought to have been about fourteen, and had already begun to make payments for a bride. For the complete narrative, see below, pp. 199–219.

I was born of a Fulani woman who was the slave of a relative of the chief of Matankari.[56] When I was captured by the Tuareg I was about fourteen years old. I was good-looking then, with large bright eyes encircled by long lashes. People said I was so handsome that my mother must have slept with a Tuareg noble. But she was also very beautiful.

Matankari was an important regional market. Our huts had straw roofs, and around them waste matter thrown out from the market piled up, stinking terribly and attracting hordes of dogs. But we were not poor, you know; around the village and in the entire valley we had very good harvests of millet, tobacco, huge sweet onions, cassava, peanuts, and indigo.

The day when I was captured there was a windstorm from the south which stirred up eddies of sand, darkening the air. We were exhausted by this sandstorm mixed with red dust which penetrated everything. Nevertheless, it was necessary to go and fetch water. So, at sunset when the storm seemed to have died down, the women emerged and went from hut to hut calling each other to go together to the wells, accompanied by any young person capable of carrying a water pot. We went there as a group, above all to tell, or to listen to, the village gossip, and to see the girls.

So we went off all together, laughing and chattering, towards the water holes. It was almost night, and we began drawing water to fill our pots, whilst some sat awaiting their turn. Suddenly a party of Tuareg threw themselves on us, shouting, gesticulating and brandishing spears and swords. Though we were initially stunned, a rapid getaway ensued, everyone trying to escape as best he could. The Tuareg tried to encircle us. Turning round we saw our village burning. Panic-stricken we did not know where to head for. My friend Makoko tried to escape by slipping in between two Tuaregs, but one of them saw him and nailed him to the ground with a spear and Makoko shrieked in pain. Another, a eunuch of the chief, had his arm severed by a sword. The Tuareg surrounded us, herding us together with blows of spear shafts, the flat side of swords, and riding crops.

The attackers hurried us off northwards until we reached a depression where there were other Tuareg, some Arabs, and some camels. They counted us, and quickly tied our hands together with previously soaked ropes of goat hair. Altogether we were 43 women, 20 young men and fifteen children of both sexes. Four old women who were with us, and whom I did not include in the above number, quite simply had their throats cut. The eunuch who had been wounded in the arm with a sword was finished off with a dagger to the stomach. In this way they would not raise the alarm.

Without further ado we set off northwards, more or less in the direction of Forkas.[57] Those driving us went on foot and hit us with their riding crops to make us move faster. Others were mounted on riding camels, in front, behind, and on both sides. In this way they could watch over us and spot any enemy who might want to take their catch away.

Towards midday [the next day] the raiding party halted in an endless plain completely devoid of vegetation to let us breathe a bit. On the horizon in the north I thought I could make out a small line of dunes. The Arabs and Tuareg again gave us a little water, but it was not enough to quench our thirst, since we had walked almost a whole night and half a day without stopping.

Off again! The women dragged their feet painfully. Blows rained thick and fast on exposed backs; the slowness of our pace annoyed the raiders, who displayed some nervousness. Suddenly the convoy halted, and there was a dense swirl of dust. Koka, the Bornu woman, one of our neighbors in Matankari, had just collapsed. The woman she was attached to crouched passively awaiting the decision of the masters.

"Leave her to die," shouted an Arab called Ali (I knew his name because he appeared to be the leader of the Arabs, who called him Ali Laouar, because he was one-eyed).[58] The Tuareg were angry. They did not want to abandon her. She was young and represented a lot of money. Finally, after many shouts and curses, they hauled her up onto a camel and the march resumed.

(3) SLAVE RAIDING TO PAY OFF MERCHANTS

Source: An account of a caravan led by a Tuareg caravan leader Cheggueun, as told by a member of the caravan to Gen. E. Daumas, and published in his *Le Grand Désert. Itinéraire d'une caravane du Sahara au pays des négres, royaume de Haoussa* (4th edition, Paris, 1860), 199–247 (selected extracts). The events described below probably occurred in the early 1830s.

We had been at Katsina for ten days, and the story having got around in the surrounding villages that a rich caravan had arrived, all the petty merchants had hastened to the town. Moreover, since those of Katsina were pressing us, it was decided to put our merchandise on sale, and Cheggueun went to tell Omar[59] what we intended to do. The response of the serki[60] was that we could do as we liked, but that he would reserve the sale of all our broadcloths, in the name of the sultan. His oukil[61] made a list the same day and took us to the palace to discuss the price with the serki himself.

"Khabir,"[62] said Omar to our chief, "according to what my agent has told me, the broadcloths of your merchants are of inferior quality and are worth no more than a single slave, negro or negress, per cubit."[63] "Sir, it shall be done according to your justice. We are your servants," replied Cheggueun, and we all put our fist on our chest as a sign of consent, for in fact we were getting a good deal. Our cloths cost us only two boujoux (3 fr. 60 c.) per cubit. We would have sold them twenty for about 36 fr; at this price a slave is not too dear. "Go in peace, then," replied the serki, "I do not have enough slaves to pay you today. But, by the grace of God, Mohammed Omar shall not fail in his word."

As we went out of the palace a regular low pitched sound, reminding me of the cannons of Abd el Kader at the siege of Aîn Mahdy,[64] caught our attention. It came from the center of the town and we made for it. It led us to the Makhzen[65] square where, from every street, a crowd came running like us. But the chaouchs[66] guarded the edges and would not let anyone penetrate the interior of the Mekhazenia. At the center of the square was placed a huge drum which a strapping Negro beat with a knobbed stick with all his might. This drum, which is called *tenbery* [Hausa: *tambari*], is covered with the skin of a "wild camel"[67] and two symmetrical holes are put in it in the upper part of its barrel to give greater sonority to the sound which comes out of it and which, if one believes the Negroes, is heard at a distance of two days' journey. This is the sultan's drum. It is never beaten for anything but assembling the army.

We had the secret of the strange noise that had moved us, and this proclamation of the chief of the Mekhazenia informed us for what purpose they were gathered: "This is the will of the serki. In the name of sultan Bello the Victorious,[68] may God bless him, all of you, people of the *Moutanin,*[69] are summoned to present yourselves here at daybreak, armed and mounted, with sufficient provisions to go, some to Zenfra[70] and others to Zendeur[71] to hunt the idolatrous Koholanes[72]—enemies of the glorious sultan our master—may God curse them." "All that the sultan orders is good," responded the soldiers, "Let it be done according to the will of our lord and master."

The Slave Raid

The following day, in fact, the Mekhazenia, prompt to the appointed meeting, divided themselves into two "goums,"[73] one taking the east and the other the southwest with orders to attack places without defenses and to carry off the inhabitants as well as seizing all peasants busy cultivating their fields. At the same time orders were given to track down the idolatrous Koholanes in the interior.

Trading in Katsina

Omar's promises were thus to be realised and, according to custom, we presented him, as a token of our gratitude, a piece of cotton fabric, four pounds of cloves, four pounds of benzoin,[74] some sembel,[75] six mirrors, six chachia[76] and some beads for his wives and children.

In the days that followed we entered into relations with the merchants of Katsina and surrounding settlements.

[There follow lists of principal items sold and purchased with prices paid in Algeria in "boujoux" and sales in Katsina in cowries and then purchases in Katsina in cowries and sale prices in Algeria in "boujoux."]

Silver coinage is not used at all in the Sudan.[77] Jewish jewellers convert it into bracelets, rings, etc. All commercial transactions take place through exchange or by *oudâas.*[78] Cowries, I am told, are taken from the Bahar en-Nil[79] which flows ten days west of Katsina. The sultan has organized a customs system which prevents individuals from bringing them to the interior without paying enormous dues. He has the monopoly.

The weights of the Negroes are the same as ours. There is no merchant who does not have balances or even a steelyard in his store, brought to them long ago by the caravans and no doubt by Arabs who have been resident among them for a long time. Measurements of volume are made with dried calabashes for oil, butter, etc.; for grains in wood.[80]

Whilst waiting for the return of the goums that Omar had dispatched to hunt Negroes, we went every day to the slave market, *Barka,* where we bought at the following prices:

A Negro with beard	10 or 15,000 cowries

They are not considered as merchandise since one has little chance of preventing them from escaping.

An adult Negress, same price for the same reasons:	10 or 15,000 cowries
An adolescent Negro	30,000 cowries
A young Negress	50–60,000 cowries

The price varies according to whether she is more or less beautiful.

A male Negro child	45,000 cowries
A female Negro child	35–40,000 cowries

The seller gives the buyer the greatest possible chance to examine the slaves and one has three days to give notice of concealed faults. Before that time one may return the following:

> One whose ankles damage one another when walking.
> One whose umbilical cord is too protruding.
> One whose eyes or teeth are in a bad state.
> One who dribbles like a child when asleep.
> A Negress who has the same defect or who snores.
> A male or female whose hair is short and in "*plique*" [81]

Moreover, one never purchases those who, for example, suffer from a peculiar sickness that is called seghemmou.[82] Seghemmou is a pustule which appears on the legs, arm or neck and which has at its end a sort of filament-like thread which has to be drawn out with caution, winding it round a piece of wood as one would do to thread on a bobbin, for if it breaks during the operation the Negro either dies or fails to get better or remains disabled. These threads are sometimes twelve or fifteen feet long.

Purchasing Slaves

One does not purchase those who, being grown up, have not been circumcised.[83] Nor does one purchase those who come from a certain land to the south of Nupe, since they have never eaten salt and they do not take well to a forced change of diet. Nor does one buy a particular species that comes from the south of Kano. They are cannibals and can be recognized by their teeth which they sharpen and are pointed like dog's teeth—we would be afraid for our children. Moreover, they eat without distaste animals that have died a natural death (djifa [*jīfa*] carcasses). They consider us pagans because we desire only animals bled in accordance with the law, for they say "You eat what you have killed and refuse to eat what God has killed."[84] Neither do we purchase those called Kabine el Aakoul. They are reputed to have the power to drain a man's health by looking at him and to cause him to die of consumption.[85] They are recognized by their having their hair twisted into two long braids on either side of the head.

The purchase of Fulanis, pregnant Negresses and Jewish Negroes[86] is strictly prohibited by the order of the sultan. The purchase of Fulanis is forbidden because they claim to be white, pregnant Negresses because the child they give birth to will be the property of the sultan if he is an idolator, and will be free if he is a Muslim; Jewish Negroes because they are all jewellers, tailors, useful artisans or indispensable go-betweens for commercial transactions, for beneath the skin in both the Sudan, in the Sahara and along the coast Jews everywhere have the same instincts and the twin gift of languages and business.[87]

To avoid cheating, no caravan leaves Hausaland without the slaves it is carrying having been closely examined, and the same is true at Tassaoua, Damergou, at Agades and among the Tuareg where Bello has agents who are responsible for the same tasks. Any merchant who went against his orders would expose himself to having all his merchandise confiscated.[88]

To sum up: slaves come from raids made on the neighboring Negro states with which Hausa is at war, and into the mountains of the land from where the Koholanes who have refused to recognize the Muslim religion are brought back,[89] and seizure of those who, having embraced the new religion, seem to hanker after their old one and are hostile to authority and commit certain misdeeds.

The Return of Omar's Goum

The goum of serki Omar had been on campaign for about a month when we learnt from a messenger that the double raid launched against Zinder and Zamfara had been completely successful and that the makhzen, bringing back two thousand slaves, would return to Katsina the next day. In a few hours this good news had spread throughout the town and at daybreak the next day the entire population crowded the gardens on the east side where the two armies that had the previous day joined up at Itooua ought to arrive.

A cloud of dust soon announced it and as they crossed the outer wall where the route was better marked and the terrain more solid, their confused mass began to make itself out from the veil of sand that they had raised on the plain. The prisoners walked at the head, men, women, children, the elderly, almost all naked or half covered in rags of blue cloth. The women and the elderly were unbound but tightly packed together; the children were piled onto camels with some sitting on their mothers' backs in a piece of cloth doing duty as a bag. The men had been chained, five or six to the same chain (el-aanaguya),[90] their necks fixed in a strong iron ring closed by a padlock and their hands bound with palm ropes. The strongest and most resistant were tied down to the tails of horses. Women moaned and children cried. Men, in general, seemed more resigned, but the bloody cuts that the whip had made on their shoulders bore witness to their tough struggle with the horsemen of the serki.

The convoy steered itself towards the palace of the kalifat[91] and its arrival was announced to Mohammed Omar by musicians, some playing the *fanfanay,*[92] others the *moulou,*[93] the *gouguy,*[94] the *karâaz,* while yet others beat the *tassa namouny*[95] and the *ganga.*[96] The fanfany is a buffalo horn which produces a low monotone; the moulou is a violin with two strings made of goat gut which is plucked with the thumb and first finger and whose sound resembles the cooing of a pigeon. The goguey is similar to the moulou in form but it only has one string of horse hair which is scraped by a bow of the same material. The karâaz is simply a reed flute with six holes on the upper side and one underneath. The tassa namouny is a long flared earthenware tube the end of which is wider and provided with a goat skin on which one beats the rhythm with the fingers; it is the derbouka of the Arabs. The ganga is a drum which is beaten with a hand on one end and with a curved stick on the other.

At the first sound of the music the serki came out of his palace followed by his agent and some dignitaries. On seeing him all the slaves threw themselves on their knees and the musicians attacked their instruments with a passion that bordered on fury. But the one who beat the tassa namouny, who was both the leader of the group and its improviser, silenced it with a gesture, took a few steps towards Omar and began to sing in guenaouïa.[97] This song was not all sung as one piece. After each couplet the improviser broke off; together with the tassa his voice gave the tone of a refrain which recapitulated the entire music. During this time he gathered his thoughts and made up the couplet which followed.

Omar, thrilled at one and the same time by the liveliness of the instruments, the verses sung in his praise, and above all by the fortunate success of his raid, had the singer given a touba of Noufia cloth[98] and several thousand cowries were given to the musicians who, stamping their feet rhythmically, went back to the town to continue the festivities there in open places and at street corners.

The serki, approaching the goum, complimented its leaders, examined the slaves, and gave the order for them to be taken to the market (barba).[99] There they were placed in two rows in sheds, women on one side and men on the other, and on the next day we were invited to go and choose those that suited us. Chegueun and the palace agent went with us and after very careful examination each of us obtained as many Negroes and Negresses as he had handed over cubits of broadcloth to the serki. Nevertheless, we only accepted those whose sound constitutions were a surety against the hazards of the long journey we had to make. The elderly, small children, and pregnant women were sold to the people of Katsina or given by Omar as gifts to the leaders of his mekharenias.[100]

Postscript. An apologia for slavery

Is it repugnant to you to have slaves? But in the fact of our servants being our property and yours being free there is only a difference in name. Though a Christian servant has the right to change master as he sees fit, he will nevertheless be a servant his whole life long, and in consequence a slave, minus the name. When our Negroes are old we grant them freedom. They are still part of us, of our tent. When old age has come to your servants what do you do with them? I don't see a single one of them with a white beard.

In your society a wife in marriage looks down on a servant woman who has given her master a child. To survive she must never say anything. In our society she is oum el-weled;[101] she has her dwelling, her son is honored and both belong to the family. You are too proud and you are not sufficiently dignified. For all good Muslims Bou Hourira[102] formulated this proposition: "Never say 'my slave' for we are all slaves of God; say rather 'my servant' or 'my serving girl.'"[103]

• VI •

The Middle Passage

The passage across the Sahara or up the Nile valley was, in many ways, as perilous and cruel as the crossing of the Atlantic. While slave merchants shared many of the perils with their slaves, and sought to preserve their human capital, the slaves were often abused (the females sexually), and attempting to run away was full of perils. Slaves invariably had to walk both for security and economic reasons. However, pregnant women, nursing mothers, and small children were sometimes granted respite by being mounted on a horse or camel.

* * * *

(1) FROM KORDOFAN TO THE NILE VALLEY

Source: Ignatius Pallme, in Madden, op. cit., 168–75. His comments follow his account of a slave raid into the Nuba mountains in the Sudan; see above, p. 53.

But the sufferings of these poor people did not end here; they had to suffer greater torments on their way to Cordofan. I was, alas, myself, eye-witness of the misery of the prisoners. No pen can describe what cruelties these poor creatures, who were already cast down on account of the loss of their goods, and especially the loss of their liberty, had to suffer on their way. Partly with the heavy sheba[104] round their necks, or tied together two and two, with strong leather strings, or their hands fastened within clasps; these poor negroes were driven along like cattle, and treated with far less indulgence, and much more severity. Most of them covered with wounds which they had received in the battle, or from the friction of the sheba, the leather strings, or the clasps, had to suffer the most excruciating pains, and if they became too exhausted to keep pace with the others, still greater sufferings awaited them.

The cries and lamentations of these unfortunate persons, as well as the weeping and crying of the children, who either had lost their parents when the village was taken by storm, or were too much fatigued to follow their mothers who were still more so; who suffered with hunger and thirst, and did not receive a morsel of bread to satisfy their hunger, nor a drop of water to quench their thirst, from the hard-hearted Turks. All this could move a heart of stone, but it made no impression on these unfeeling capturers. They walked indifferently by the side of their prisoners, and only stimulated them to advance, by blows and strokes. As all who were found alive were carried off; there was a great number blind, lame, old, or otherwise feeble people, respecting whom they knew beforehand, that they would either perish on the way or fetch no price.

But this was not regarded, all were unmercifully taken from their homely hearth and left to their fate, their only care was to procure the requisite number of slaves demanded by government.

About ten o'clock in the forenoon they halted, the slaves were arranged into different divisions after their ages, and received their food, which consisted of boiled maize (dohna,)[105] no salt is given, and the maize is boiled so hard, that it is scarcely possible for adults to chew it; the children whose teeth are too tender to chew this kind of corn, swallow it like pills, and afterwards perish most miserably, as they cannot digest what they have swallowed, which makes their bellies swell. I frequently saw that mothers chewed it for their children.

When the division of the prisoners was made in the camp according to their ages, no allowance was made for the children, who anxiously embraced their parents, the sick and the wounded; the former were violently torn from the arms of their parents, in order that they might accustom themselves to eat alone; and the sick received the same food as the healthy; several of them preferred to throw themselves crying into the sand, and endeavoured to refresh their weak limbs, refusing to take any food. If any one became so exhausted that they saw no possibility of driving him any further, or if he was already dying, they would throw him aside like a piece of wood, and let him either perish from exhaustion or be torn by wild beasts. Bread is not even heard of, although there is a possibility of baking some on their march; this, however, would in their opinion, be superfluous for the poor slaves, and they must content themselves with food which is too bad for cattle. As soon as the signal of decampment was given, every one was obliged to hasten to his detachment. Whoever came only one minute too late, was beaten with whips and the butt ends of the guns. Old men and women, who, bent with old age, could scarcely creep along, suffered the same ill-treatment, and were left behind in the sand, if they were not able to advance; and the children were not allowed to take leave of their dear relatives; with tears in their eyes, they could only look at them, and leave them to their fate. In order not to see the father left behind in so miserable a situation, wives and daughters took him between them and helped him on, while he had his arms round their necks, and he was sometimes carried by them.

Children from six years, and even from four years of age, were obliged to run. But they could seldom bear the fatiguing march, and were obliged to be carried by their mothers and sisters. I even saw mothers with a sucking babe in one arm, a child of two years of age in the other, and at last an exhausted boy on their backs, sink under this threefold burden.

Officers who are charged with such a transportation, are the chief cause why the soldiers treat the poor slaves so cruelly—either riding at some distance before the caravan, or behind it, they care nothing about the condition of the captives, and leave them entirely in the hands of the soldiers; and it is soon perceived when a humane officer conducts the caravan, for then only few perish. I saw one of them particularly attending to the children and the sick, and as soon as he perceived that one of them lost his strength, and could not go on with the rest, he ordered that he should be put on one of the beasts of burden: he even took one or two on his own horse.

Such an officer can lie down on his couch with a good conscience, and has not to reproach himself with having increased the misery of his fellow-men, which is already sufficiently great; while so many of his comrades have the miserable death of hundreds on their conscience.

An hour before sunset, they halted again, and distributed boiled corn (dohna) among the slaves. But during the night, the misery of the slaves reached its highest pitch. In the month of January, in which the change of the temperature is generally keenly felt, as the thermometer frequently falls to eight degrees [46° F], the cold was so intense, that it might be compared with the cold of Northern Germany, when four to five degrees below the freezing point. Let the reader remember that the poor negroes are naked, without any covering, exhausted within hunger and fatigue, and he can judge what these poor people had to suffer; fires were, indeed, kindled; but as there was a deficiency of wood, they were not sufficient to protect against the cold. The wailing and moaning of the children, sick, wounded, and dying, were therefore terrible; and one morning they found a sucking child frozen to death, still on the breast of its mother. The negroes have, indeed, no covering when in their villages, but are quite naked, with the exception of a cotton girdle round their loins; but during the night they lie in their huts and cover themselves with skins, all of which they were deprived of on their march.

Those who wore the sheba, round their necks could not sleep on account of pain, their necks were so pressed together, that they could not move them, and thus not one was free from suffering. A woman near her confinement was delivered, one night, without any assistance, The new-born babe was wrapped up in a shirt which I had given to the mother, and safely brought to Lobeid.[106] I gave my donkey to the mother to ride on.

It is, indeed, impossible for me to describe all the misery which I witnessed during the time I remained within them. Language fails; the sufferings which the slaves have to undergo is beyond conception, and no words can describe the pain which a sensitive heart feels when witnessing such scenes. I did all in my power, partly by kind words, and partly by small presents, to make the soldiers as well as the country people who had to escort the slaves more compassionate; the consequence was, that many of them would take a poor child that could not move his wounded feet any longer in the sand, or that was a burden to his exhausted mother, on his arms and carry it nearly the whole of the way. But it was impossible for me to put a stop to all the acts of cruelty, and I was obliged, one day, to see an unfeeling soldier knock down with the butt end of his gun, a poor man whose feet were quite inflamed on account of the wounds which he had received in battle, and whom pain prevented from keeping step with the others.

I was no longer master of my feelings; I drew my sword, and would have hewn this tiger into pieces if my servant had not stopt me, by wrenching the sword out of my hand, he likewise took my pistols from me, and did not return either, until he saw that my anger had cooled.

On the eighth day the whole expedition arrived at Lobeid, where the distribution of the slaves took place, and this is the chief reason that the soldiers treat the slaves so unmercifully; for as they are obliged to take these instead of the arrear pay, and that at a very high price, and as the slaves frequently die before they have sold them again, and the soldiers consequently lose all, they try all they can to let the old and feeble perish before they reach Lobeid. If the troops in Cordofan, and in other provinces, received their pay in ready money, I feel convinced that they would treat these unfortunate people with more humanity.

(2) A COMMERCIAL SLAVE CARAVAN (1830s)

Source: Gen. E. Daumas, *Le Grand Désert,* extracts of pp. 226–43. The following account describes the first stage of the trans-Saharan caravan journey from Katsina; see above, p. 57. Several caravans joined together for the initial stages: one making for Ghadames, one for Ghat, and one for the Fezzan, as well as the narrator's caravan, making ultimately for Mtlili in Algeria.

At daybreak our camels were loaded, the Negro children perched atop the baggage, the male Negroes secured by their chains in the center of the convoy and the Negro females grouped in eights or tens under the watch of men carrying whips. The departure signal was given and the first caravan moved. It was at this point that suddenly a confused noise of cries and sobs passed from one group of slaves to another and reached our own. All, together, wept and moaned, called out and uttered farewells. They were terrified of being eaten during the journey. Some rolled on the ground, clung to bushes and absolutely refused to walk. Nothing had any effect on them, neither kind words nor threats. They could only be got up with mighty lashes of the whip and by rendering them completely bloody. Despite their obstinacy, no one of them resisted this extreme measure. Moreover, joined together as they were, the less fearful or more courageous, struggling with the weaker ones, forced them to walk.

Little by little order was finally restored, but those of Ghadames were already at the first halt while we still had not moved. For, beyond the time necessary to file down the narrow paths of the gardens of Katsina, each of the caravans as it passed through the gate of the perimeter was searched by the chaouchs[107] of Mohammed Omar who had been given the task of ascertaining that we were not carrying off either Fulanis who were Muslims or Jews. A man of Ghat had a Fulani who was immediately recognized and set at liberty. "How is it that you have bought this man?" said the chief of the chaouchs, "He is a Muslim, he is your brother in religion. Like you he recognizes only one God. Do you not know our laws? Could you not have recognized him by his color?" The foolish man objected that having bought him during the night he had been deceived and that the next day he had not been able to find the person who had sold him to him. Despite these clever denials he had to pay a fine of fifty douros.[108] Moreover he was very lucky not to have had his merchandise confiscated and then been put in prison, but his good faith, whether genuine or pretended, saved him from this plight.

The first day we halted at only three leagues[109] from Katsina on a huge plain where we found pools and plenty of grass and wood. It had rained a few days earlier and vegetation in the Desert is so vigorous that it often takes only one very rainy night to change the sand and the prairie from one sun-rise to another. Conversely, however, the sun may devour one day what it made grow the previous one.

Each caravan established its camp separately. As soon as our camels had crouched down and after having, first and foremost, chained up our Negresses by the foot in groups of eight or ten, we forced our Negroes to help us, using their left hand which we had left free, in unloading our animals, marking out a circle with our loads and putting up the ox-hide tents we had brought from Katsina within this perimeter. Two or three of the older Negresses whom we had not chained together, but who nevertheless had their feet shackled, were set to preparing something for us to dine on. They made hacida[110] for everybody and, as on the outward journey, we ate in fours. When this sorry supper was over we placed guards around our camp and sent both our male and female slaves to bed, chained up as I have said.

The next day we loaded up early and this time the Ghat caravan took the lead. Although calmer than they were the evening before, our slaves were still very irritable. To tire them out and weaken them we made the slaves carry their irons, their dishes (*guessâa*)[111] and the mortars (*maharaz*)[112] for pounding maize and millet. And so that our entire attention could be concentrated on them, each of us tied his camels together in a single file. Watching over them thus became easier and if one of them fell down or a load fell off, we could in this way halt them all at once and we avoided the whole group bolting as we got one on its feet or reloaded another.

Childbirth en route

[p. 229] We would have arrived early before Tassaoua[113] where it was our intention to spend the night if, during the journey, one of the Negresses of a certain El-Hadj Abd-er-Rahman [*al-ḥājj* ᶜAbd al-Raḥmān] had not been overtaken by the pangs of childbirth. Despite the interdiction of our khebir, Abd-er-Rahman had bought this woman, knowing full well she was pregnant, because she was beautiful, tall and strong, and we all had to suffer the inconvenience of his bad faith. Cheggueun, though very annoyed with this man, made the caravan halt until the woman had given birth. She and her child were then put on a camel and only then could we resume our journey. This is the usual practice of caravans in such cases, because it is a Muslim who has just been born.[114]

The First Runaway

Outside the walls of Tassaoua, where our companions were already established when we arrived, we made the same arrangements for our camp as the previous evening, though we took even greater precautions since we were coming close to the Tuareg. When making his evening round Cheggueun, out of humanity, ordered Abd-er-Rahman not to chain up the Negress who had given birth, but to give her some meat for supper and to let her sleep warmly on a mat. Abd-er-Rahman willingly complied with these measures, but whilst he was asleep the mother put her child in a basket full of ostrich feathers, placed this on her head and escaped. El-Hadj Abd-er-Rahman noticed this the next morning and ran immediately to Cheggueun who, without wasting precious time on futile reproach, asked the other khebirs to delay their departure until he had caught the fugitives. They consented with good grace, since in such a long and arduous journey it is in the common interest to show solidarity one with another and to seek to obtain the goodwill of everyone. Some of the most energetic and best mounted men of each caravan came forward to offer to help Cheggueun in his search. He accepted their generosity and divided them into small bands and sent them off in different directions while he took yet another direction with Abd-er-Rahman and his friends.

The Negress, still weak, could not have been far away. In fact, a few hours walk from the camp she was found huddled in a bush, breast-feeding her child. Two shots fired [in the air] brought all the searchers back to camp. No one complained of this delay which, however, forced us to stay at Tassaoua. But our khebirs took advantage of the situation to get everyone to double their watch and public criers announced that if other slaves escaped through their owners' negligence they would be left to their fate and lost to the careless.

The next day the Fezzan caravan led off the march. Passing before Tassaoua, which we left on our right, we were again inspected by the chiefs of that town and by the agent representing the sultan of Hausa.[115] This time, however, no smuggled slaves were found and we continued our journey to one day's march short of Damergou[116] where we camped in a somewhat marshy plain which had excellent pasture for our camels. At dawn it was the turn of our caravan to lead the march and we stopped early near Damergou. The last camels of the rear caravan, however, did not arrive until 5 p.m. We stayed there the next day as much to rest as to replenish in town the provisions which were exhausted.

Official Inspection

The chiefs of Damergou gave us a good welcome, but like those of Tassaoua, they went through all our tents. Some of their own people, they told us, had been carried off by horsemen from Zinder and no doubt sold at Katsina where we might have bought them. Whether they were telling the truth or not, they recognized, or pretended to recognize, as being among those they were looking for, two of the best looking Negroes of the Ghat caravan. Whatever the case, it would have been difficult for us to resist and by common accord our khebirs decided that justice would be done to the claimants. For the owner of the slaves it was a real loss and I was astonished not to find him considerably affected. "God willed it," he said, "Perfect resignation to God's decrees consists in receiving both good and ill fortune with the same tranquillity." I later learnt that this saintly man was a marabout of Trabless.[117]

More Runaways

[*En route four days northwest of Agades*] From our last resting place a very short stage should have brought us to Aghezeur and we would have arrived there during the morning if, during the night, my slave Mebrouk and five Negroes of the Ghadames caravan had not run off. Since I had chained him up securely, Mebrouk had shown himself as submissive as a child. He always called me *Abi,* my father, and when camped he was the first to set to work. He told me that he realised that I did not want to eat him, that the Touraoua[118] were good people and that he would be better fed, better clothed and happier than he was in Oumbouroum where the Fulani would have either killed him when he was young or when he was old. When I performed the prayer he repeated the *chehada*[119] and often asked me to get him circumcized so that he could boast of being a good Muslim.

His tongue was golden, and since his service was also useful to me I first moved him from the center of the chain to its end; next I had set him completely apart and since Agades, his two hands free and only his feet fastened, he had followed me like a good servant. At the camp where we had arrived early, I went to visit the Ghadames caravan and Mebrouk, who was always at my side, had recognized there five Negroes from his land who had been carried off in the same raid as him. Their owner and I had left them to chat together and on our return Mebrouk said to me, "Abi, you should buy my friends. Their owner wants to sell them and they are physically strong and their hearts are without malice. They would serve you just as I do since they already like you because of your good reputation and what I have told them about you."

These words gave me greater confidence, but Mebrouk was the "night-bird" (bat):

> I say to the rats: I am your brother;
> I say to the birds: I am your brother.
> Come the rats, he bares his teeth;
> Come the birds, and he takes flight.

What he had said to his friends was that he would come when I was asleep and help them to break their chain. Next day all six were free.

When news of this event was noised abroad, our khebirs, each followed by fifteen horsemen, set off at a gallop and explored the countryside far and wide. But it is full of scrub and so dotted with hillocks that they could only find two of the fugitives. Injured by the irons on their legs they had thrown themselves into a swamp, being no longer able to follow their companions. Neither of them was Mebrouk. What had become of him only God knows!

Back at the camp, our leaders were exhausted and in high dudgeon. Under the influence of these two feelings they called us together and had the following warning bawled out to us:

"O children of sin, you do not want to listen! Every day we repeat the same thing: never sleep without inspecting your slaves' irons and wake up frequently in the night to look again. You are indeed crazy, for the Negro who cost you ten boujoux is already worth fifty! For the last time we warn you: we shall not halt the caravans again to run after your slaves. Whoever allows his own to escape should consider himself like a man who, having driven off some camels in a raid, shamefully lets them be taken back."

All at once we protested that this had not happened through fault of our own, but by the will of God. In truth there was none among us whom fatigue and wakefulness had not reduced to half his normal weight. However, I was to blame for the excessive liberty I had allowed Mebrouk and I had to confess my shame and humbly endure the remonstrances of Cheggueun. But I understood that no matter how roughly he spoke to me, he did so in my interest and I harbored no rancor towards him.

A Flogging

As a lesson for the future, it remained for us to learn from the two recaptured fugitives by what clever means they and their companions had slipped their chains. But neither kindness nor patience on the part of Cheggueun who was interrogating them, could make their tongues wag and, seized by anger, he ordered that they should be flogged in front of the other slaves. In no time all these pagans were lined up on the side of a hillock. Two powerful men seized one of the two Negroes, threw him to the ground and sat astride his heels and neck. At the same time two chaouchs had taken up their stations, canes in hand, one on the right and the other on the left of the guilty one.

"Go to it," said Cheggueun. At the first blow the canes were white. At the fiftieth they were red and blood ran on the thighs and sides of the victim. But the obstinate fellow had still said nothing. Only his fitful breathing and some movement of his loins bore witness to the fact that they were not beating a corpse. Finally he cried out, "Abi! Serki! I will tell all. Stop the beating." A gesture from Cheggueun brought the chaouchs to a halt.

"Speak," he said to the Negro. "What did you do to break your chains and what happened to them?"

"O Serki! I touched them with my kerikeri[120] (amulet) and made them melt."

"Chaouchs!" responded Cheggueun, "Beat him harder. He lies."

The canes descended on the liar so hard that they removed a strip of his skin.

"Abi! Serki! I will talk. I will talk," he cried.

"Dog of a pagan," said Cheggueun, "I will have you killed if you lie to me again."

"By my father's neck," replied the slave, "Here is the truth. During the night, by slithering on the sand, Mebrouk came over to us. He had some hot water in a calabash and he poured some of this in the lock of our chains. Thus wetted, when we tapped it on its side we made the bolt slide and we opened it. Out of the five, however, two had to escape attached to one another, carrying the chain with them."

"O my children," Cheggueun said to us, "You hear him. Above all, those of you whose Negroes are chained up with old chains, never go to sleep without seeing with your eye and touching with your hand the padlocks which protect your fortune. Let this be a good lesson to you all!"

The slave was seated and the chaouchs helped him to stand up. Limping and groaning he dragged himself to the feet of his master, prostrated with his face on the ground and poured sand over himself as a sign of his repentance and submission.[121] It had taken no less than one hundred and twenty strokes of the cane to drag out his secret from him, and good justice would have required that his accomplice receive the same. But his owner objected that two such wounded men would be an embarrassment for everyone, that they might die of exhaustion and that his loss was already great. Cheggueun, who had a heart of gold, was easily convinced by these good reasons and he gave orders that on departure the next morning the sick man should be put on a camel.

No sooner was this performance finished than two men from the Ghat caravan who had gone off to practise antelope hunting came to tell their leaders that they had found tracks of two Negroes to the northeast. They had followed these to the middle of some dense thickets which the tracks had entered while veering sharply to the south. "We did not dare go any further," they added, "but we are convinced that good horsemen, properly guided, could catch the runaways, since they have not been able to break their chains and are walking chained together side by side as is shown by their footprints which are always the same distance the one from the other."

Search for the Runaways

The authority of these two men, who were famous as experts in *El-Kyafat*,[122] convinced Cheggueun to send off twenty horsemen under their direction and they left immediately with orders that if necessary they should spend the night on the trail of the Negroes, and start out again at dawn and continue until midday.

When night came we had to rest, but at sunup we set off again and at eight o'clock our guides called out, "Keep your weapons close. There is a lion around." At this terrible word more than one of us regretted having left his tent, but all the guns were primed. "His tracks follow the tracks of the Negroes," added one of our guides. "Be brave, for the lion cannot be very far away."

At that time we were walking in a wood, or rather through dense bush out of which tall trees rose here and there. In the successive clearings the large paw marks of the lion were intermingled with the tracks of the Negroes; he had evidently hunted them as a dog hunts game. Bunched together as tightly as possible and as tightly as the clumps of bushes allowed, we went forward in silence, with guns held high, led by the two guides who all of a sudden fell back on us. "Look!" they said, and we beheld a fearsome spectacle. A huge lion was sleeping at the foot of a tree in which a Negro was hidden, his foot attached by a chain to his companion, or rather the remains of his half devoured companion. Our frightened camels turned tail and carried us off scattering us in the forest. Little by little, however, we were able to calm them down and we regrouped in a clearing. It was decided that we should go on foot, slowly and carefully and all together fire our twenty guns at the head of the lion. The lion, however, no doubt woken by the noise we had made, was no longer there when we arrived. The Negro alone, trembling in all his limbs, maintained the terrible posture in which we had found him.

He told us that his companion had not been able to break the chain which linked them together by their feet, but they had nevertheless continued their march. The reason they took a northerly direction was that they fully expected a search would be made for them and that it would be supposed they had gone south. A few steps away from the place where we had found them a lion had attacked them and both had tried to take refuge in a tree. But with a leap the hungry animal had thrown himself on them, his claws had seized the less agile of the two who had fallen head first and been devoured under the eyes of his companion. After this hideous meal the lion had slept and it was at this moment that we had arrived.

It was not without difficulty that we managed to free the foot of this mangled corpse from the shackle to which it was attached and we had to use the yatagan.[123] The fright of the poor Negro who escaped was so great that he died at the camp the same evening.

Next day as soon as we arrived at Aghezeur we went to visit the marabouts who had been looking after our things. Everything we had left with them was scrupulously given back, and to pay these good people for their kindness we made them a present of perfume, honey and sayes[124]. . . .

We had to spend some time at Aghezeur so as to obtain provisions and repair our equipment. Our negroes, more docile the more distant they became from their land and the more they lost all hope of escape and, moreover, the better they became acquainted with us, helped us in these tasks openly and without ill humor. By the grace of God, death had not taken a single one of us and we had not lost a single camel.

• VII •

Slave Markets

(1) SLAVE DEALING IN KUKA [BORNU], 1870

Source: Gustav Nachtigal, *Sahara and Sudan*, vol. 2, *Kawar, Bornu, Kanem, Borku, Ennedi*, trans. Allan G. Fisher and Humphrey J. Fisher (London: C. Hurst & Company, 1980; reprinted by permission), 215–18. Gustav Nachtigal was born in Germany in 1834, and trained as a medical doctor. His *Sahara und Sudan* was published in three volumes between 1879 and 1889, containing accounts of the people, politics, and natural history of the Fezzan, Tibesti, Bornu, Bagirmi, Borku, Wadai, and Darfur, resulting from five and a half years of travel starting from Tripoli; each volume contains observations on slavery as witnessed by him. He was an exceptionally acute and scientific observer, and was fortunate enough, almost a century later, to have his work translated into English by an academic father and son team, assisted in the annotation by numerous Africanist colleagues. He died in 1885.

In the eastern section of the south side of the market slave dealers have set up large stalls where, protected from the sun and rain, their wares, with or without chains, are displayed in long rows. There await their fate slaves of both sexes—*kinji* means slave without regard to sex, *kalia* means male slave, *kir* female slave—of every age and price from the most diverse Pagan countries to the south of the states of the Sudan.

Old men, tired of life, sit alongside small children snatched away from the tender care of a loving mother before they could retain any picture of her in their memories. Among repulsive-looking women, whose faded skin hangs loosely on their fleshless bones, and who have become apathetic through toil and misery, there are bright young girls, their full well-rounded figures in the first bloom of youth, with coquettish head-dress, washed clean and glistening with butter, who look hopefully into the future.

The most marketable category of human merchandise is the so-called *sedâsî*, that is a male slave who measures six spans from the ankle to the top of the head, a measurement corresponding to an age of about 12 to 15, and whose price is an indicator of market conditions for slaves as a whole. A foreign merchant who wishes to inform himself about the prices of slaves in a country asks, How much are *sedâsî*? and from the answer he deduces for himself the prices of the other age groups.

There is also a great demand for the *khomâsî,* or *khomâsîya*, the group nearest to the *sedâsî*, male and female slaves whose height is five spans, with ages ranging from 10 to 13, for they already have a certain capacity to resist the effects of a changed climate and an unfamiliar way of life, and yet, both physically and morally, are still exceptionally adaptable. The 15–20 year-old *sebâ'î*'s, that is those who measure seven spans, who can adjust even better to unaccustomed climatic conditions, are likewise easy to sell. It is, however, more difficult to train them than those who are still children, and if they have not been habituated to slavery perhaps over many years, they are more easily tempted to run away. For this reason, adult men, *gurzem*, are not much in demand, especially if they have not been tested, and have not been put up for sale only because of special circumstances. Least valued are the older men, over whom the older women, *shômalîya*, have at least the advantage that they can more easily be employed in household work. The price of mature young girls who are suitable as concubines is understandably a good deal above that of the *sedâsî*, but they constitute a less marketable and rather uncertain article of commerce, since their value fluctuates very much according to the degree of their beauty and the taste of the bargainer for them.

The lot of these young girls or women—in Arabic, *surrîya*, plural, *serrârî*, probably from *sirr*, the secret—is usually the happiest among the slaves. They take over completely the place of a housewife, and are much more zealous than she is to gain and to maintain the goodwill of their master by their industry and amiability, so as not to pass from hand to hand. If also in cases where they gain too much influence over their master, they easily become arrogant, demanding and too fond of dress, still on the whole the costs of maintaining them, and thus too the housekeeping costs, are much smaller than for lawful wives. For men without means and people who are compelled to great journeys and long absences, they are a real blessing, for lawful wives are seldom inclined to leave their home and kinsfolk, and according to the religious law, they cannot even be compelled to do so. If, however, a slave girl is blest with children, she is nearly as secure in her position as a lawful wife, for it is only the most compelling circumstances that can bring even a moderately upright Muslim to the point of parting with the mother of his children by selling her.[125]

Eunuchs, *adim*, have an exceptional value, but they scarcely ever come on to the open market. The demand for them on the part of foreign merchants who seek them for the great men of the Muhammedan world of Europe, Asia and Africa is so great, while indeed the supply of them can only be limited, that they are very quickly sold privately. Most of the eunuchs who come up for sale in Bornu are from Bagirmi,[126] but many a mighty man of Bornu itself has not been ashamed to increase their number, either with a view to immediate profit, or in order to keep them in readiness as a costly present for the Shaykh. Lamino[127] too appears to have been sufficiently devoid of conscience to collect from time to time hundreds of boys, and to subject them to castration, condemned though this is by Islam. Under the pretext of wanting to circumcize the boys, the barbers who perform the operation are accustomed with a quick grip to grasp the whole of their external genitals in the left hand, and with the right to amputate them with a sharp knife. Boiling butter is kept in readiness and poured on the fresh wound to staunch the bleeding of the unfortunate boys. Very many of them, of course, succumb to the horrible operation.

Deaf and dumb slave girls, though not as high priced as eunuchs, are also much in demand, as servants for their wives, by the magnates of the more highly civilised countries of Islam, and high prices are paid for them. Dwarfs, *wâda*, if possible trained as court jesters, are still a favourite plaything for Mohammedan princes. I have seen both of these sold in Kuka for export to the north.

(2) SLAVES AND SLAVERY AT SHENDI

Source: John Lewis Burckhardt, *Travels in Nubia* (London, 2nd edn., 1822), 290–300, 326–28. Original foototes by Burckhardt are followed by the indication [JLB]. Not all of his footnotes, however, have been retained. Often Burckhardt wrote Arabic terms and names in the Arabic script. These have been transliterated and placed within parentheses.

Born Jean Louis Burckhardt in Switzerland in 1784, he took refuge from revolutionary French encroachment by taking up residence in England, after a period of study in Germany. In 1808 he volunteered his services to the African Association, which was looking for someone to find a way to Timbuktu by crossing the Sahara from Cairo. To train for this he then went to Aleppo to learn how to speak Arabic and there become acquainted with Arab culture. He also learned how to pass himself off as a Muslim. After a journey to explore Petra in 1812 he set off from Cairo to explore the Nile valley as a further stage of preparation for his major journey. At the 6th Cararact he joined a caravan going to Suakin on the Red Sea coast. He crossed the sea to Jeddah and decided to move on, first to Mecca and then to Medina. Returning to Egypt in June 1816, he took a small boat containing passengers afflicted by the plague. He died in Cairo sixteen months later. His accounts of this journey, and of his Syrian experiences, were published posthumously in 1830 as *Notes on the Bedouins and Wahábys.*

I calculate the number of slaves sold annually in the market of Shendy[128] at about five thousand, of whom about two thousand five hundred are carried off by the Souakin merchants, and fifteen hundred by those of Egypt; the remainder go to Dongola, and to the Bedouins who live to the east of Shendy, towards the Atbara and the Red Sea. I have already made some mention of the places from whence these slaves come. Those brought from Kordofan to Darfour are, for the greater part, from the idolatrous countries of Benda, Baadja, Fetigo, and Fertit, to the south and south-west of Darfour, from twenty to forty days from Kobbe;[129] each of these countries speaks a separate language. The Darfour merchants trade with Fertit, which lies about twenty days distant from Kobbe, in a southerly direction: the country is mountainous, and its inhabitants are wholly ignorant of agriculture; but they have tasted the luxury of Dhourra and Dokhen;[130] and are said, in cases of a dearth of these grains, to sell even their own children to procure them.

Far the largest proportion of the slaves imported into Shendy are below the age of fifteen. All of them, both male and female, are divided by the traders, with reference to age, into three classes: namely, Khomasy (*khumāsī*), comprising those apparently below ten or eleven years; Sedasy (*sudāsī*), those above eleven and below fourteen or fifteen; and Balegh (*bāligh*), or grown up, those of fifteen and upwards. The Sedasy are the most esteemed; when I was at Shendy a male of this class was worth fifteen or sixteen dollars, provided he bore the marks of the small-pox, without which a boy is not worth more than two-thirds of that price;[131] a female was worth from twenty to twenty-five Spanish dollars. The price of the male Khomasy was twelve, of the female fifteen dollars. The male Balegh seldom sells for more than eight or ten dollars; and there is but a small proportion of this class, because it is thought both in Egypt and Arabia, that no great dependence can be placed upon any slave who has not been brought up in the owner's family from an early age. Hence there is a great reluctance to the purchasing of grown-up slaves for domestic purposes, or even for labourers. The Baleghs are chiefly bought by the Bedouins, who employ them as shepherds. The Bisharein[132] have many of them in all their encampments. Grown-up female slaves, although past the age of beauty, sometimes sell for as much as thirty dollars, if they are known to be skilful in working, sewing, cooking, &c. In Syria few slaves are kept; those which I have seen there are, for the greater part, imported by the caravans from Bagdad, or come from Souahel on the Mozambik coast.[133]

Few slaves are imported into Egypt, without changing masters several times, before they are finally settled in a family; for instance, those from Fertit are first collected on the borders of that country by petty merchants who deal in Dhourra. These sell them to the traders of Kobbe, who repair to Fertit in small caravans for that purpose. At Kobbe they are bought up by the Darfour, or Kordofan traders, who transport them to Obeydh[134] in Kordofan. Here they generally pass into the hands of other Kordofan dealers, who carry them to Shendy, for the Soudan merchants commonly limit their speculations to a single market; thus the Kordofan people who trade to Darfour are different from those who visit Shendy, while, on the other hand, the Egyptians who trade to Shendy only, are different from those who proceed forward to Sennaar; and, in like manner, the Soakin traders are divided into Shendy and Sennaar merchants. At Shendy the slave is bought by some Egyptian or Ababde.[135] Upon his arrival in Upper Egypt he is disposed of either at Esne,[136] Siout,[137] or Cairo. In the two first places, entire lots of slaves are taken off by merchants, who sell them in retail at Cairo, or in the small towns of Upper Egypt, in each of which they stop for a few days, in their passage down the river. Even at Cairo they are not always finally disposed of in the first instance. The Khan of the slave-traders, called Okal-ed-djelabe,[138] which is near the mosque El Azher,[139] is crowded with pedlars and petty traders, who often bargain with the merchants of Upper Egypt for slaves immediately after their arrival, and content themselves with a small profit for the re-sale. Again, there are merchants from Smyrna[140] and Constantinople residing constantly at Cairo, who deal in nothing but slaves; these persons export them from Alexandria, and it often happens that they pass through three or four hands, between Alexandria and their final destination in the northern provinces of Turkey. Such is the common lot of the unfortunate slave, but many instances happen of a still more rapid change of masters. At Shendy and Esne I have seen slaves bought and sold two or three times before they were finally removed from the market; after which, perhaps, if the master at the end of a few days trial did not find them answer his expectations, he would again put them up for sale, or exchange them for others. In fact, slaves are considered on the same level with any other kind of merchandize, and as such are continually passing from one merchant to another. The word Ras (head) is applied to them as to the brute species; and a man is said to possess ten Ras Raghig [*ra'ˀs ragig*][141] or ten head of slaves,[142] in the same manner as he would be said to possess fifty Ras Ghanam [*raˀs ghanam*], or head of sheep. When the buyer is desired to take the slave away, it is usual to say, Soughe, [*sūg'hu*] drive him out, an expression which is applied only to cattle, as Soug el ghanam go damek.[143]

I have seen among the young slaves on sale at Shendy, many children of four or five years old without their parents; others of the same age are met with in the market, with their mothers; and the traders so far show humanity, that they seldom sell them separately; when such a thing is done, the vendor is in general reproached with being guilty of an act of cruelty.

The traders, in buying slaves, are very attentive to their origin, because long experience has proved to them that there is little variety of character amongst individuals of the same nation. Thus the Noubas who come from Sennaar are said to have the best dispositions next to the Abyssinians and Gallas, and to be the most attached to their masters. Of the Abyssinians, those from the northern provinces, called Kostanis, are said to be treacherous and malicious, while the Amaaras[144] are noted for their amiable tempers. Of the western Negroes, those from Benda[145] are the most esteemed, and next to them those imported into Darfour from Borgho, a Mohammedan country, whose inhabitants carry off their pagan neighbours.[146] The slaves from Fertit[147] are said to be ferocious and vindictive, and stand the lowest on the list.

Few slaves arrive at Shendy who have not already passed a considerable time in a state of slavery. The strongest proof of this fact is, that I never saw any who could not make themselves understood in Arabic; and the greater part of those imported from Darfour and Kordofan, besides their own native tongue, and Arabic, have some acquaintance with the idioms of those countries.

As soon as a slave boy becomes the property of a Mussulman master he is circumcized, and has an Arabic name given to him. They are seldom honored with a true Mussulman name; such as Hassan, Mohammed, Selim, Mustapha, &c. Most of them bear such names as these: Kheyr el illah [Khayr Allāh]; Fadil 'ilah [Faḍl Allāh]; Fadil Elwasia [Faḍl al-Wāsiᶜ]; Jaber Wadjed [Jabr Wājid]; Om Elkheyr [Umm al-Khayr], and the like. Sometimes the names are more extraordinary, as Sabah el Kheyr [*Sabāḥ al-khayr*] (good morning), Djerab [*jirāb*] (leather sack), &c &c. It very rarely happens that any uncircumcized boys come from the west; and I never knew any instance of a Negro boy following the pagan worship of his father, and refusing to become Mussulman; though I have heard it related of many Abyssinian slaves, who, after having been converted from idolatry to the Christian religion, by the Abyssinian Copts, were sold by them to the Mussulman traders. I have been told of several of these slaves, particularly females, so steadily refusing to abjure their faith, when in the harem of a Mohammedan, that their masters were finally obliged to sell them, in the dread of having children born of a Christian mother, which would have been a perpetual reproach to the father and his offspring. In Soudan, the slaves, though made Mussulmans by the act of circumcision, are never taught to read or to pray: and even in Egypt and Arabia this instruction is seldom given to any but those for whom their masters take a particular liking. It may be observed, nevertheless, that they are greater fanatics than the proudest Olemas,[148] and that Christians and Franks are more liable to be insulted by slaves than by any other class of Mussulmans.

I inquired at Shendy whether any of the slaves were eunuchs, but I was informed that no eunuchs were imported into that place during my stay, and that Borgho, to the west of Darfour, is the only country in eastern Soudan where slaves are thus mutilated for exportation. Their number, however, is very small; a few are carried to Egypt from Darfour, and the remainder are sent as presents by the Negro sovereigns to the great mosques at Mekka and Medina, by the way of Souakin.[149] The great manufactory which supplies all European, and the greater part of Asiatic Turkey with these guardians of female virtue, is at Zawyet ed-deyr [*Zāwiyat al-dayr*], a village near Siout [Asuyūṭ] in Upper Egypt, chiefly inhabited by Christians. The operators, during my stay in that part of the country, were two Coptic monks, who were said to excel all their predecessors in dexterity, and who had a house in which the victims were received. Their profession is held in contempt even by the vilest Egyptians; but they are protected by the government, to which they pay an annual tax; and the great profits which accrue to the owners of the slaves in consequence of their undergoing this cruel operation, tempts them to consent to an act which many of them in their hearts abhor. The operation itself, however extraordinary it may appear, very seldom proves fatal.[150] I know certainly, that of sixty boys upon whom it was performed in the autumn of 1813 two only died; and every person whom I questioned on the subject in Siout, assured me that even this was above the usual proportion, the deaths being seldom more than two in a hundred. As the greater number undergo the operation immediately after the arrival of the Darfour and Sennaar caravans from Siout, I had no opportunity of witnessing it, but it has been described to me by several persons who have often seen it performed. The boys chosen, are between the age of eight and twelve years, for at a more advanced age, there is great risk of its proving fatal. *The boy is seized by some strong men and held over the table. Then the emasculator binds the genitals with silk threads, lubricated with soap, and cuts them with a barber's razor as quickly as possible (while the boy faints with pain). To stop the bleeding they cauterize the wound using dust and dry sand, and after several days they treat it with warm oil. Then the wound is cared for with a certain concoction which is a secret among the Copts, for forty days until it heals. Nowhere else in the world have I heard of such a practice.*[151] The operation is always performed upon the strongest and best looking boys; but it has a visible effect upon their features when they arrive at full age. The faces of the eunuchs whom I saw in the Hedjaz appeared almost destitute of flesh, the eye hollow, the cheek bones prominent, and the whole physiognomy having a skeleton-like appearance, by which the eunuch may generally be recognized at first sight.

A youth on whom this operation has been successfully performed is worth one thousand piastres at Siout; he had probably cost his master, a few weeks before, about three hundred; and the Copt is paid from forty-five to sixty for his operation. This enormous profit stifles every sentiment of mercy which the traders might otherwise entertain. About one hundred and fifty eunuchs are made annually. Two years ago, Mohammed Aly Pasha caused two hundred young Darfour slaves to be mutilated, whom he sent as a present to the Grand Signor.[152] The custom of keeping eunuchs has greatly diminished in Egypt, as well as in Syria. In the former country, except in the harems of the Pasha and his sons, I do not think that more than three hundred could be found; and they are still more uncommon in Syria. In these countries there is great danger in the display of wealth; and the individual who keeps so many female slaves as to require an eunuch for their guardian, becomes a tempting object to the rapacity of the government. White eunuchs are extremely rare in the Turkish dominions. In Arabia, I have seen several Indian eunuchs of a sallow or cadaverous complexion, and I was informed that slaves are often mutilated in Hindostan. Almost all the eunuchs of Siout are sent to Constantinople and Asia Minor.[153]

Among the slave girls who arrive at Shendy and Siout, there are several who are called Mukhaeyt[154] from an operation[155] which has been described by Mr. Browne.[156] I am unable to state whether it is performed by their parents in their native country, or by the merchants, but I have reason to believe by the latter. Girls in this state are worth more than others; they are usually given to the favourite mistress or slave of the purchaser, and are often suffered to remain in this state during the whole of their life.

The daughters of the Arabs, Ababde and Djaafere, who are of Arabian origin, and inhabit the western bank of the Nile from Thebes, as high as the cataracts, and generally all of those people to the south of Kenne and Esne as far as Sennaar, undergo circumcision, or rather excision,[157] at the age of from three to six years. Girls thus treated, are also called Mukhaeyt but their state is quite different from that of the Negro slave-girls, just mentioned.

The treatment which the slaves experience from the traders, is rather kind than otherwise. The slaves are generally taught to call their masters Abouy,[158] and to consider themselves as their children. They are seldom flogged, are well fed, are not over-worked, and are spoken to in a kind manner; all this, however, results not from humanity in the traders, but from an apprehension that, under different treatment, the slave would abscond; and they are aware that any attempt to prevent his flight by close confinement would injure his health; for the newly imported slaves delight in the open air, and reluctantly enter houses, which they look upon as prisons. But when they are once in the desert, on the way to their final destination, this treatment is entirely changed; the traders, knowing that the slaves have no longer any means of escaping, give a loose to their savage temper. At Shendy, I often overheard my companions, who, although savage enough, were certainly not of the worst class of slave-merchants, say to each other, when a slave had behaved ill, and they were afraid of punishing him, "Let him only pass Berber, and the Korbadj[159] will soon teach him obedience." The Souakin traders with whom I afterwards travelled, showed as little humanity, after we had passed Taka. The health of the slave, however, is always attended to; he is regularly fed, and receives his share of water on the road at the same time that his master drinks; and the youngest and most delicate of the females are permitted to ride upon camels, while all the others perform the journey on foot, whether it be to Egypt or to Souakin, as they had done from Darfour to Shendy. The hardiness of the young slaves is very extraordinary; after several successive days march at the rate of ten or twelve hours a day, I have seen them in the evening, after supper, playing together as if they had enjoyed a long rest. Females, with children on their backs, follow the caravan on foot; and if a camel breaks down, the owner generally loads his slaves with the packages. If a boy can only obtain in the evening a little butter with his Dhourra bread, and some grease every two or three days, to smear his body and hair, he is contented, and never complains of fatigue. Another cause which induces the merchants to treat the slaves well, is their anxiety to dissipate that horror which the Negroes all entertain of Egypt and of the white people. It is a common opinion in the black slave countries, that the Oulad er-Rif[160] [*Awlād al-rīf*], or children of Rif, as the Egyptians are there called, devour the slaves, who are transferred thither for that purpose.[161] Of course, the traders do everything in their power to destroy this belief, but notwithstanding all their endeavours, it is never eradicated from the minds of the slaves. Another terrible apprehension which they have is of a small jumping animal, which they are told will live upon their skin, suck their blood, and leave them not a moment's rest. By this description they mean fleas, which are entirely unknown in the interior parts of Soudan, and of which the most curious stories are told by the people of the country, in enumerating the superior advantages of their own country over those of Egypt. Other vermin, however, more to be dreaded than fleas, are too common among them. The fear of being mutilated on their arrival in Egypt, operates powerfully also upon the minds of the young slaves.

Slave-boys are always allowed complete liberty within the yard of the house; but the grown up males, whose characters cannot be depended upon, or whose dispositions are unknown, are kept in close confinement, well watched, and often chained. On the journey they are tied to a long pole, one end of which is fastened to a camel's saddle, and the other, which is forked, is passed on each side of the slave's neck, and tied behind with a strong cord, so as to prevent him from drawing out his head; in addition to this, his right hand is also fastened to the pole at a short distance from the head, thus leaving only his legs and left arm at liberty; in this manner, he marches the whole day behind the camel; at night he is taken from the pole and put in irons. While on my route to Souakin, I saw several slaves carried along in this way. Their owners were afraid of their escaping, or of becoming themselves the objects of their vengeance: and in this manner they would continue to be confined until sold to a master, who, intending to keep them, would endeavour to attach them to his person. In general, the traders seem greatly to dread the effects of sudden resentment in their slaves; and if a grown up boy is only to be whipped, his master first puts him in irons.

It is not uncommon to hear of a slave-dealer selling his own children born of Negro women; and instances occur daily of their disposing of female slaves who are pregnant by them; in such cases, the future child of course becomes the property of the purchaser. Most of the traders have old slaves who have been for many years in their service; these are placed over the young slaves bought in trade, and become very useful in travelling; but even these, too, I have seen their masters sell, after they had become members as it were of the family, merely because a high price was offered for them. It is vain to expect in a slave-trader any trace of friendship, gratitude, or compassion.

• VIII •

Eunuchs and Concubines

*It is a curious irony that the best path to an easier life for male slaves was to be deprived of their sexuality, whereas for females it was to have their sexuality exploited. Male eunuchs were the most expensive type of slaves, due to the high mortality rate of those who underwent the operation. They were therefore purchased by wealthy owners who needed them to oversee their women's quarters (*ḥarīm *—harem), and were often clothed and outfitted luxuriosly as a reflection of their owners' wealth. Within the harem they often enjoyed considerable authority, and were in part responsible for bringing up their owner's children. Some ended up as guardians of the great mosques of Islam's holy places (*al-ḥaramayn*)—Mecca and Medina.*

Any female slave could be used as a sexual partner by her master, and some became regular concubines, having then almost the status of a junior wife. This enabled them to assimilate into the dominant society to some extent, especially if they bore children for their master. Such children were, of course, free, so the concubine became the mother of free men, even in some cases of rulers. A woman who bore such children could not thereafter legally be sold, and was automatically free on her master's death.

(1) EUNUCHS IN NINETEENTH-CENTURY EGYPT

Source: G. Tournès, *Les Eunuques en Egypte* (Genève, 1869), 9–13. G. Tournès was at one time physician to the Suez Canal Company, and to the French Consulate in Cairo. His pamphlet on eunuchs in Egypt was a part of a longer unpublished work, *Notes sur l'Egypte.*

Their Place of Origin

It is not, as one might have thought or rightly supposed, among barbarous hordes and cannibals that greedy speculators—executioners of humanity, have pitched their tents and set up their bloody establishments. No, it is only a few days' journey from Cairo, up the Nile towards Assiout, in and around Asna, that those horrid mutilations are performed every year, creating so many victims. It is from there that the eunuchs who are destined to fill the harems of Egypt, Syria and Turkey begin their journey.

Coptic priests are reputed—and rightly so—to have the monopoly of this type of mutilation. Sennar, Dar Fur, Kordofan and Abyssinia are the countries which normally supply the persons fated for castration. In the wars between tribes and peoples, children are carefully spared by the victors. They are then taken as captives to the banks of the Nile where they are sold to slave merchants of Upper Egypt who have them mutilated.

This is how the operation is carried out, on children of seven to nine years old, and sometimes on much older boys.

Details of the Operation

The operator seizes the penis, the scrotal sacs and the testicles and ties them together tightly with a thin but tough cord. Then, with a single razor stroke, he cuts off everything below the ligature. The huge wound is then covered with ashes to stop the bleeding, then boiling oil is poured on and finally, if the first two methods have proved ineffective, it is cauterised with a red-hot iron. This having been done, a crude probe of metal, usually of lead, is inserted in the urethra right up to the bladder to facilitate the flow of urine. This probe is held in place by a harness of the most primitive type which remains in place until healing is complete.

When all these measures have been taken, the patient is immersed to the waist in the muddy silt of the Nile and left there for five or six days to help the formation of scar tissue. The Nile—that supreme god—ought to heal all ills. These details are horrible, but true. Therefore, I have no fear of exposing them in all their hideousness and fearfulness.

The general appearance of eunuchs after the operation.

This is the appearance most generally presented by the genitals, or rather their place, after the operation: a huge broad scar of very irregular shape, with raised edges, the scar tissue being of a lighter colour than the surrounding skin, full of folds and wrinkles. There is a purulent discharge, mixed for a long time—often several months—with a great deal of matter tinged with blood. There is almost continuous pain in the perineum, sharp and stabbing at first, later dull. Then come loss of appetite, nostalgia, strange dreams, terrible nightmares; the brain becomes empty, ideas flee, thought is wiped out. The eunuch turns into a brute. The man has disappeared.

Incontinence, especially during the night during sleep, is almost always one of the inevitable results of castration. From the accursed day henceforth the wretched eunuch always has with him, at home or on his person, a probe which he uses to project his urine to a distance. Sixty percent die during the operation or as a result of it. Those who survive receive assiduous attention and usually attain to more or less complete healing towards the end of the third month after the operation. From then on they are merchandise having a value and are soon sent off to Cairo to become the property of beys and pashas, or towards Alexandria from where they are sent on to Syria and Turkey. A young eunuch is then sold for about 25 purses, the value of a purse being 80 francs.

Physical state

People generally think that eunuchs are fat, obese, excessively rounded. This is a great mistake; the exception has been taken for the rule. Eunuchs, so numerous in Cairo, are almost all tall and very slender. Their legs and arms are of disproportionate length, especially the legs. Their hands are long, dry and nervous; their fingers recall the monkey. They have thick protruding lips with the lower lip hanging down; their hair is thick, strong, dry and fuzzy; their teeth are sparkling white, widely spaced and jutting out, standing out in a half circle against their ebony face. Their face is sometimes thin, dry and elongated, sometimes fat, heavy and rounded. The forehead is always narrow and receding, the eyes glassy and lifeless, devoid of vigor and energy. Their back is arched with the head leaning to one side. One would think them old men.

In a word, everything in them hints at an incomplete man, an abnormal being deprived of the life force in its very principle. Almost all of them are black in color, except however the Abyssinians who are of a very handsome type.

Their way of life, their tastes, their habits. Their functions in the harem

An unbridled passion for luxury dominates them totally: a taste for jewels, a love of horses, precious stones, diamonds and rich clothes absorbs them completely, sums up their life, their entire existence.

To ride superb thoroughbred Arabian horses with trappings resplendent with gold and laden with embroidery, sometimes decorated with fine and precious stones; to dress in silk or in fine clothes of the most diverse colours, bright or dull—black, orange, cherry, apple-green, chocolate brown or coffee-coloured, head wrapped in a gilded *kūfiyya*[162] with glittering fringes, the chest covered in enormous chains, always in solid gold, fingers covered in rings set with diamonds, pearls, emeralds and sapphires— these are the pleasures, the very life, of the eunuch.

They walk out, mixing with the crowds, amid carriages, mounted men and pedestrians, passing along the most frequented streets of Cairo and along the road to Shubra,[163] a huge avenue lined with majestic sycamores leading to the towns made up of palaces and gardens belonging to Prince Halim. There they follow, with a look of envy mixed with hatred, the groups of young women and girls, lolling in graceful carriages, and seem happy to show off to all eyes their luxury, their horses, their impotence and their persons.

The Arabs respect them, admire them, almost venerate them. They mysteriously seem to think they have a supernatural power, given by heaven to these unfortunate beings as a compensation for the tortures which men have made them suffer—in exchange for those earthly pleasures they have been denied. The crowd parts at their arrival . . . . The eunuch belongs to the pashas and the Arab never forgets it. Perhaps also at the bottom of his heart, the wretched peasant comes to envy them their rich adornment, their evident good fortune, their artificial happiness and even their positions in the great houses.

One sees them seated before the gates of the palaces of pashas, continually smoking a *shibbūk*[164] with a gilded head and a long pipe, or a Spanish cigarette, or better still, the traditional *narghīla,* with its flexible rolled-up pipe like a huge snake. For them it is a serious occupation, the only one which totally absorbs them—or the horse or the divan—no happy medium.

Into those sumptuous dwellings of which they are the guardians, none can penetrate, either as visitor or as friend of the household or on any other pretext, without being preceded and accompanied by one or several eunuchs. They go ahead, striking the echoing flagstones with their sticks and emitting loud cries so that the serving women who might find themselves in the path of the strangers can withdraw. They are, at one and the same time, ushers, chamberlains and masters of ceremony in the palaces of the pashas. It is they who preside over all events in the private, intimate life of the harem—meals, baths, excursions, visits, walks etc. One of their main tasks is to accompany the women on excursions outside when they go out in carriages. Riding on fine horses, two eunuchs go ahead of the carriage to clear people from its path. A third is always seated next to the coachman, holding in his hand a huge cane with a silver knob. Two others run beside each carriage, each with a hand resting on the door to proclaim its inviolability, and ready to lower the blinds which a well-made hand, light and indiscreet, may sometimes try to raise in order to enjoy a view of the passers-by and the bustle of the street.

At the destination, when the carriage cannot enter an interior courtyard, they make sure, above all, that the women who have been entrusted to their care can step down without being the object of any audacious glances. Woe to the *giaour,*[165] infidel and indiscreet who would hamper them in carrying out this task.

Imagination in the eunuch

If the senses have been extinguished in the eunuch, the same cannot be said for the imagination—that "madwoman in the house" as a famous fabulist put it.

Continual contact and constant residence among women induces in the eunuch a strong tendency to look back on his past. He realises that he, too, could have been a man, and that men in pursuit of a goal of unqualified egotism, have made him descend below the level of the brute while nevertheless retaining the attributes of his sex. Thus, in his weakness, he looks for one who is yet weaker than him to give free rein to his notions of rancor and vengeance. And it is woman, that woman whose guardian and protector he should be, who becomes his victim.

The eunuch is king in the harem and in its dependencies. He reigns as absolute master, as despot, over the women who inhabit it. For the least fault, the least forgetfulness, the slightest oversight, these unfortunate creatures are subjected to his anger, his brutality, his ill treatment. This is literally true: they manage the women with a stick. Only the legitimate wife and the favorite of the moment can escape their ill humor and caprice. Hard, proud, haughty, and insolent with all, they are nevertheless humble, submissive, servile and grovelling before their lord and master. He has power over their lives and can with a signal obliterate them from the ranks of the living—they are slaves.

Like the slave in ancient Rome, the slave is part of his master's household. He is a thing—*res*—but he is the essential and indispensable "thing." Without the eunuch there is no peace, no repose for the pasha, since the eunuch is entrusted with that which is most precious, most dear to the pasha—the women of the harem. The eunuch thus identifies himself with his position, and considers himself at home in his master's domain. He refers to my women, my horses, my carriages, my palace, my harem. The eunuch is an integral part of all of it. He has been brought up in the harem, has lived there and it is there that he ought to die.

One has seen eunuchs who have gained their liberty, either

through the death of their master or some other means and have attained an independent position. Well, it is not long before these same eunuchs get fed up with this new existence, this life of liberty forgotten by them. They soon return to the harem to take up their old profession as guardians of women and their easy, unending idleness.

(2) CASTRATION IN THE DESERT

Source: F.J.G. Mercadier, *L'Esclave de Timimoun* (Paris, 1971), 41ff. Mercadier was commandant of Timimoun, the chief locality of the Saharan oasis of Gourara, from July 1944 to the end of 1947, a post he took up after serving as a *méhariste*, or camel corps commander, in the French Algerian Sahara. He says that he spoke Arabic and some Tamasheq. His book is derived from extensive discussions with Griga, a former slave, then in his late 90s, who worked in the oasis gardens of a certain Si Hamou ben Abdelkader. For the complete narrative, see below, p. 199. The narrator is Griga, a slave who was part of the caravan traveling from Matankari (in far northeastern Hausaland) to Mtlili in Algeria.

The Chamba were inclined towards castrating three of the children who had fallen to their lot.[166] Naturally they chose the most robust and least exhausted of their share. It was important to operate immediately since only those who survived the operation would be taken away. To delay castration would mean giving food and water for several more days to creatures who might perhaps die. It was better that they should die right away. This would cost less.

Ali Laouar, crouched like a tailor close to his saddle, sharpened his knife—the knife which he otherwise used to shave his head—on a fine grained stone that he wore hanging from his neck together with a huge string of amulets. He spat on the stone to give it more bite. When he judged the knife to be sufficiently sharp he tested the cutting edge on the nail of his left thumb, whilst two of the Chamba brought one of the children and laid him down on the ground. One of the Arabs held down the arms of the boy with his knees, while he used his hands to press down the hips of the victim, who, in his fright, struggled, twisting, turning, and flexing his muscles. The other Arab took hold of the patient by the ankles and pulled his legs apart. The young Negro boy at first screamed, then wept, and finally moaned softly. Ali Laouar got up and crouched down beside the child. He uttered the ritual prayer: "In the name of God, the Beneficent, the Merciful," seized the testicles in his left hand, made them slightly taut, then cut. Inhuman screams of pain! We were all completely distraught, but unfortunately could do nothing. Ali Laouar wiped the blade of his knife on his patient's thigh, then stuck the blade into the ground. He dressed the wound with wood tar and powdered it with ground camel dung to stop the bleeding. The child screamed! Two Arabs raised him up, each one taking an arm, and forced him to take a few steps, to relax his muscles so they said. Then they let him fall down beside their baggage, and went on to the next child, who tried to bite them, and twisted about like a snake.

Do you think anyone could forget that? Even in my tomb I shall see once again the frightful spectacle of those tortured children.

Unmoved in the face of this inhuman suffering, the Chamba calaculated for each one of the boys operated on the chances of his survival and the fabulous price that the merchants of Ghadames who export Negroes to the kingdoms of the east would pay for him.

When, after several hours, the bleeding of one of the emasculated boys had not stopped, his wound was cauterized with a red-hot iron. Hideous new screams! The smell of burnt flesh! He nevertheless died in the night.

(3) EUNUCHS AT THE PROPHET'S MOSQUE IN AL-MADINA

Source: J. Burckhardt, *Travels in Arabia* (1829), 342–44. For information on Burckhardt, see above, p. 88.

The police of the mosque, the office of washing the Hedjra[167] and the whole of the building, of lighting the lamps, etc. etc. is entrusted to the care or forty or fifty eunuchs, who have an establishment similar to that of the eunuchs of the Beitullah[168] at Mekka; but they are persons of greater consequence here; they are more richly dressed, though in the same costume; usually wear fine Cashmere shawls, and gowns of the best Indian silk stuffs, and assume airs of great importance. When they pass through the Bazar, every body hastens to kiss their hands; and they exercise considerable influence in the internal affairs of the town. They have large stipends, which are sent annually from Constantinople by the Syrian Hadj caravan; they share also in all donations made to the mosque, and they expect presents from every rich hadjy, besides what they take as fees from the visitors to the Hedjra. They live together in one of the best quarters of Medina to the eastward of the mosque, and their houses are said to be furnished in a more costly manner than any others in the town. The adults are all married to black or Abyssinian slaves.

The black eunuchs, unlike those of Europe, become emaciated; their features are extremely coarse, nothing but the bones being distinguishable; their hands are those of a skeleton, and their whole appearance is extremely disgusting. By the help of thick clothing they hide their leanness; but their bony features are so prominent, that they can be distinguished at first sight. Their voice, however, undergoes little, if any change, and is far from being reduced to that fine feminine tone so much admired in the Italian singers.[169]

The chief of the eunuchs is called Sheikh el Haram: he is also the chief of the mosque, and the principal person in town; being consequently of much higher rank than the Aga, or chief of the eunuchs at Mekka. He is himself a eunuch, sent from Constantinople, and usually belonging to the court of the Grand Signor, who sends him hither by way of punishment or exile, in the same manner as Pashas are sent to Djidda. The present Sheikh el Haram had been formerly Kislar Agassi,[170] or prefect of the women of the Emperor Selym,[171] which is one of the first charges in the court. Whether it was the dignity of his former employ, of which the eastern grandees usually retain the rank through life even if they are dispossessed of it, or his new dignity of Sheikh el Haram, that gave him his importance, I am unable to say; but he took, on every occasion, precedence of Tousoun Pasha, whose rank was that of Pasha of Djidda, and of three tails; and the latter, whenever they met, kissed the Sheikh's hands, which I have seen him do in the mosque. He has a court composed in a manner similar to that of a Pasha but much less numerous. His dress is given with the most minute accuracy in D'Ohhson's work:[172] it consists of a fine pelisse, over a rich embroidered silk gown, made in the fashion of the capital; a khandjar, or dagger, set with diamonds, stuck in his belt; and a kaouk, or high bonnet, on his head: whenever he walked out, a number of servants, or Ferráshyn of the mosque, armed with large sticks, walked before him.

The person of Sheikh el Haram was respected by the Wahabys: when Saoud took Medina he permitted the Sheikh, with several other eunuchs, to retire to Yembo,[173] with his wives, and all his baggage and valuables; but would not receive another into the town; and the eunuchs themselves appointed one of their number to preside over them, till after an interval of eight years, when the present chief was sent from Constantinople; but his influence over the affairs of the town is reduced to a mere shadow of what it was.

A eunuch of the mosque would be highly affronted if he were so termed by any person. Their usual title is Aga. Their chief takes the title of Highness, or Sadetkom,[174] like a Pasha, or the Sherif of Mecca.

(4) THE EGYPTIAN HAREM (19TH CENTURY)

PART 1

Source: William Edward Lane, *Manners and Customs of the Modern Egyptians, written in Egypt during the Years 1833, -34, and -35*, 5th edition, with numerous additions and improvements, from a copy annotated by the author, edited by Edward Stanley Poole (London, 1860), 133, 183–86. Lane was a distinguished scholar of Arabic who spent the years 1825–28 in Egypt. His *Manners and Customs* is still being reprinted, as is his massive and authoritative Arabic lexicon. Lane married a Greek ex-slave woman, and may thus have gained some authentic insights into life in a harem.

Before I describe the ordinary habits of the master of a family, I must mention the various classes of persons of whom the family may consist. The ḥareem [*ḥarīm*], or the females of the house, have distinct apartments allotted to them; and into these apartments (which, as well as the persons to whom they are appropriated, are called "the ḥareem,") no males are allowed to enter, except the master of the family, and certain other near relations, and children. The ḥareem may consist, first, of a wife, or wives (to the number of four); secondly, of female slaves, some of whom, namely, white and (as they are commonly called) Abyssinian (but more properly Galla) slaves, are generally concubines, and others (the black slaves) kept merely for servile offices, as cooking, waiting upon the ladies, &c.; thirdly, of female free servants, who are, in no case, concubines, or not legitimately so. The male dependents may consist of white and of black slaves, and free servants; but are mostly of the last-mentioned class. Very few of the Egyptians avail themselves of the licence, which their religion allows them, of having four wives; and still smaller is the number of those who have two or more wives, and concubines besides. Even most of those men who have but one wife are content, for the sake of domestic peace, if for no other reason, to remain without a concubine-slave: but some prefer the possession of an Abyssinian slave to the more expensive maintenance of a wife; and keep a black slave-girl, or an Egyptian female servant, to wait upon her, to clean and keep in order the apartments of the ḥareem and to cook. It is seldom that two or more wives are kept in the same house: if they are, they generally have distinct apartments. Of male servants, the master of a family keeps, if he can afford to do so, one or more to wait upon him and his male guests; another, who is called a "saḳḳà," or water-carrier, but who is particularly a servant of the harem, and attends the ladies only when they go out;[175] a "bowwáb," or doorkeeper, who constantly sits at the door of the house; and a "sáïs," or groom, for the horse, mule, or ass. Few of the Egyptians have "memlooks," or male white slaves[176]; most of these being in the possession of rich 'Osmánlees (or Turks); and scarcely any but Turks of high rank keep eunuchs: but a wealthy Egyptian merchant is proud of having a black slave to ride or walk behind him, and to carry his pipe. . . .

Some wives have female slaves who are their own property, generally purchased for them, or presented to them, before marriage. These cannot be the husband's concubines without their mistress's permission, which is sometimes granted (as it was in the case of Hagar, Sarah's bondwoman); but very seldom. Often, the wife will not even allow her female slave or slaves to appear unveiled in the presence of her husband. Should such a slave, without the permission of her mistress, become the concubine of the husband, and bear him a child, the child is a slave, unless, prior to its birth, the mother be sold, or presented, to the father.

The white female slaves are mostly in the possession of wealthy Turks. The concubine-slaves[177] in the houses of Egyptians of the higher and middle classes are, generally, what are termed "Ḥabasheeyehs," that is, Abyssinians, of a deep brown or bronze complexion. In their features, as well as their complexions, they appear to be an intermediate race between the negroes and white people: but the difference between them and either of the above-mentioned races is considerable. They themselves, however, think that they differ so little from the white people, that they cannot be persuaded to act as servants, with due obedience, to their master's wives; and the black (or negro) slave-girl feels exactly in the same manner towards the Abyssinian, but is perfectly willing to serve the white ladies. I should here mention, that the slaves who are termed "Abyssinians" are, with few exceptions, not from the country properly called Abyssinia, but from the neighbouring territories of the Gallas.[178] Most of them are handsome. The average price of one of these girls is from ten to fifteen pounds sterling, if moderately handsome; but this is only about half the sum that used to be given for one a few years ago. They are much esteemed by the voluptuaries of Egypt; but are of delicate constitution: many of them die, in this country, of consumption. The price of a white slave-girl is usually from treble to tenfold that of an Abyssinian; and the price of a black girl, about half or two-thirds, or considerably more if well instructed in the art of cookery. The black slaves are generally employed as menials.[179]

Almost all of the slaves become converts to the faith of El-Islám; but, in general, they are little instructed in the rites of their new religion; and still less in its doctrines. Most of the white female slaves who were in Egypt during my first visit to this country were Greeks; vast numbers of that unfortunate people having been made prisoners by the Turkish and Egyptian army under Ibráheem Báshà, and many of them, males and females, including even infants scarcely able to walk, sent to Egypt to be sold. Latterly, from the impoverishment of the higher classes in this country, the demand for white slaves has been small. A few, some of whom undergo a kind of preparatory education (being instructed in music or other accomplishments, at Constantinople), are brought from Circassia and Georgia. The white slaves, being often the only female companions, and sometimes the wives, of the Turkish grandees, and being generally preferred by them before the free ladies of Egypt, hold a higher rank than the latter in common opinion. They are richly dressed, presented with valuable ornaments, indulged, frequently, with almost every luxury that can be procured, and, when it is not their lot to wait upon others, may, in some cases, be happy: as lately has been proved, since the termination of the war in Greece, by many females of that country, captives in Egyptian ḥareems, refusing their offered liberty, which all of these cannot be supposed to have done from ignorance of the state of their parents and other relations, or the fear of exposing themselves to poverty; though not a few of them may probably have been induced to remain in bondage by a sense of the religious and moral degradation to which they had been forcibly subjected, and by their having borne children to their masters. But, if some of them are undoubtedly happy, at least for a time, their number is comparatively small: most are fated to wait upon more favoured fellow-prisoners, or upon Turkish ladies, or to receive the unwelcome caresses of a wealthy dotard, or of a man who has impaired his body and mind by excesses of every kind; and, when their master or mistress becomes tired of them, or dies, are sold again (if they have not borne children), or emancipated, and married to some person in humble life, who can afford them but few of the comforts to which they have been accustomed. The female slaves in the houses of persons of the middle classes in Egypt are generally more comfortably circumstanced than those in the ḥareems of the wealthy: if concubines, they are, in most cases, without rivals to disturb their peace; and if menials, their service is light, and they are under less restraint. Often, indeed, if mutual attachment subsist between her and her master, the situation of a concubine-slave is more fortunate than that of a wife: for the latter may be cast off by her husband in a moment of anger, by an irrevocable sentence of divorce, and reduced to a state of poverty; whereas a man very seldom dismisses a female slave without providing for her in such a manner that, if she have not been used to luxuries, she suffers but little, if at all, by the change: this he generally does by emancipating her, giving her a dowry, and marrying her to some person of honest reputation; or by presenting her to a friend. I have already mentioned, that a master cannot sell nor give away a slave who has borne him a child, if he acknowledge it to be his own; and that she is entitled to her freedom on his death. It often happens that such a slave, immediately after the birth of her child, is emancipated, and becomes her master's wife: when she has become free, she can no longer lawfully supply the place of a wife unless he marry her. Many persons consider it disgraceful even to sell a female slave who has been long in their service. Most of the Abyssinian and black slave-girls are abominably corrupted by the Gellábs, or slave-traders, of Upper Egypt and Nubia, by whom they are brought from their native countries: there are very few of the age of eight or nine years who have not suffered brutal violence; and so severely do these children, particularly the Abyssinians, and boys as well as girls, feel the treatment which they endure from the Gellábs, that many instances occur of their drowning themselves during the voyage down the Nile.[180] The female slaves of every class are somewhat dearer than the males of the same age. Those who have not had the small-pox are usually sold for less than the others.[181] Three days' trial is generally allowed to the purchaser; during which time, the girl remains in his, or some friend's, ḥareem; and the women make their report to him. Snoring, grinding the teeth, or talking during sleep, are commonly considered sufficient reasons for returning her to the dealer.—The dresses of the female slaves are similar to those of the Egyptian women.

(4) THE EGYPTIAN HAREM (19TH CENTURY)

PART 2

Source: Huda Shaarawi, *Harem Years: the Memoirs of an Egyptian Feminist*, translated by Margot Badran (London: Virago Press, 1986; reprinted by permission), 39. Huda Shaarawi was born into an upper-class Egyptian family in 1879, and was brought up and educated in a family harem. She stood up boldly for women's freedom, and symbolized this by publicly unveiling herself at age 44. She became head of the Egyptian Feminist Union, and was also involved in Egypt's struggle for independence from British overrule. She died in 1947. The eunuch whom she mentions, Bashir Agha, was an Ethiopian slave, who was freed in 1884 on the death of Huda's father.

Bashir Agha, the oldest of my late father's eunuchs, a merry man with a deep laugh, was an awesome and venerable personage, held in high esteem by friends of the family and all others who knew him, but not so much by my brother and me, as he used to take us to task. He had numerous friends of all ranks and classes. His lightheartedness and praiseworthy virtues earned the nickname "Abu al-Bashir," Father of Mankind. An inveterate better on horse races and ram and cock fights (he owned a number of animals himself), he tried to interest my brother, of whom he was very fond, in these pursuits. I feared it would distract from his lessons, but my mother's maid, Fatanat, entrusted to look after my brother when his Sudanese nursemaid died, tried to persuade him he had no need for learning because he was rich. I threatened never to speak to him again if he didn't pay attention to his studies.

Said Agha, a younger and more severe man, was charged to watch over us and all who came to the house. He accompanied us everywhere and was even present during our lessons. The household staff feared him because he observed every minute detail. He was "master of life and death" over the servants and tutors.

(5) CONCUBINAGE IN MECCA (1880s)

Source: C. Snouck Hurgronje, *Mekka in the Latter Part of the 19th Century* (Leiden, 1931), 106–9. Hurgronje spent 1884–85 in Arabia, for six months of which he was in Mecca. Here the concubine seems to play the role of lover, at the expense of the lawfully wedded wife. The prized African concubine is the "Abyssinian" woman, because she is light-skinned, and perhaps viewed as more "Arab" than "African." However, there seems also to have been some attraction towards the "sexual exoticism" of much darker-skinned African women. Although the more fortunate of such concubines could find an honored status, it is also clear that owners of such young women could exploit them sexually, deflowering them at the onset of puberty, or "loaning" them to young male relatives.

If the Mekkan marriage is in many cases, in our view, equivalent to concubinage, so on the other hand many connexions which approach nearest to European marriage, are regarded in Mekka as concubinage. If the Mekkan expresses himself openly, he will confess that his heart can belong to hardly any Mekkan woman but can well belong to a slave woman. An imprudent man once expressed himself before me with real enthusiasm in this sense, while his wife was walking up and down in the next room; when she then began to cough nervously, he changed his tone and said that everything was only relative and that there was nothing more precious than the freeborn daughter of the people (*bint en-nâs*—which in the language of Mekka denotes freeborn female, while *wèlèd en-nâs* denotes a freeborn male). All this, however, was mere make-believe, and that was not misunderstood even by the wife.

The physical advantages of the slave-women are here generally recognised, and indeed the darker the color the higher is the degree of sexual attractiveness. I have known a very rich man, who could get almost anything in the way of *harîm* that he wished, dissolved in tears because a pitch-black negress whom he has shortly bought was willing to comply with his wishes in almost all things, but in one thing not. And here with decent people the principle holds good: all can be got by force except one thing. The above mentioned[182] pitch black son of the rich Indian merchant was the fruit of the more fortunate inclination of this man towards his black kitchenmaid. In short in the purely sexual regard, all Mekkans are full of the praises of the daughters of Ham. Only the low culture and certain peculiarities of the negro character put a limit after some time to this inclination. The negress who has excited this passion of her master generally profits by it for her whole life, for each pregnancy makes the slave woman inalienable and free after her master's death, but this concubinage has no resemblance to a marriage.

Though the Mekkan may sometimes run after Mekkan women or get infatuated with negresses, yet his real enthusiasm is reserved for Abyssinian women *(hubûsh).*[183] If the ordinary Mekkan followed his inclination, he would unite himself only to Abyssinians; it is, however, part of the "convenances"[184] that a man should at least once in his life marry a freeborn woman, and people of small means can pay a few dollars as dowry for a wife but not a hundred or two for a slave. So it comes about that a man either brings up a slave girl from her youth or gets one out of a good house. Elderly ladies of good position, especially such as are mistresses of their houses (*bint* ^{c}*amm*)[185] but not of the hearts of their husbands, are glad to buy several quite young girls in order to occupy themselves with their education. They send them to school, have them taught spinning, knitting and so forth, and treat them as their daughters. When some of these girls have grown up together on this footing, disagreements gradually arise between them, and their mistress sees that the time has come to get a situation for this one or the other. A good "situation" for an Abyssinian girl is concubinage with a good master. These girls themselves generally prefer to enter a large and fashionable household, for they there find many companions and a cheerful life full of variety, but their lot is in the long run happier if they find a master with a somewhat elderly wife and, besides her, only menial slaves, male or female. With the man of comparatively humble position who has just enough to buy and keep an Abyssinian woman, she must at the same time fill the position of wife and work slave, and this is too hard in this climate. If her master brings her into the house of a spouse who still has pretensions, then the Hagar meets an often very cruel Sara, and has to fear bad treatment every time that the master leaves the house. Therefore such a master hires a small separate dwelling for the concubine so that the lawful wife (*bint al-ᶜamm*) may know nothing of her. Only in large houses must the wife be tolerant in this regard; there the girls distribute between themselves all kinds of work, and the space conditions withdraw the master's amours from all control of the wife. No matter how fleeting his connection may be with one of the many handmaidens (*jawâr* plur. of *jâriyah)*, he would be condemned by public opinion if he sent her away after such connexion.

A slave girl who has not been brought up by her master from her childhood in his house is never bought as a virgin, even if she has not had a situation before. Her owner or some relation of her mistress deflowers her as soon as she has reached the age (12 to 14 years), and the buyer would look upon it as suspicious if that had not been done. Now no man may live with a slave girl who does not belong to him and transgressions of this law are even practically regarded as grave misdemeanours; so a rigid distinction is made between the slave girls of the wife and those of the husband, and in ordinary families the wife takes care to have ugly ones. An exception however is made for slave girls brought up by their mistress, or the fiction is resorted to that she has bestowed her girl on her son, cousin, nephew, or the like, and has then taken her back the next day.

In other matters too the holy law of concubinage is much transgressed. Thus a man who has bought a concubine should, as is well known, wait a certain time before cohabitation so that there may be no doubt about the parentage of children.[186] This rule is however confessedly too hard for the Mekkans: it is much for them to wait even two or three days, though the rule of allowing a woman an interval between two marriages is practically respected.[187] Furthermore, it happens that the harmony between master and concubine is not lasting while, on account of pregnancy the connexion is indissoluble. In this case the man should set the concubine free so that she may later contract a marriage; only scoundrels deny their children so as to be able again to sell the slave girl. It is not rare, however, for the denial to be made at the urgent request of the girl herself, for if she gets married she is exposed to the daily danger of a divorce and would perhaps fall into serious trouble.[188] She prefers to remain a slave until she finds a sympathetic master and he and she have reared children together. And so concubines are often inclined to use the temporary preservative against fruitfulness but not the perpetual ones.

Of a black female slave (negress) the highest ideal is to work in a good house so long as her strength allows it, for then in her old age she is affectionately cared for; to attract the passing inclination of her master whereby in the case of pregnancy a fairly happy existence is secured for her; to be given as a wife to a freed slave whereby she gets an opportunity to obtain an independent position; or again to be married to another free man, which is not so rare as might he supposed.

The aim of the Abyssinian woman is a lasting connexion with a Mekkan to whom she, if her good intellectual and moral gifts have not been spoilt by her upbringing, becomes a true life companion. She has not, like the wife, interests contrary to those of the husband, and her thoughts are far from exploitation. Her highest wish is to attach the man to her and to prepare for him a happy home. The well brought up Abyssinian women are excellent house-keepers, modest, unpretending women, and they put all their good qualities at the service of their lord. The high esteem in which they are held by the Mekkan men is most clearly shewn by the many cases in which an Abyssinian woman has borne him from five to twelve children, and the children are the best pledge of the continuance of their parents' happiness. As mother of one or more Mekkans she belongs to Mekkan society as a virtually free member, though nominally her slavery continues. If her master sets her free, then she marries only on condition that her position is equal to that of a free born Mekkan woman, and as such a free born woman in case of need flees to her relations, so does the Abyssinian woman find a safe refuge in her children.

Theoretically these children stand on an equal footing in every way with those born from free mothers;[189] in practice they are generally preferred to the latter. In general it may be said that in every well-to-do family sons of both kinds of mothers, the free and the slave woman, are represented, but no difference in appearance nor in mutual behavior can be observed by the stranger.

Former members of Ottoman sultan Abdulhamid's harem
with two eunuchs (1929).
Alev Lytle Croutier, *Harem: The World behind the Veil*, 141.

(6) THE "NEGRESS OF THE BED"

Source: Jérôme and Jean Tharaud, *Fez, ou les bouregeois de l'Islam* (Paris: © Librairie Plon, 1930; translated by permission), 28–31. Jérôme and Jean Tharaud were celebrated literary brothers, whose real names were Ernest and Charles Tharaud. They were born in 1874 and 1877 respectively, and wrote many books together, including novels, biographies and travel books. In 1906 they won the Prix Goncourt, and both were eventually elected to the Académie française, Jérôme in 1938 and Jean in 1946. In 1917 General Lyautey invited them both to Morocco, and they made several extended visits there, producing as a result books on each of the major cities: Marrakech, Fez, and Rabat. Jean Tharaud died in 1952, and Jérôme the following year.

In the world of slaves—who to untrained eyes are only differentiated by their faces or their age—life, law, and custom have ended up creating quite a hierarchy.

First, there is the Negress of the bed. Rather than marry, many people prefer Black concubines, who are allowed by the Qur'ān. There is no dowry to pay, no wedding ceremonies involving ridiculous expenses—as I will speak of later on; there is no family obstacle, and it is very convenient to take these women with you when you travel. It even happens frequently that the mother of a family who wants to retain her authority in the house, pushes her son to satisfy himself with one or more Negresses in the hope of keeping them under her thumb. The slave is always more docile, more prone to admire the master, and of a more obliging nature. Says the *ḥadīth*: "There is no Negress who would refuse love when it is offered." And if the lover is deceived, he always has a source of consolation in thinking "The Prophet told us so."

But what binds the man of Fez to his Negresses above all is that their skins, it would seem, are warmer than those of white women.[190] For a Moroccan all illnesses spring from coldness, and conversely all cures come about through the effect of heat. A burning black skin is a remedy for all ills. . . Furthermore, white women raised in the houses of Fez, which are generally badly ventilated, are pale, sickly, with poor constitutions, whereas the Negresses, despite the little work they do, still retain some energy, are less feeble and more healthy. In any case, the climate affects them less perceptibly; it doesn't turn them into cucumbers, as one says over there of women who have lost their color. In Rabat and Salé, where the sea air is more lively, and the dwellings less damp and gloomy, white women get worn out less quickly; and so, contrary to the people of Fez, the men of Rabat and Salé never take on black concubines. Not to mention the fact that, as they say, the son of a Negress that one can put up with is the eighth wonder of the world.

To the Negresses of the bed also belong the concubines of the sons, or the married sons who often continue to live in their father's house. To these should be added the Negresses that well-off burghers are in the habit of giving to a son as soon as he reaches the age of puberty. The boy does not always wait to have one chosen for him, but takes any one in the house that he fancies. Only his father's concubines are strictly forbidden to him. It is the law of the Orient, as one already sees in the Bible, which is full of stories of sons who, disdaining the Lord's orders, have stolen the favorites of their father's flock. In Fez, these ancient stories are the stuff of everyday life. And it is no small matter for fathers of families to keep their harem out of the hands of their offspring!

Should this bed slave bear a child, she is by this act freed.[191] Henceforth she occupies in the house a room which belongs to her, and which, if the master dies, cannot be taken away from her. Her son has all the rights of a legitimate child, since the law makes no difference between the children of the same father, so that it often happens that this child of a slave becomes the principal heir, and the guardian of the whole family.

• IX •

Domestic Service

*Although no statistics are available, it is generally agreed that the majority of African slaves in the Mediterranean Islamic world were used as domestic servants; and most of these were probably women. It has been estimated that two-thirds of the slaves who crossed the Sahara in the nineteenth century were female. Only a minority would have been formal concubines, though any female might be called upon for sexual services. Formal concubines might have relatively easy lives, especially if they became mothers of their master's children. Other female slaves were not so fortunate, though as will be seen below, in a trusted occupation such as child-nurse (*dada*) they did better than the average. It will also be noted that Ethiopian women often fared better than others.*

* * * *

(1) WOMEN SLAVES IN 19TH-CENTURY TURKEY

Source: Frederick Millingen, "Slavery in Turkey," *J. Anthropological Society of London* (1870), 102–3. Major Millingen was a Fellow of the Royal Geographical Society of London.

Let us now see what befalls the generality of negro slaves when they once make their début on the market-place. Some twenty years ago on their arrival at Constantinople the slaves used to be stored up within the precincts of an imperial slave market, as at that period the slave-dealers were patentee-merchants. Such a scandal could not, however, be patronised any longer and the Turks have continued the trade in an underhand way. Non-official markets were then opened at Sultan-Mehemet, at Tophaneh, and in some of the cafés and shops of Stambul.[192] One of these places is opposite the mosque of Suleimanieh in the bazar named Teriaki-teharshisi, the third shop to the left, looking west ward, if my memory does not fail me. In those markets slaves are sold daily, the hours of brisk business being from eight to twelve a.m., Turkish time. Up to A.D. 1869, this state of things was in existence. The thirty or forty girls that come on the market at the same period, all find customers quickly enough: the Abyssinians on account of their good looks are the first to be disposed of; they are taken as upper servants in the harems of those whose limited means forbid them to indulge in a thorough-bred Circassian. The Abyssinians are also taken as economical odalisks by the lower class of amateurs. The genuine negro girls with flat noses and thick lips are doomed to the kitchen and the rough work of the house.

On being raised from the market the new master sends the slave to the bath, and gives her a clean set of linen and a calicot suit of clothes. If the master happens to be a good-hearted man, the slave has a chance of being properly fed and clad; besides this she may obtain two or three shillings a month pocket money. On these terms she may go on for years till her frame gives way. There are cases in which negro slaves become old servants, loved and considered by their masters, and pass thus happily their old age. It happens sometimes that slaves are freed by the master, and are established in life by marrying some old servant of the house; such cases are not, however, frequently met with.

As a rule, the lot attending these creatures is sad. They pass through the hands of ten or twenty masters, who make them lead the life of cab-horses, beat them at intervals, and at last sell them. Such treatment irritates the temper and inflames the passions of the African destitute who, driven to despair, becomes a fury, wages war against her oppressors, and ends by becoming a hater of the white species. It is not to be wondered, then, if negroes have often been known to set fire to the wooden houses of Stamboul, as being the best means of retaliation they could devise.

After having been sold and re-sold over and over again, the negro slave gets at last in a condition to be not even worth feeding; then she obtains her freedom, and she is let loose on the streets of Stamboul, without the means of subsistence or the power to provide for herself. Her lot then is to roam about town a cripple and a beggar. Many of them, however, knowing what is in store for them, do not wait for the arrival of the bad season, and try to provide for themselves beforehand. Either through the assistance of their kinsmen, or with the money which they have been able to save or somehow to steal, they manage to buy themselves free from the market. Alarmed at the consequences which might result from the existence in the capital of numbers of freed negroes, destitute of everything, the Turkish Government formed of these fellows a regiment some six or eight hundred strong. The special duty of these men is that of storing into the arsenal the timber which comes to Constantinople in rafts from the Black Sea. Two queer sorts of trade practised by freed negro-males are those of sorcerers and of chemical confectioners. The sorcerers manage to get a good living by working on the credulity of a superstitious population. They employ sacred fumigations and beverages, and distribute talismans (*nuskha*s) good for all evils. The chemical confectioners go about the streets selling a miraculous jam, which is highly patronised by the impotent proprietors of harems.

(2) DOMESTIC SLAVERY IN FEZ

Source: Jérôme and Jean Tharaud, *Fez, ou les bourgeois de l'Islam* (Paris: © Librairie Plon, 1930; translated by permission), 25–26, 31–33. For information about the authors see p. 119 above.

What is most striking to a foreigner in the houses of Fez is the multitude of slaves. At the door of a rich house there are always at least two slaves: a porter and a runner of errands. Often there is also a mule slave, who, seated on the mounting platform, waits with his animal for his master to go out. All of these are very neatly dressed (each one gets a new garment on the great feast-days), and gossip throughout the day. If the house owner is some senior official of the government (*makhzen*), you see not two or three, but seven or eight slaves at the entrance wearing the pointed red hat of the sultan's livery. As you enter the abode you encounter equally idle slaves everywhere. Finally, you get to the master of the house. He receives you with good oriental grace, and immediately there begins a parade of Negresses to perform the tea ceremony. One busies herself boiling water; another brings the cups, the teapot or the silver samovar; yet another brings pastries made in the kitchens by other invisible Negresses. Brilliantly dressed, with the wide sleeves of the caftan rolled up on their naked arms and held in place by silken cords, their dresses hitched half way up their legs and drooping over their rumps like a bunch of multi-colored feathers, they silently bustle about whilst their master, without allowing anything to be seen, watches their work, or follows with a sensual thought, the undulations of their haunches.

* * * *

After discussing concubinage, the authors move on to two other uses to which African women slaves were put in Morocco

* * * *

Another type of slave is the *dada*, the nurse, a person of great importance in these households, where people are accustomed to pampering children a great deal. A householder of Fez told me that he has in his house an old Negress, an intolerable character at odds with his wife, who has not said a word to her for four years, and also at odds with his mother, who died without saying farewell to her. She has taken charge of one of his daughters, is raising her in her own fashion, spoils her, and lives in the house despite all opposition. Often her master declared, "You are free. Get out of here!" wishing with all his heart that she would take him at his word. But every time she would reply, "I am your children's Negress. I love them and I can't part from them. You can get out if you wish." In the houses of Fez there is no lack of such devoted and despotic old slaves whom one would wish to be rid of, and who hang on, resist, and attach themselves to that abode, outside of which nothing exists for them. If one talks of selling them, they throw themselves at the feet of their child (the one they have raised), and seize a fold of his robe, thereby making themselves untouchable.

There is yet another type: the dowry slave. In important families (and naturally everyone in Fez thinks they are important), when a girl marries it is specified in the contract that the husband should give her a slave. She is most often purchased by the husband from the girl's parents. She is either her *dada*, or a slave of the same age as her, who has grown up alongside her. This dowry slave belongs to the wife as her property. If her husband dies, the slave woman can in no way be part of his estate. If her mistress divorces, she also leaves the house. Neither the husband nor the sons can take her as a concubine, unless the mother agrees to give her to one of her boys when he has reached manhood. She is the living link between the young wife and her family. She constantly shuttles between one house and the other, giving an account of what is going on. In household disputes, or quarrels her mistress might have with other women, she always takes her part. In her secret love affairs she is the messenger and the bearer of gifts (a woman sends her lover pastries, garments, perfumes, a handkerchief, or a piece of gum she has chewed). She is the living letter between lovers, and is, of course, as unable to read a love letter as she is to sew or knit. In short, to sum it up in a word, she is the confidant in the ancient comedy.

Slave woman bath attendant, Moroccco.

Frederick Arthur Bridgman, *Winters in Algeria* (New York: Harper & Brothers, 1890), 107.

Black slave woman (*négresse esclave*), Morocco.

Oskar Lenz, *Timbouctou. Voyage au Maroc, au Sahara et au Soudan* (Paris: Librairie Hachette, 1886), vol. 1, 395.

• X •

Agricultural Labor

Relatively few slaves were employed in agricultural labor, as there were no large expanses of fertile virgin land waiting to be opened up, as there were in the Americas. However, there was a demand for slave labor in the date groves and gardens of the North African oases. Slaves were especially needed for dangerous tasks, such as cleaning out wells or underground irrigation systems.

(1) LABOR IN A SAHARAN OASIS

Source: F.J.G. Mercadier, *L'Esclave de Timimoun* (Paris, 1971). For information about this source, see pp. 55 or 105 above. For the full narrative, see pp. 199–219 below. The narrator is an ex-slave called Griga.

Soon I was initiated by Barka [a senior slave] into the horticultural tasks. I now knew the various types of palm, and learned how to pollinate female trees. O.K., I'll tell you about this because it was very tough. First of all you had to climb up the palm tree, but then when you got to the branches you had to seek out the most open pathway between the palm leaves, slip in there slowly with infinite precaution so as to avoid being pricked by the enormous spikes that bristle along their underside, and reach the heart of the tree. I then powdered the clusters of female flowers with pollen, and sometimes left there a small branch of male flowers.

When I had finished I climbed down, with legs, arms, the whole body scratched to the point of bleeding by the thousands of spikes, and then I went on to the next tree.

You know, pollinating palm trees is an art, but even more, it is a ritual. If there is the least moment of inattention, the smallest wrong movement, one or more spikes, a dozen or so centimeters long, very hard and fluted, sharp and wounding, will penetrate deeply into a limb or the abdomen and cause wounds that are difficult to heal....

That year the owners decided to refurbish the Amraïer foggara. Seven kilometers [4 miles] long, it was made up of 300 wells interconnected by an underground tunnel that brought water drained from the sandstone of the plateau down to the town's gardens. Its rate of flow had considerably diminished through obstruction of its canals, due no doubt to collapses. The owners of the foggara, who did not own enough slaves to carry out the necessary repairs with rapidity, asked for a "touiza," or work party, from the various quarters of the town.

Two days later at dawn, the drum went up and down the streets summoning to work the Negroes who had been detailed the night before. Everyone—men with short-handed hoes, women and children with palm-frond baskets—gathered together at the place where the foggara emerged, where the Zenata elders discussed the best way to accomplish this task.

They organized teams of ten Negroes, each of which had to clean out, cleanse, and rehabilitate ten wells. I and ten other Negroes under Barka's command were alloted to the wells of the plateau, which were more than 80 cubits [120 feet] deep.

We quickly made a hoist with the help of three palm trunks and attached to it a pulley carved out of acacia wood. I went down into the first well, without a rope, putting my hands and feet in the rough crevices of the sides of the well to stop myself falling. After a descent that was long and painful, since I was hit on the head by falling stones, I reached the water and bent myself down in the narrow tunnel that joined the two wells, whilst another slave followed me, preceded by a shower of stones. The Blacks who remained on the surface sent us down a basket on a rope, in which were a pick, a hoe, an oil lamp and a flint. As soon as the lamp was lit, work began. It was cold and humid. I cleaned out the canal, filled the basket with soil and gravel and passed it to my comrade, who fastened the rope. Once it had gone up to the top, the receptacle was emptied and sent down again.

You know, it often happens during this mole-like work that a lump of clay gets loose, obstructs the passage and entombs or crushes the workers. Then there is an incredible, superhuman effort, in a narrow, dark, and humid tunnel, to create a passage through this stopper of sticky, clayey paste, behind which the water rises inexorably.

Exhausted, my comrade and I went back up to the suface with the help of the rope, whilst our place was taken by two other slaves.

Suddenly, farther down around the one hundredth well, we hear cries. Everyone runs, gathers together, and discusses. It seems to me that someone is calling for help. We run there. The slaves explain that while descending the well, Moumen, the slave of Abdelali, had slipped and fallen forty cubits [60 feet]. Two men had just gone down to try and bring him up. Si Abdelkader and Abdelali, having been immediately informed, show up.

By using two ropes placed under his armpits, Moumen is hauled to the surface. He breathes with difficulty. He is laid out on the ground. Si Abdelkader bends over him, prods him, then slowly, then straightens up, shaking his head.

"He will die," he said, "His thighs and his ribs are broken. Take him to the village, and the rest of you, instead of looking and doing nothing, get back to work!"

* * * *

The cleaning out of such irrigation systems seems to have become a hereditary occupation of descendants of such slaves. An American traveler in the 1920s describes such an operation near Temacin in the Algerian Sahara. While he does not characterize the men as black Africans, the photograph he provides clearly shows them to be so. They were locally called in French les plongeurs, *and Hull describes them as "survivors of a medieval occupation." If this passage does not directly speak to slavery, it does, at least, provide a glimpse into the condition of black Africans in post-slavery in Algeria.*

(2) WELL DIVING

Source: E. M. Hull, *Camping in the Sahara* (New York, 1927), 17–19.

Their function is to descend to the bottom of wells that are fed by underground rivers, and clear away the accumulation of mud and fibrous matter which collects at the mouth of the inlet and chokes the steady inrush of water. . . .

Stripped to a loin-cloth, standing already waist-deep in water on a rope ladder, the diver was bending forward with his hands gripping the edge of the well, taking deep breaths and clearing his throat and lungs of all fluid and matter, while hanging over him was the chief of the little company, muttering prayers and incantations and massaging him vigorously between the shoulders.

Then, almost before we could set out watches to time him, the diver slipped down the ladder and the water closed over his head. It seemed hours before he reappeared. In reality it was three and a half minutes. Seven minutes is said to be the limit these men can remain immersed, though the late Messaoud ben Akli, who was with us at the time, told me that five minutes was the longest time he had ever seen. The obstructing rubbish collected from the inlet of the well is put into a skin bag which the diver carries tied round his waist.

When at last our man's head rose above the water again the filled bag was taken from him, and he was caught and held by the headman, who thumped and massaged and prayed over him once more, while he gasped and coughed and spat until he had recovered sufficient breath to half clamber, half be dragged out of the well. Hastily smothered in thick coverings, he was then laid down beside a blazing brushwood fire.

The diving exhausts them, and for half an hour or so afterwards they are more or less in a state of collapse. One reason for this may be the fact that they are ordinarily very small eaters, and when actually at work fast for twelve hours before starting operations, with the result that they are incredibly thin—walking skeletons, in fact. If there is a real necessity for this abstinence, or whether it is part of the ritual of their calling, I was not able to discover.

* * * *

In Arabia, agricultural labor was generally considered an inferior type of work, especially by the nomadic peoples. Hence, it was frequently carried out by slaves, though in the following passage we learn that slaves could be treated almost like sharecroppers.

(3) AFRICAN SLAVES IN ARABIA

Source: T.E. Lawrence, *The Seven Pillars of Wisdom* (New York: Doubleday, Doran & Co., 1935), 89. The passage below was originally written in 1919, but refers to the situation some two years earlier.

At the most, the tribal Arabs of Wadi Safra lived in their villages five months a year.[193] For the other seasons the gardens were entrusted to slaves, negroes like the grown lads who brought in the tray to us, and whose thick limbs and shining bodies looked curiously out of place among the bird-like Arabs. Khallaf told me the blacks were originally from Africa, brought over as children by their nominal Takruri fathers, and sold during the pilgrimage, in Mecca.[194] When grown strong they were worth from fifty to eighty pounds apiece, and were looked after carefully as befitted their price. Some became house or body servants with their masters; but the majority were sent out to the palm villages of these feverish valleys of running water, whose climate was too bad for Arab labour, but where they flourished and built themselves solid houses, and mated with women slaves, and did all the manual work of the holding.

They were very numerous—for instance, there were thirteen villages of them side by side in this Wadi Safra—so they formed a society of their own, and lived much at their pleasure. Their work was hard, but the supervision loose, and escape easy. Their legal status was bad, for they had no appeal to tribal justice, or even to the Sherif's courts;[195] but public opinion and self-interest deprecated any cruelty towards them, and the tenet of the faith that to enlarge a slave is a good deed,[196] meant in practice that nearly all gained freedom in the end. They made pocket-money during their service if they were ingenious. Those I saw had property, and declared themselves contented. They grew melons, marrows, cucumbers, grapes and tobacco for their own account, in addition to the dates, whose surplus was sent across to the Sudan by sailing dhow, and there exchanged for corn, clothing and the luxuries of Africa or Europe.

• XI •

Military Service

*Slaves were used as soldiers from early times in north Africa. The earliest known incidence of this comes from 9th-century Tunisia under the Aghlabids. In Morocco the use of black military slaves dates from the 11th century under the Almoravids, a Berber dynasty originating from the southern Sahara. After the Sa*ᶜ*dian conquest of Songhay in 1591, Mūlāy Aḥmad al-Manṣūr established a black slave corps in his army. Later, under the* ᶜ*Alawī ruler Mūlāy Ismā*ᶜ*īl* (reg. *1678–1727), the practice was revived, expanded and institutionalized, as may be seen from the passage below on the* ᶜ*Abīd al-Bukhārī. This represents the apogee of such a practice in the Muslim world, though slaves continued to be used for military purposes down to the 19th century, notably in the Sudan.*

(1) THE MOROCCAN ROYAL SLAVE ARMY

Source: Aḥmad b. Khālid al-Nāṣirī, *Kitāb al-istiqṣāʾ li-akhbār duwal al-maghrib al-aqṣā* (Casablanca, 1955), vol. 7, 56–58, 71. The *Kitāb al-istiqṣāʾ is* a chronicle of Moroccan history from early Islamic times until the late 19th century.

[p. 56] This army was one of the greatest armies of this auspicious kingdom, as we shall see. The reason for its composition was as was found detailed in the notebook *(kunnāsh)* of the secretary and chief vizier of the Ismāᶜīlī kingdom,[197] the jurist and man of letters Abū 'l-ᶜAbbās Aḥmad al-Yaḥmadī—may God have mercy upon him. He said: When the sultan Mūlāy Ismāᶜīl b. al-Sharīf conquered Marrakesh and entered it for the first time, he would enlist his soldiers from among the free tribes. And then there came to him the secretary Abū Ḥafṣ ᶜUmar b. Qāsim al-Marrākushī, called ᶜAlīlīsh, whose household had been a leading one from ancient times. His father had been a secretary with al-Manṣūr al-Saᶜdī,[198] and later with his sons. This Abū Ḥafṣ joined the service of Mūlāy Ismāᶜīl and informed him about the register in which were the names of the slaves who were in the army of al-Manṣūr. The sultan asked him if any of them remained and he said, "Yes, and many of their descendants and they are scattered about in Marrakesh and its region (*ḥawz*) and the tribes of the *dīr*.[199] If our lordship orders me to assemble them, I shall do so." So Mūlāy Ismāᶜīl put him in charge of this and wrote on his behalf to the leaders of the tribes ordering them to support him and strengthen his arm as regards what he was about. ᶜAlīlīsh set about searching for them in Marrākesh and making inquiries about their ancestry until he had assembled those of them who were there. Then he went out to the *dīr* and gathered those who were there. Then he went to the tribes of the *ḥawz* and exhausted whomever was among them until there was left no black among all those tribes, whether slave or *ḥarṭānī*, or free black.[200] The drive became irreversible. In a single year he assembled 3,000, some married and others bachelors. Then he recorded them in a register and sent it to the sultan in Miknāsa [Meknès]. The sultan looked through it and was pleased with it, and he wrote to him ordering him to purchase [p. 57] slave women for the bachelors, and to pay the price of the slaves to their owners and to clothe them from the taxes (*aᶜshār*) of Marrākesh, and to bring them to him in Miknāsa.

ᶜAlīlīsh worked hard at that and purchased as many slave-women as he could, and collected up a number of *ḥarṭānī* women until he had fulfilled the task, and he clothed them and forced the tribes to transport them to the royal abode (*al-ḥaḍra*). They were carried from one tribe to another until they reached Miknāsa. The sultan gave them arms and appointed leaders over them and send them to the place known as al-Maḥalla in Mashraᶜ al-Ramla,[201] one of the provinces of Salé.

Then the sultan sent his secretary Abū ᶜAbd Allāh Muḥammad b. al-ᶜAyyāshī al-Miknāsī to the tribes of the Gharb and to the Banū Ḥasan, and ordered them to assemble all the slaves (*al-ᶜabīd*) who were in them.[202] Those who had no owners would be taken without payment, and those who were owned by someone, their owner would be given their price and permission [to possess him] from [the owner]. Ibn al-ᶜAyyāshī left and went round those tribes and took out every last black from them. The sultan had also written to the governors of his cities telling them to purchase slaves and slave women from Fez, Miknāsa and other settled places of the Maghrib at the rate of 10 mq. for males and the same for females. They took all they could find so that there remained no slave man or woman with anyone. The total purchased by the governors was a further 3,000. The sultan clothed them and armed them and sent them to al-Maḥalla after appointing them their commanders.

Then Ibn al-ᶜAyyāshī arrived with the register in which were 2,000 slaves, some married and some bachelors. The sultan wrote to the commander Abū 'l-Ḥasan ᶜAlī b. ᶜAbd Allāh al-Rīfī, ruler of the land of al-Habaṭ,[203] ordering him to purchase slave women for the bachelors and to clothe them and provide them with arms from Taṭāwīn [Tetuan] and to appoint them their commanders and send them to al-Maḥalla. The total then became 8,000, which is the number he [the sultan] first mustered. Then the sultan forced the tribes of Tāmasnā and Dukkāla[204] to bring the royal slaves (*ᶜabīd al-makhzan*) which they had with them, and they had no option but to comply. They assembled every slave from their land and added more by purchase from among them, and gave them horses and arms and clothed them and sent them to him. From Tāmasnā came 2,000, and from Dukkāla 2,000. The sultan encamped them at Wajh al-ᶜArūs in the environs of Miknāsa until he constructed the fortress of Ād-Khasān, where he installed the male slaves (*ᶜabīd*) of Dukkāla, while the *ᶜabīd* of Tāmasnā were installed at the *zāwiya* of Dilāʾ.[205]

Then in 1089/1678 the sultan Mūlāy Ismāᶜīl raided the desert of Sūs and reached Āqā and Ṭāṭā, and Tīshīt and Shingīṭ and the borders of the [Bilād] al-Sūdān. Arab tribes of the Sāḥil and the Qibla—Dalīm, Barbūsh, al-Maghāfira, Ūdāy, Maṭāᶜ, Jirār and other Maᶜqil tribes—sent delegations pledging allegiance. In one of the delegations was the shaykh Bakkār al-Maghāfirī, father of the free woman Khanāthī (?), mother of the sultan Mūlāy ᶜAbd Allāh b. Ismāᶜīl, who presented his daughter to the sultan [at that time], and she was a woman of beauty, [with knowledge of] jurisprudence, and literature. The sultan married her and consummated the marriage.

In that campaign in those regions 2,000 *ḥarāṭīn* and their children were brought back, and he clothed them and armed them in

Marrakesh, appointed a commander in charge of them, and sent them to al-Maḥalla, while he returned to his abode in Miknāsa. The total number of al-Bukhārī troops assembled was 14,000—10,000 at Mashraᶜ al-Ramla, and 4,000 at Ād-Khasān and its surrounding Berber territories. Then they were pardoned, and they produced offspring and multiplied, until by the death of Mūlāy Ismāᶜīl their number had reached 150,000.

The reason for their being called the ᶜAbīd al-Bukhārī is that when Mūlāy Ismāᶜīl—may God have mercy on him—had assembled them and instilled in them a spirit of solidarity as he wished, he made exclusive use of them instead of using the tribes to fight one another. Then he praised God and lauded Him, and gathered his notables and brought a copy of the *Ṣaḥīḥ* of al-Bukhārī,[206] and said: "You and I are slaves of the *sunna* of the Messenger of God—may God bless him and grant him peace—and his law is enshrined in this book. Whatever he ordered us we do, and whatever he forbade us from doing, we eschew, and for this we fight." They gave him their pledge to that, and he ordered them to preserve that copy and to carry it when they mounted [for battle] and to carry it before them in their battles like the Ark of the Covenant (*tābūt*) of the Israelites. This they have been doing from that time until this, and hence they were called the *ᶜAbīd al-Bukhārī* ["Al-Bukhārī's slaves"].

[p. 71] In the year 1100/1689 the sultan ordered those slaves to bring him all their sons and daughters over the age of ten. When they were brought he divided up the girls among the matrons (*ᶜarīfāt*) of his household—one group per palace—to be educated and taught good manners. He divided up the boys among the builders and carpenters and other craftsmen to serve them and work with them, and he sent others to drive donkeys and learn to ride them. A year later they were transferred to driving mules that carried bricks, tiles, wood, etc., and after a further year they were transferred to the service of the central palace to make prefabricated bricks. The following year they were transferred to the first[207] rank among the soldiery, and were given uniforms and trained in the military arts. After a further year they were given horses which they had to ride bareback and bring out to the arena to learn how to handle them. In the last year of their training, when they had mastered their mounts, they were given saddles to ride on and were taught to charge and retire, how to be skilful in thrusting with lances, and how to hurl javelins from on horseback. After this they were enrolled in the army of active service.

Then he brought forth the girls who had come with them earlier and married one to each of them, giving each man 10 mq. [of gold] as dowry for his bride, and each girl 5 mq. for her trousseau. One of their older relatives would be given charge of them and he would be given sufficient funds to build a house for them and huts, known among us as *nawāwīl*, for his companions. Then he sent them off to join the army after their names had been recorded in the army register.

• XII •

Religion and Community

Although most African slaves became Muslims, either before or after reaching their Mediterranean destinations, many retained religious practices derived from their original communities. The Hausa possession and healing cult, bori, *was widespread in North Africa, as were other similar cults, sometimes assimilated to bori. Some of these cults came to incorporate Islamic elements, such as invoking the name of the Prophet Muḥammad, or the Ṣūfī "saint" ᶜAbd al-Qādir al-Jīlānī.*

(1) THE BORI CULT IN 19TH-CENTURY TUNIS

Source: Aḥmad b. *al-qāḍī* Abī Bakr b. Yūsuf, a Fulani Muslim from Timbuktu, returning from the pilgrimage to Mecca, stayed for a while in Tunis and was scandalised by what he saw and heard. In July 1813 he therefore penned a small treatise addressed to the Bey of Tunis in which he deplored the existence of such "paganism" in the lands of Islam and called upon the Bey to root it out, *Hatk al-sitr ᶜammā ᶜalayhi sūdān Tūnis min al-kufr* ["Piercing the Veil: Being an Account of the Infidel Religion of the Blacks of Tunis"]. The text from which the passage below has been translated was published in Abdeljelil Temimi, *Etudes d'histoire Arabo-Africaine* (Zaghouan, 1994 [Publications de CERMODI]), 80–82, 84–85. In 2000 an edited text with English translation was published by Muḥammad al-Manṣūr and Fāṭima al-Ḥarrāq, together with another text by the same author deploring black African religious practices in Morocco, under the title *Muṣliḥ Fūlānī fī bilād al-Maghrib* (Rabat: Institute of African Studies, Muhammad V University [Series: Texts and Documents, no. 6]).

Know—may God favor us and you with the best of acts—that a description of their worship is an inexhaustible subject, but I shall speak of that part of it of which I have knowledge. The first thing I observed of their worship was when I was sitting one day at the house where I dwelt before going on pilgrimage when suddenly a slave woman entered and went to the room in which their idols were and prostrated. When I saw her do that I was perplexed and I asked what was going on. People told me that that was their mother, I mean the old woman whom they worship. I was extremely troubled by this. One day before this incident they had said to me:

"Will you not pay a visit to your mother?" And I said, "Where is she?" So they led me to a place which was like a tomb, upon which were some cloths. I said to myself, "Perhaps this is the tomb of some holy woman." And I was glad at that and continued on until I drew close to that place. There I recited some parts of the Qur᾿ān with the intention of making the occasion a visitation[208] and went away happy. Then my companion turned to me laughing, for he was aware of the *fitna*[209] that was in that place. He said to me, "Are you visiting an idol?" And I said, "Indeed, no. I am visiting a holy woman." He said, "No, by God. You visited nothing else but an idol." Then he told me the true story.

When I came back from the pilgrimage I was sitting in the shop of a man from Timbuktu when a slave woman came to me and said, "Give some money." I said to her, "Young woman, what will you do with the money?" And she said, "I will go and play[210] at the place of the old woman," meaning their idol. I said to her, "If you were going to the mosque I would give you money, but as for the old woman, I know her not." She said, "Yes [that is true], because you have been too haughty in her regard and but for this you would have got to know her. If any one who comes from al-Sūdān[211] fails to enter with them upon the worship of their gods they will infallibly show hostility and hatred towards him and will have him locked up if he is within their jurisdiction. Look, brother, at those people and call them to the mosque. They are calling me to the idol."

One aspect of their worship is that if they wish to worship their idols they take a hen which is red, black or white according to the idol. Then they bring coriander seeds and other grains and pass incense over and sprinkle the hen and feed those grains to it. If it eats the grains they ululate and place their hands in a begging position behind them[212] and prostrate to their gods and claim that their gods have accepted their offering from them and is pleased with it. If the hens do not eat it, they take it ill and claim that their gods have rejected their offering and are angry with them. Then they humble themselves before them and say: "O masters, why is it you are angry with us? Why is it you do not accept our offering?" If the hen then eats it, they do as was described before.

After this they slaughter it without invoking God's name; sometimes they slaughter it by cutting the nape of the neck.[213] At the time of slaughtering they drink its blood. If the hen refuses to eat altogether they bring another one and claim that their gods were not satisfied with that offering.

If a sick person or one in need comes seeking health or the satisfaction of a need, they tell him to bring a hen of such and such type, then they do with it as has been described and rub the man over with the blood if he is sick. Then the sick or needy one prostrates to their gods and if the one in charge of the ceremony is a slave woman who commands the jinn, the patient prostrates to the jinns, who are in her head. Then they say to him: "Your requests are granted," and they order him to make slaughter to their gods every year on the same day. Every year they take from him what he has, and he may sometimes grow poor by this means.

Another aspect of their worship is their sacrificial slaughter to the granaries[214] at the beginning of every year, and making pious visitation to them every Friday, which also involves slaughtering and other acts. If they make sacrificial slaughter to the granaries they eat as much of the meat as they can, then they bury the rest of it and the bones in the granaries, but without breaking any of the bones. No one enters that place with them unless he is in a state of ritual purity. Despite this, we never see any of them bow except to pick up something from the ground, or prostrate except to an idol.[215] In addition, they always light fires in those granaries for the whole night, undoubtedly because there is some form of sorcery in them. Do you not see that they cut their stomachs and their faces with knives during their worship of the jinn and claim that the metal does not enter into their stomachs. I swear by my life, if they put the knife in my hand I would plunge it into their stomachs until it came out of their backs. This is a form of sorcery in addition to their unbelief.

Another part of their worship is making sacrificial slaughter to their demons at the end of Shaᶜbān, asserting that if they did not do so they [the jinns?] would flee from their heads. . . .

All this came upon them because they abandoned the five [daily] acts of worship which God prescribed for them. When they prostrate [to their idols] they say: "Anyone who says anything else but this"—meaning by this their gods—"is a liar." When asking their gods for something they say: "If those who are in the heaven and those who are on the earth will it," meaning by "those who are on the earth" their gods. And God knows best what they mean by "those who are in heaven."

Another aspect of their worship is drinking blood when they make sacrifice to their gods, alleging that it is the jinn that drink that blood. Even if there were nothing more in their *fitna* than this it would be enough to have it done away with, since blood which comes forth during a sacrifice is forbidden.[216]

[p. 84] Be aware, O most auspicious Emir, that there is not to be found in the entire lands of Islam any place set aside and dedicated to an idol. How much more fitting that such a thing should be absent from your land, since people praise and laud you for your good deeds, and especially do they do so from the pulpits of the Muslims. Know then . . . that your doing away with this reprehensible business will bring greater [divine] reward than building a thousand mosques and a thousand schools, and giving away a thousand dinārs a day to the poor and making *jihād* against the Christians. . . .

Do you not see that many Muslim women enter with them into this reprehensible business and their husbands cannot restrain them, for it is no secret to you that the men of this age are under the thumbs of their womenfolk and this is one of the greatest scourges (*fitan,* pl. of *fitna*)? Have these men not heard the *ḥadīth*: "A people who are governed by a woman shall never be successful"? Do you not see also, my lord, that weak-minded men have also entered with them into this reprehensible business? Do you not see, my lord, that the behavior of these slaves leads them astray and causes others to be led astray and that they will perish [spiritually] and cause others to perish and that they devour the wealth of your land unjustly and falsely? Do you not see that they take uncountable sums of money at the hands of women for the worship of the jinn and for lesbian acts? Muslim women have begun to steal money from their husbands to pay for the sport of idol worship and lesbianism. Do you not see that women have exchanged their men folk for slave-women? Do you not see that whoever embraces one of the slave women, if she is beautiful or wealthy, no one can marry her and she can be married to none but *bori*? The slave women will take her money if she is wealthy or will make her a wife [of *bori*] if she is beautiful. If she wants to marry [a man] they will tell her she is married to *bori*, who is the jinn that is in their heads. If she rejects what they say, they will report her case, or the case of the one who wants to marry her, to their leaders, who will order her to be imprisoned and her fortune to be seized. May God fill their bellies with fire!

This is all because of this *fitna*. O brethren, beware of eating what they have slaughtered to their gods, for it is a carcass.[217] Though they mention the name of God when they slaughter it, do not be deceived, since their offering is to the devil and the devil does not accept that over which the name of God has been uttered.

O our lord, if you do not do away with this reprehensible business, no one else will do so during your life time, let alone after your death, since few like you would be found. Thus we pray for your life to be prolonged in obedience to God and His Messenger. It is incumbent and binding upon you, O Emir, to seize the Dār Kūfa and build over it a mosque, as the Prophet—may God bless him and grant him peace—did with all the churches when the lands of the polytheists were conquered, or a school for the pursuit of knowledge, or a hostelry for the soldiers of the believers who make *jihād* in the path of God. For it is not right that any house or other place should be devoted to idol worship so that their gods may be adored in it. It is also incumbent upon you to take every idol from the Dār Kūfa and from all the other houses of their community and burn them, and to fill in the granaries in their houses. You should also send out a crier to announce in every town that whoever sees slave-women "playing" together in their house of assembly, or in the house of any man of your land, other than for a wedding etc., should inform you so that you seize them and administer to them a painful chastisement from which they can scarcely recover, since they cannot be guaranteed not to be performing acts of paganism during their assemblies and in any case gatherings of women are absolutely condemned by holy law. You should also say that anyone who sees a slave-woman fall possessed should take her and imprison her after beating her soundly. If she repents thereafter, well and good, but if not, she is to be put to death. You should also forbid them from going out to the wool-carder and other such places of worship and you should appoint for this purpose a specific official who has knowledge of the Book and the Sunna. All this should be after you have ordered them to repent. If they refuse to do so, put them to death, since they are apostates and the apostate can not be confirmed in his religion. If they say that they are following their original paganism and there exists no proof or circumstancial evidence proving their lie, force them into Islam now, for they are *majūs*[218] having no scripture and the *majūsī* is to be forced into Islam by threats and beating, unconditionally. You should order the people of your kingdom to close their gates against these demons for they are a *fitna* worse than the *fitna* of the Anti-Christ (*al-dajjāl*).[219] Do you not see that they have introduced polytheism to the wives of the believers and to the weak-minded among the men? [They should be thus excluded] until they make their commitment to Islam manifest and are of good conduct.

* * * *

The next text is a description by the French anthropologist of Islam, Emile Dermenghem, and probably refers to the 1930s. What he is describing is clearly a post-slavery situation, though it is clear from what he says that it represents a continuing tradition from earlier days of slavery.

(2) THE BLACK DIWANS OF ALGERIA

Source: Extracted and translated from E. Dermenghem, *Le culte des saints dans l'Islam maghrébin* (Paris: © Editions Gallimard, 1954; used by permission), 259–74.

It is difficult to get a precise idea of black demographic evolution in Algeria. Official statistics do not distinguish skin color. Old figures are vague and only deal with freed blacks in the occupied territories. According to the "Table of the Situation," there were no more than 418 in Algiers in 1855, which is few, if it is true that there were 2,000 in 1830, and that at that time 600-800 were being imported annually into the province of Algiers. M. Lespès says that in the view of the City Sanitation Department there were no more than 150 in 1930. In addition many came from the South for only two or three years. Moreover, they are often confused with the people of Warghla, the Mzab and Tuwat who are dark-skinned but may be of *ḥarāṭīn* origin. The black population thus seems to have shrunk considerably and moreover not to have tolerated being transplanted very well. Even when mixed marriages have noticeably lightened the skin color, a consciousness of race is retained, supported by the ritual institutions of which we shall speak. The most important and well-knit black communities are in the South and in the Province of Oran, especially in recently created towns where they have found work. This is where we find the best organized diwans.

Nothing we have just said is, in fact, irrelevant to our subject, since black worship is closely linked to their economic and social history. The cruel situation, at least in regard to its origin, of the blacks of North Africa has fostered the life of the brotherhoods and the maintenance of a Sudanic ritual adapted to Islam, and it is the liturgical activity of the brotherhoods that has encouraged the maintenance of racial consciousness and mutual self-help.

The religious phenomena characterized by the words *zār* and *bori* (spirit possession) and by *dīwān* (assembly) are widespread in Ethiopia, North Africa, Hausaland and among the Bambara and Songhay. Beneath the symbolism of the spirits the deeper goals, beyond the social effects, are a catharsis, a purification of [psychic] energy, the healing of sicknesses of nervous origin, and the calming of the soul through ecstasy.

The spirits of Black Africa, having come to North Africa, found there Arab and Berber spirits with whom they could get along well.

Both these and those became *rijāl Allāh*—"men of God"—and the brotherhoods which cultivated their presence placed themselves under the clientship of Sīdī Blal: Bilāl, the muezzin of the Prophet, the Ethiopian ransomed by the Prophet from the persecutors of Mecca, one of the first Muslims, one of the most revered Companions. One could find no more venerable Islamic referent.

Around 1900 there were seven *diyār* ("houses," pl. of *dār*) of Sīdī Blal in Algiers, based on lands of origin: three for eastern Hausa Sudan[220] (Borno, Katsina, Zouzou[221]), four for the west (Bambara, Songhay, Tombo, Gurma[222]). Today there remains only the Dār Bambara, the most important of them, run by the only black born in the Sudan, and the Dār Zouzou which has integrated the *diyār* of the east. The latter, however, is run by a white and is hardly distinguishable from one of the white possession-divining societies that have themselves perhaps adopted some of the rites that are strictly speaking negro.

The brotherhood shows itself off publicly in two ceremonies that have been described quite often: the Wednesday morning sacrifices at the Seven Fountains[223] and the annual bull sacrifice in the Spring. But the most interesting rituals are those that take place in the fairly restricted festivals inside the house, during the second fortnight of Sha^cbān and on the major dates of the Muslim lunar calendar. The month of Shaᶜbān is the one which comes before the great mystical renewal of Ramaḍān. It is on the night of 15 Shaᶜbān, according to popular belief, that the fortunes of the year are fixed. It is at the end of that month that "Those People," "Those Other People"—the spirits—are shut up in their mysterious retreats until the end of the fasting. This fortnight continuously resounds with the noise of the great iron castanets and the drums.

The Ceremonies of Mid-Shaᶜbān

A large house in the upper part of town, which the Europeans call the casbah and the Muslims the *jabal* [mountain]; a house much finer and more spacious than one would imagine when one passes through the labyrinth of narrow streets. The zig-zag entrance leads into a huge rectangular courtyard, on three sides of which are eight white columns with green corniches supporting the galleries. On the right hand side pilasters frame the small windows of rooms which the stairway at the end of the courtyard leads to. At the far end of the courtyard a huge room stretches crosswise—the *bayt rijāl Allāh*—"the house of the men of God." These "men of God" are none other than the spirits in whose honor the ceremony will take place. Normally this place looks like the back vestry of a village church, with benches, chairs piled up, musical instruments, etc. This evening it is the holy of holies.

In front of it, underneath the gallery, is the orchestra, made up of a large drum held between the legs and beaten on top with two large curved sticks instead of being carried on a shoulder strap and beaten from both ends; a small Sudanic drum, the *kourketou,* a truncated cone of terra cotta, the larger end of which is covered by a henna-stained skin beaten in flat fashion by two straight sticks of olive wood; a *guinbri,* a curious rectangular guitar with three plucked strings whose long neck, decorated with shells and metal rings that tinkle gently, ends in a large thin sheet of white metal bedecked with rings which, at moving moments, vibrates completely by itself with a sound like silk paper being crumpled; finally, the classic *qarqabou,* large double castanets of iron of deafening sound whose metallic ringing joins the imperious booming of the large drum.

In front of the musicians is a large candle fixed on a high chandelier, some silk scarves, incense burners, various instruments, knives and clubs. Opposite, in the middle of the courtyard, marked out by benches and the women sitting on them, is another rectangle, specially consecrated, and reserved for the *jdeb.*[224] One can only venture there barefoot, as also among the orchestra or in the *bayt rijāl Allāh,* for it is full of spiritual presences. In the entire courtyard it is forbidden to smoke or drink.

It is the night of 17 Shaᶜbān, the month preceding Ramaḍān.[225] This fortnight is the great liturgical period for the blacks of Algiers who claim they would be ill if they did not celebrate their *der-*

débas.[226] Today there will be a long ceremony of music, dance and sacrifice. The woman who feels herself "possessed" will get up and move herself in various ways. Each jinn has its own accredited tune and in certain cases they are played successively until the subject finds the one which "fits." There are certain psychic states which ought to find their harmony in certain rhythms and sounds, the individual seeking to unite himself by "exiting" from the self, through ecstasy.

Lalla K. leads the performance. She is strong, ample-bosomed and tireless. Upon her head, as on the heads of other women in trance and that of the old shaykh, are placed 10-sou coins that begin to pile up like golden seed on a cloth spread out in front of the candle. A smile is always flitting across the face of Lalla. Her dance is lively, but not too vigorous. She changes her gestures and her scarf and a new "guest" enters her welcoming soul and docile body. But towards midnight—and she has been dancing without rest for three hours—her smile becomes a grimace, she rolls on the ground like a barrel, she rushes wildly here and there. She makes as if to go out of the holy arena and is brought back; she kneels before the incense burners, she goes on all fours, shakes her frizzy head in all directions, rolls her face on the ground, then recaptures her calm smile and goes off up the stairs at the back to one of the rooms to take a well-earned rest.

Sick children are brought. The Shaykh takes them by both hands and throws each one onto his back to dance for a few moments with him. Boys are massaged on the arms, shoulders, neck and back by a black *ᶜarīfa* [matron]. Rouina, that is, roasted corn that can be made into a paste by soaking it in cold water, is brought and the old women lard their faces and arms with it. The spectators are tremendously attentive. The iron castanets make your ears, bones and head vibrate, the drum beats seize your heart and make your arteries tremble. A cloud of incense befogs everything.

At about 1 a.m. the master of ceremonies clears the courtyard. Seven small blue saucers, some incense-burners, a sprinkler, a bowl of milk and a box containing two big knives are brought. The *chaouch* with the curved black profile comes to the corner close to the gate where a small hole normally serves to drain water from rain or from washing the yard out to the gutter. On the light blue plastered wall an open hand has been painted in dark green. Above the hole he affixes to the wall seven small candles by melting their ends on the embers. A black women places herself on one side with the saucers on a tray; another holds the sprinkler.

Shaykh al-Ḥusayn, head of the Bambara *dār*, a tall, thin, boney old man with a gentle kindly face, born in West Africa, moves forward facing the *bayt rijāl Allāh* and the array of candles and kneels down. An assistant takes off his robe (*ᶜabāya*) and replaces it with another brand-new one, just as one would put a cope on a priest when he goes up to the altar and takes hold of the monstrance. Then a large red and black apron is put round his waist. Still kneeling, the Shaykh passes the knives through the smoke of the incense, then puts his hands behind his back. In each hand is then placed the feet of two chickens. He rises, puts his back to the light, huge and haunting amid a cloud of smoke, circles his arms slowly three times swinging his victims around his shoulders. Then he goes into the house [of the "men of God"] and passes the fowls in front of the women who have offered them, makes for the corner where the seven candles are burning and swiftly cuts the throat of six fowls whose bodies are piled up in a hamper while their blood, mixed with scented water, flows towards the gutter.

A plaintive cry like that of a child is heard. A black kid now makes its entry followed by four others. The victims are soon consecrated; they are thurified by passing the incense-burner (*kānūn*) about them and are made to drink milk. The master-slaughterer awaits them and cuts the carotid artery of each in turn and casts them into another corner. Six fine sheep now emerge from a little door that leads to the stable. They are likewise thurified, coaxed forward, and put to death. A heap of anguish shaken by convulsions arises before us. One of the sheep has enough strength to rise and seems to want to charge us with his huge horns and sprinkles us with his blood. Half of the door of the courtyard is red; a thick stream flows slowly towards the hole in the wall. A black woman throws the remaining milk on it, another empties the contents of a packet of henna, while a third passes the incense pot over the heap of dying animals. The woman who was holding the blue saucers fills them with blood from the arteries themselves. This will then be dried and made into a powder for medicine.

The sacrificer, now holding the knife in his left hand, takes some drops of blood from it with his right index finger, applying them to the wall in two lines close to the candles. Children are thrust towards him and mothers come with babies in their arms. Taking more blood from his knife he marks their foreheads, chins and throats. . . .

These black cults are naturally rather badly viewed by official Islam. It is said that Sīdī ᶜAbd al-Raḥmān, patron saint of Algiers, cursed them, whence the decrease in the black population. Nevertheless, these cults remain alive and prosperous. . . . Arab husbands look askance at their wives spending their money and scheming with black women, who are very influential and aware of everything that is going on, since they are often masseuses in the public baths, just as those of Fez are *neggāfāt,*—organizers of wedding ceremonies.

The black males of the *dīwān,* moreover, make much of proclaiming their Islamic faith, never failing to offer prayers for the Prophet Muḥammad and to invoke Arab saints. Their society, as we have seen, has both a social and a racial *raison d'être.* From the economic point of view, it deals in substantial amounts of cash through its festivals, consultations, sacrifices and the soliciting of alms. It knows how to foster enthusiasm in its clientele. It has a name for promoting good health, happiness and fertility. One custom, which can be found in the Sahara as well as in Kabylie, is that of the "purchased child." A barren woman, or one of those whose first children have not survived, will go to the blacks who make a mark on her leg. The child who is born will then be fictively purchased for a small sum of money by the brotherhood. It will become one of its clients and will naturally bring periodic offerings.[227]

(3) BORI IN TURKEY

Source: Leïla Hanoum, *Le harem impériale au xixe siècle* (n.p. [Brussels]: Editions Complexe, 1991), 76–80.

The great pitfall for the negresses is contact with other, corrupt, women of color, who get into their heads with an incredible ease, give them all the vices and then exploit them for their own profit. These naive and ignorant girls are in fact an easy prey for the *Abla*s and the *Godia*.[228]

The *Abla*s are older and more experienced negresses, who use and abuse their influence on the young and untried. The name *Abla* is often given to any negress when one wants to be nice and show her some respect. The word *abla* means elder sister.

The Godia, she is a real power. It is an old negress who is considered to have hidden dealings with the spirits, the departed, and who is herself perhaps convinced; it is something like the sorcery of the tribe. All the negresses, although they are Muslims, and probably through some remaining paganism, have a great veneration mixed with terror for the Godia.

The Godia wears a fur cape, and on her head a headgear called *cache-basti* (eyebrow squeezer), made up of a scarf rolled round the head, tightly fastened over the temples and coming down over the eyebrows; she is seated majestically, full of gravity, by a *mangal* (brazier), with a woollen blanket on her knees. She receives loftily the homage of the negresses who come and kiss her hands and knees respectfully and bring presents to obtain her good grace, and sometimes to ask for her intervention with the spirits.

To summon the spirits the Godia throws a little incense into the brazier, and the room is filled with a dense smoke and a penetrating odor. Then she rubs her palms on the ground and utters unintelligible words in a raucous but muffled voice; sometimes she rolls on the ground, and strikes herself while giving out strange little cries and giving the onlookers more or less clear orders, among which however one manages to discern that it is necessary to offer the Godia a sheep with black eyes and a black hen without marks for sacrifice, some sugar and syrups for the libations, and many other things besides.

Personally, I have never seen the Godia, but I have witnessed one of the nervous crises that are quite common among the negresses, and which are called the *baba.* It was in Crete. I was sitting one evening with my father chatting when we suddenly heard a strange uproar on the floor below. I ran to find out and was told: —it is Hoche-Kadem, the negress of a woman visitor who is having her *baba.* I asked my father permission to go and have a look, and he replied: "These are theatricals, hoaxes. There is nothing worth the trouble of seeing. But you may go and see if you wish."

Here is how this nervous crisis began. At table—I know not how—the noise that is made by hitting copper platters with their covers irritated the negress who, in common with her likes, had very sensitive nerves. She pleaded: "Don't make a noise, you are going to give me a nervous crisis." Then the mischievous and teasing girls began to joke and mock her and to rock her head, which is the most disagreeable thing for a negress. At the same time they continued to make even more noise and threw some incense on the brazier fire, and some aromatic herbs, anything that came to hand. With this infernal din, this thick and enervating smoke, the negress became more and more excited and went into a frenzy. When I arrived I found her on her knees beating the ground with her hands. I drew the girls away and made them keep quiet. Then the negress began to utter in a peculiar voice like the warbling of birds, some strange and unintelligible words. It was, it seems, a conversation with Roukouche Hanoum, the old and powerful Departed One. We ended up understanding that Roukouche had a weakness for the color red, and since I had a red ribbon in my hair the negress jumped on me to snatch it. I was terrified. But she immediately reassured me, saying in her negro accent, "Don't be afraid, I like you."

At the same time she did not forget to ask—always on behalf of Roukouche—for numerous things, among them a scarlet silk dress. One of the girls had a red dress and brought it and gave it to her, but the negress rejected it with disdain, saying to her, "I don't want your rags, take your old dress." Roukouche wanted something new and beautiful! After Roukouche Hanoum it was the turn of her brother Yavrou Bey: it was by him that the negress was possessed. This time her voice imitated a young man. She put her fingers on her lips to curl imaginary mustaches. Next she was possessed by a bearded old uncle—what next I wonder? She tried thus long enough to mystify us, striking attitudes that were sometimes tender and at other times threatening.

• XIII •

Freedom and Post-Slavery

The freeing of slaves was built into the Islamic understanding of slavery. Setting a slave free was an act of piety for which the owner could expect to be rewarded by God, or at the very least, spared from the tortures of Hell. An anonymous manual of guidance for writing letters and documents gives a manumission formula that reflects precisely this.

(1) FREEDOM FORMULA

Source: J.O. Hunwick, "Falkeiana III: The Kitāb al-tarsīl, an anonymous manual of epistolatory and notary style," *Sudanic Africa,* 5 (1994), 179–84. The manual gives templates for types of documents, of which the following is an example. Its usage is confirmed in many manumission documents drafted in Timbuktu.

So-and-so, son of so-and-so has granted his slave complete freedom for the sake of God the Generous, and in hope of His mighty reward. He has caused him to become classified with the free Muslims, partaking of both their privileges and their responsibilities. May God free from the fire of Hell a limb of his corresponding to the limb he set free [of his slave], even his genitals for the genitals [of the slave].

* * * *

Although, as the above text states, the freed slave is to be "classified with the free Muslims, partaking of both their privileges and their responsibilities," this was not necessarily the case in terms of social practice. Even from the legal point of view, a freed slave remained a client of his former master, though this could have advantages as well as disadvantages. The social and economic status of a freed slave clearly varied in accordance with both local and personal circumstances. Some masters might set their freed slaves up in business; some might help them to find marriage partners. In some places the stigma of slavery always remained; in others, the burden of former slavery was more easily overcome, as the following account relating to late 19th-century Mecca demonstrates.

(2) POST-SLAVERY IN 19TH-CENTURY MECCA

Source: C. Snouck Hurgronje, *Mekka in the Latter Part of the 19th Century*, 12–13.

House servants are almost invariably set free at about the age of twenty, one reason being that their occupation would otherwise bring them almost daily in contact with many free and unfree women. Also the well-to-do owner feels himself bound when possible to set up the faithful servant in a household of his own, and the liberation is itself a very meritorious work; the family tie remains as before.

There is hardly an office or position that is unattainable to such freedmen. They compete with the free-born on a footing of perfect equality, and the result shows that they are not the worst equipped for the struggle as they are numerously represented among the influential burghers and the owners of houses and business establishments. A reason why his colour is no handicap to him is that the free man also rears black children from his black concubine.

* * * *

Another witness of the fate of freed slaves in the 19th century comes from an English traveler.

(3) FREEDMEN IN ARABIA, 1862–63

Source: William Gifford Palgrave, *Personal Narrative of a Year's Journey through Central and Eastern Arabia* (1862–3), 5th edn. (London, 1869), 270–72.

Palgrave was born in 1826, and after a distinguished graduation from Oxford, served as an officer in the Bombay regiment of indigenous soldiers. Whilst in India he converted to Roman Catholicism and trained as a Jesuit missionary. In 1853 he moved to Syria to undertake missionary work there. In 1862–63 he traveled through central Arabia, financed by Napoleon III, with the task of assessing Arab attitudes to France, and to look into the possibility of obtaning pure Arabian horses for importation into France. He also wanted to see whether the area might be suitable for Christian missionary work. On his journey he posed as a Syrian

Christian doctor and merchant. Later in life he undertook some British consular missions, during the last of which he died in Uruguay in 1888. He was made a Fellow of the Royal Geographical Society in 1878, and was also a fellow of the Société Géographique Française and the Royal Asiatic Society.

Palgrave introduces the topic of Africans in Arabia as part of a discussion of "the general character and principal elements of the population of Ri'aḍ itself and of the surrounding districts." Reflecting the social Darwinism of his day he begins his discussion: "We will observe a due gradation in this important matter, and accordingly begin from the lowest in the human scale—its negro type."

Throughout Arabia we had frequently met with negroes—in Djowf, Shomer, Ḳaseem, and Sedeyr. But we had only met with them in the condition of slaves, and rarely in other than in the wealthier households, where these Africans were living, contented indeed and happy, fat and shining, but invariably under servitude, and in consequence entitled to no share in the political, or even in the civil, scheme of Arab society. Similar is their condition throughout Nejed itself so far as 'Aareḍ. But here a change takes place; not only are negro slaves much more numerous than in the north, but even a distinct and free population of African origin comes into existence, along with its unfailing accompaniment of mulatto half-castes, till at last they form together a quarter, sometimes a third, of the sum total of inhabitants. Ri'aḍ abounds with them, Manfooḥah and Selemee'yah yet more, while they swarm in the Ḥareek, Wadi Dowāsir, and their vicinity. This is the result of several causes: firstly, the nearness of the great slave-marts, whether on the eastern or on the western coast, like Djiddah in Ḥejāz, and the numerous seaports of 'Omān on the other side; nor is this a nearness of space only, but of commerce. Hence the first draught of slaves to Central Arabia, whether from the starting point of Mecca or from that of Hofhoof, passes directly through 'Aareḍ, and many of them find a master here without going any farther. Alongside of this cause, and dependent on it, is the comparative cheapness of price: a negro here fetches from seven to ten pounds English in value; at Ḥā'yel or the Djowf it would be thirteen or fourteen. The climate also of Southern Nejed, which exhibits a certain similarity to the African, renders this part of Arabia more suited to negro habits and constitutions than are the high lands of Ṭoweyḳ or Shomer, and thus contributes to their multiplication. Lastly, there exists in the indigenous population itself a certain bent of character inclining to sympathy with the dusky races; this originates in a fact of extensive historical and ethnological bearing, and meriting more elucidation than my present limits allow.

The number of negro slaves in these provinces gives rise to a second stage of existence for the black, common in the East, though not equally compatible with his condition in the far West. I mean that not of emancipation only, but of social equality also, with those around him—not by Act of Parliament or of Congress, but by individual will and public feeling. Nothing is more common for a Mahometan, but above all for an Arab, whether Mahometan or not, than to emancipate his slaves, sometimes during his own lifetime, on occasion of some good success, of a religious obligation, of a special service rendered, nay often out of sheer good will, and sometimes on his death-bed, when he often strives to ensure a favourable reception in the next world by an act of generous humanity (at his heir's expense) done at the moment of quitting this. Another cause in operation is one readily imagined in a land where morals are lax, and legal restraint on this point yet laxer—I mean the universality of concubinage between the master and his female slave. In Nejed,[229] at least, the boys sprung from this union are freeborn, and so, I believe, are the girls, at least in the eye of the law.

These new possessors of civil liberty soon marry and are given in marriage. Now, although an emancipated negro or mulatto is not at once admitted to the higher circles of aristocratic life, nor would an Arab chief of rank readily make over his daughter to a black, yet they are by no means under the ban of incapacity and exclusion which weighs on them among races of English blood. Accordingly, negroes can without any difficulty give their sons and daughters to the middle or lower class of Arab families, and thus arises a new generation of mixed race, here denominated "Khoḍeyreeyah" or "Benoo-Khoḍeyr," the which being interpreted means, "the Greens," or "the sons of the Green one." My readers must not, however, suppose that mulatto flesh in Arabia is so literally grass as to bear its actual hue. The colours green, black, and brown are habitually confounded in common Arabic parlance, though the difference between them is, of course, well known and maintained in lexicons, or wherever accuracy of speech is aimed at. These "green ones," again, marry, multiply, and assume various tints, grass-green, emerald, opal, and the like; or, in exacter phrase, brown, coppercoloured, olive, and what Americans call, I believe, yellow. Like their progenitors, they do not readily take their place among the nobles or upper ten thousand, however they may end by doing even this in process of time; and I have myself while in Arabia been honoured by the intimacy of more than one handsome "Green-man," with a silver-hilted sword at his side, and a rich dress on his dusky skin, but denominated Sheykh or Emeer, and humbly sued by Arabs of the purest Ismaelitic or Ḳaḥtanic pedigree.[230] Ri'aḍ[231] is full of these Khoḍeyreeyah shopkeepers, merchants, and officers of government; and I must add that their desire, common to all parvenus, of aping the high tone and ruling fashion, makes them at times the most bigoted and disagreeable Wahhābees in the city; a tendency which is the more fostered by hereditary narrowness of intellect.

(4) SLAVERY AND FREEDOM IN GHADAMES

Source: Gordon Laing, "Notes on Gadamis," located in the British Public Records Office, CO. 2/15, 956, and reproduced in *Missions to the Niger*, ed. E.W. Bovill (Cambridge: University Press, for the Hakluyt Society, 1964), i, 384–85. Alexander Gordon Laing, a Scotsman born in 1794, served as a military officer in the West Indies and in Sierra Leone and the Gold Coast. He developed an ambition to explore the interior of Africa, and in particular to reach Timbuktu and then trace the path of the river Niger to where it entered the ocean. In pursuit of this he arrived in Tripoli in 1825, where the British consul, Col. Hanmer Warrington, who enjoyed influence with the Pasha of Tripoli, was able to help him set up an expedition to cross the Sahara diagonally towards Timbuktu. His route took him through the Fezzan and the oases of Ghadames and Tuwāt. In the desert north of Timbuktu his camp was attacked and he was severely wounded. He nevertheless pressed on and visited Timbuktu, but was killed in a second attack in the desert on his way back. Information about his travels and what he observed is known only from letters he sent back to Tripoli from various points on his trans-Saharan route.

The slaves in Gadamis are treated with so much kindness and have so many privileges that the remark which some have made regarding the condition of the slaves in our West India Islands, *"that Slavery is but a name"* might almost apply here. They are permitted by the savings of their labour to purchase their own freedom which is estimated at fifty Dollars! sometimes an indulgent master will give a slave his whole time to himself, the slave finding himself in everything, and purchasing his liberty by installments; at other times by the payment of a certain sum (if unable to make good the whole) he will receive a written document securing his freedom after the expiration of a certain period, and so forth in various ways may a slave become accessory to his own manumission, and affords a powerful incentive to industry.[232] They are permitted at certain periods to indulge in the wild extravagant amusement peculiar to the country from which they have been transported, in the same manner that the West Indian slaves, but particularly those of Jamaica, exhibit at Christmas—at which times the giddy and thoughtless will sometimes squander away the hard earned savings "*the sair won penny fee*" of the preceeding year. At the end of the *season of pleasure*, when the dates are ripe, they have one particular day, a sort of harvest home, on which they demand from their master the Keys of the date gardens, and pulling the best cluster they can find, in every enclosure in the country, they assemble at night, and have a glorious *festa*. This species of thraldom has existed in the early history of all states, and seems by nature to be attendant upon society in its early stages, but althought it is of the mildest description, and although its ancient existence can be proved by annals both sacred and profane, yet such proof can afford no justification or shelter from reprobation, for those who wou'd desire that peacable nations shou'd wage war for the purpose of making prisoners whom they might sell for transportation from their own, native land. It is a great satisfaction to learn at any time, that the condition of such unhappy people as have been so unfortunate as to become slaves, is meliorated by kind treatment, but no argument for increasing their number; and the pastoral characters in the Idyls of Theocritus, or Eclogues of Virgil wou'd have lost all their sentiment if transplanted from their "sweet home" to labour at the cane hole or in the sugar house.

(5) SĀLAM, A HAUSA SLAVE IN TRIPOLI

Source: Charles Wellington Furlong, *The Gateway to the Sahara* (New York: Charles Scribner's Sons, 1909), extracts of pp. 53–76. Furlong was an American who was a Fellow of the Royal Geographical Society, and made a visit to Tripoli (now the capital of Libya) in 1904, at a time when it was still part of the Ottoman Empire. He stayed in the city in a hostelry *(lokanda)* run by an Italian family. The ex-slave Sālam evidently worked there as a servant.

It was one hot August night an hour after the evening prayer had wavered from the minarets across the housetops of Tripoli. I was sitting alone; my doors opened on the broad balcony which surrounded the inner court . . . I must admit I was inwardly startled as I looked up from my writing at a white burnoosed figure,[233] which had suddenly emerged from the darkness and now stood beside me. It was Sālam. I remember how black his hand looked in contrast with the white note from his master. . .

His short well-built figure was wrapped in six yards of baracan.[234] From this bundle beneath the red fez, his face like polished ebony mirrored the candle flame in brilliant high lights, and below a heavy beak-like nose, his white teeth glistened and his deep-cut tribal scars criss-crossed in blacker shadows his cheeks and temples. He received my answer: again the light flickered and Sālam disappeared as quietly as he came.

Far away to the south, six to eleven months as the camel journeys, south where the caravans end their long voyages and the Great Desert meets the forests, is the land of the Hausas, that great organized Black Empire.[235] There, in the town of Merādi Katsena,[236] Sālam was born. His town was like thousands of others which lie scattered over the width and breadth of the Central Sudan,[237] their mud walls and thatched roofs baking under the tropical sun of Hausaland.

Though short in stature, the Hausas, figuratively speaking, are head and shoulders above any of the numerous Black tribes of Africa. They have a written language resembling Arabic and the traveller through the Sudan who speaks Hausa can be understood almost anywhere. [238]

Sālam, a Hausa ex-slave, Tripoli.
Charles Wellington Furlong, *The Gateway to the Sahara* (New York, 1909).

Despite the fact that the Hausas are a commerce-loving people, slavery from time immemorial has been a national curse. For centuries the noiseless tread of laden slaves has worn deep-rutted paths below the forest level, packing them hard as adamant and weaving an intricate system of narrow highways through the jungles of Hausaland. Incomprehensible as it may seem, it is nevertheless a fact that only a few years ago at least one out of every three hundred persons in the world was a Hausa-speaking slave.

Notwithstanding horrible atrocities committed by slave-holders, slaves have always had certain rights of their own. Sometimes their condition is better than before captivity, and it is not unusual for head slaves to be slave-owners themselves and to be placed in positions of high trust. One noted instance is that of Rabbah, an ex-slave of Zubehr Pasha, who by direction of the Māhdi became governor of the great eastern Hausa state of Darfur.[239]

The slave traffic, based as it is on a tribute-paying system, has had a most demoralizing effect, and until the recent extension of the British sphere of influence permanent security of life and property was unknown. Slaves sent out with the *garflas* [caravans][240] often travel as far north as Tripoli and other towns in Barbary where freedom could be had for the asking, but through fear or ignorance many return south again to their bondage. The sum necessary for a slave to buy his freedom, subject as he would be to arbitrary taxation and recapture, is prohibitive, so only escape remains with its attendant risks.

As Sālam trudged beside me through the oasis of Tripoli, or during quiet hours spent together in my lokanda, he told me of himself and his people. In order to appreciate the circumstances surrounding Sālam's capture, one must understand the conditions in his country. A state of feudal warfare between many neighboring towns is a chronic condition throughout Hausaland. The tribute-paying system rather than a state of war was responsible for slave raiding, for vassal chiefs and towns were obliged to include large numbers of slaves in their annual tribute. The powerful Sultan of Sokoto demanded from the Hausa states three-fourths of his tribute in human beings—and got them—ten thousand coming from the King of

Adamawa alone.[241] It was in one of these slave-raiding expeditions that Sālam was first made a slave. At the time he lived at Midaroka, where he had been taken by his brother-in-law, Lasunvadi, after the death of his parents.

"I was cutting fodder in the open with Lasunvadi's slaves," said Sālam. "We had stopped work to await the approach of a great number of horsemen, thinking they were some of our own people. 'They are warriors of Filahni!' suddenly cried a slave and we fled for the brush. I was among those captured and taken to Filahni.[242] The journey was hard; some of the slaves attempted to escape and were clubbed to death. I was then fourteen years old and valuable, so I became the property of Durbee, the Bashaw's son. Durbee was just to his slaves, and we fared well. He had a great many horses which means wealth and power in my land, for every horse means a mounted warrior.

"My work was about my master's compound, but often I would steal away and sleep in the shade of a papaw tree, or watch the scarlet-breasted jamberdes flit about, and the monkeys chase and swing among the branches. Sometimes Durbee himself would find me and shake me awake. 'For what do I give you yams and *dawa?*' [bread][243] he would say. I would reply, 'Haste is of the devil and tardiness from the All Merciful.'

"'Hubba! thou lazy mud fish,' he would shout, and it would be many days before my back would heal from the welts of his rhinoceros hide."[244]

Working when made to, sleeping when he could, a year passed. In the evening he watched the slaves gamble about the fire, often staking anything of value he might have acquired. As slaves and cowries[245] form the chief currency of the people, these are naturally the principal stakes in games of chance. The little white cowrie shells found on certain parts of the African coast are, so to speak, the small change of the country. Several years ago the value of a single cowrie was about one-eightieth of a cent, i.e. two thousand equalled a quarter of a dollar. The inconvenience of this "fractional currency" is evident, considering that three-quarters of a million, weighing over a ton and a half, were paid by a king to an explorer for a few rolls of silk. Consequently, the check-book of wealthy Hausas, when travelling, is an extra number of slaves, one of which from time to time they cash for cowries.

The shells are also worn about the person as a protection from any evil influence, or the "evil eye." Five selected cowries, for gambling, may be found in the possession of most Hausas. Hardly second to the curse of slavery in Hausaland is that of gambling and the passion for it among these people is unrestrained. It takes its most insidious form in the game of "chaca," played by tossing up the five cowries, the result depending upon the way they fall. At times there is no limit to the stakes, and the escutcheon of Hausaland might well be five white cowrie shells on a field of black.

Sālam once told me that a friend of his master was playing one evening after much lakby [a palm wine] had been drunk. "Everybody was excited," said he, "for the 'evil eye' was on him, and time after time his cowries fell the wrong way. Losing first his wives, then his horses, he turned to his opponent and cried, 'Throw again; if I lose I am your slave.' The evil spirit of the hyena appeared in the darkness—and he lost."

In Hausaland, as in the rest of native Africa the Bashaws[246] and powerful natives are generally the judges, and not only the poor Hausa, but the owner of too many horses, slaves, and wives, must be careful how he treads, lest he arouse the apprehension or envy of his Bashaw, who loses no time in presenting "requests" for gifts. These demands are continued until his subject is sufficiently weakened or ruined.

Now Durbee had a cousin who had been unfairly appointed Bashaw by the Sultan of Sokoto. Despite the feeling of injustice which rankled in Durbee's breast, he loyally complied with his cousin's demands for horses, until his favorite black horse, his *akawali*, alone remained. One morning as Sālam sat in the porch of Durbee's house, a giant negro arrived to take the akawali and to summon Durbee before the Bashaw.

"My master," said Sālam, "was not feeling sweet, and seizing his war spear said threateningly, 'Take him if you can! Bur-r-ro! Go, tell my cousin a Bashaw does not go to a Bashaw, and my akawali stays with me. Tell him that before the shadows of the date-palms have darkened the doorway of his house I will meet him to fight.'

"That afternoon Durbee mounted his horse, took his shield and weapons, and went out alone. Some of us followed to the edge of the palm grove, and as the appointed time drew near he rode out in the open. There on the hot sands he awaited his enemy. The hour of the challenge passed, but the coward never came. Durbee kept his akawali, and before the annual fast of Ramadan gathered his retainers about him and supplanted his cousin."

Shortly after this Durbee made a journey to Sokoto to make his peace with the Sultan and left Sālam with a friend in a neighboring town. This man treacherously sold him for two thousand cowries [$25] in Kano, the great emporium of Central Africa.[247]

[p. 62] On his way to Kano, Sālam passed many slave caravans. Some of the wretches came in bound with thongs under heavy yokes. One method was to fasten ten to twenty slaves together, one behind the other, by shoving their heads through holes cut every few feet in a long wooden yoke. Sometimes one of these human strings thus fastened together would make futile attempts to escape, pathetically jogging in step through the bush or forest until soon run down by their merciless pursuers. Now and again, as they staggered by, Sālam saw a slave too weak and exhausted to walk, hanging limp by his neck, his feet dragging along the ground, his dead weight adding to the insufferable tortures of the others hitched to the same yoke.

At such times, unless near a market, the sick are despatched by their drivers who, not wishing the trouble of unshackling a wretch, resort to the simple expedient of decapitation, thus releasing soul and body at one cruel stroke.

In the fifth month of the dry season, during Sālam's stay in Kano, the caravans bound north being in haste to leave before the rains began, his master gathered his men and goods together, the camels and donkeys were loaded, and they started their journey across the Desert, the Great Solitary Place. They took plenty of kola nuts packed between damp leaves in baskets. These they chewed to give strength to travel far without food.[248]

[p. 65] At last they reached Ghadāmes, and in the course of a year, having passed through the hands of several other masters, Sālam was sold to an Arab by the name of Hadji Ahmed, who sent him into the desert to raise camels.

It was one night in my lokanda that Sālam told me of his escape.

"From time to time," began Sālam, "my master made journeys to distant towns, even as far as Tripoli, leaving the slaves for months without food save what we could gather ourselves. One morning while the stars were still bright and the dried grass wet with the night dews, I left on a *mehari* [running camel]. By midnight of the second day I arrived outside the walls of Ouaragla,[249] among some tents. Near one of these the mehari stopped of his own accord, and dismounting, I hobbled him and lay down under a palm-tree to sleep.

"I was startled the next morning at the sound of a voice I knew well, and peered out from under my baracan. Within six camel lengths of me stood Hadji Ahmed, my master, and his head slave.

"'Hubba!' said he to the mehari, 'thou lump of swine's flesh! How came you here?' I knew then that the mehari had led me into a trap.

"'Gibani! the mehari is hobbled. What does this mean?' said my master to the head slave. Seeing I was about to be discovered, I jumped up and ran angrily toward them exclaiming. 'Who should have brought it here but me, whom you left without food!'

"'Who showed *you* the road?' cried he, laying hold of me.

"'My hunger!' whereupon they both set upon me and flogged me and the next day I was conducted back home.

"Before my master returned from Ouragla, I planned again to escape with Bāko, another slave; we would avoid the towns and go far north, so one day when we were alone branding camels, we selected the fastest *mehara* [running camels] in the herd and started.

"For seven days and nights we travelled without stopping. . . .

"One midnight we skirted the outlying palms of an oasis. Everything was very clear in the moonlight, and *water was there*, but we dared go no nearer the habitations for fear of capture, knowing

Ahmed was not far behind us.

"We tightened up the saddle straps, for the mehara had grown thin and the soft parts of their humps had almost disappeared. Bāko's saddle, made for loads, was hard to ride and had produced boils, so he often sat behind it to vary the motion.

"As we were sick and weak, every stride of the mehara sent pain through us. We knew that we could not much longer cling to our saddles, so we lashed each other on. The last time that Bako fell to one side I was too weak to help him, and he rode with his head hanging lower than his heels. The camel ticks burrowed into our skin, our tongues were cracked and bleeding when the mehara at last staggered into Ghadāmes.

"Some days after the Turkish governor of that place sent us here to Tripoli with a caravan, to be taken before his brother the Bey [Redjed Pasha]. Many in the towns came to the Tuesday Market to see the caravan come in, and among them I saw the fat form of one of my former masters Sāla Heba—the one who sold me to Hadji Ahmed. He watched us enter the Castle, where we obtained our release, and as I came out a free man approached me: 'You are a stranger in the town. I live here now. Come and work for me.' So I did, though I well knew the old pig had heard of my escape. . . ."

• XIV •

Abolition of Slavery

There was never any formal movement for the abolition of slavery, or even the suppression of the slave trade, in the Muslim world. Slavery had long since been an integral part of the social hierarchy in the Mediterranean lands of Islam, despite the fact that slaves did not constitute a vital element in any clear means of production. After all, slavery had been tacitly acknowledged, if not endorsed, by such Qurʾānic phrases as "those whom your right hands possess," and the Prophet Muḥammad and several of his Companions had owned slaves. Furthermore, the institution was acknowledged and regulated by sharīʿa*—the sacred law. Since the freeing of a slave might be a way for an individual to be freed from the torments of Hell, to abolish slavery would be to eliminate a possible path to redemption.*

In the nineteenth century, however, a global atmosphere of abolition began to prevail, pressed by the British Anti-Slavery Society, which had been instrumental in having the legal status of slavery abolished in Britain and its colonies in 1833. British influence in the Arab world and with the rulers of the Ottoman Empire steadily increased in the nineteenth century, as Britain's naval power and its colonizing ability increased.

*The first Mediterranean Muslim government to move towards abolition was that of Tunisia under Aḥmad Bey (*reg. *1838–1855), technically a province of the Ottoman Empire, but one that was anxious to demonstrate its autonomy. Aḥmad Bey thus managed to suppress the slave trade and then abolish slavery in Tunisia before this became the official policy of the Ottoman Empire. In 1841 he ordered the slave market in Tunis closed, and abolished the government tax on slave sales. Next, he prohibited both the importation into, and the exportation of slaves from, Tunisia, and in 1842 issued a decree declaring that any person born in Tunisia thereafter was automatically free. Finally, in January 1846 a decree ordered the immediate liberation of all slaves in Tunisia.*

Why did Aḥmad Bey initiate such moves? Were they simply the result of European pressure? Leon Carl Brown, in his unique study The Tunisia of Aḥmad Bey, suggests that the situation was more complex than that, though the looming presence of an expanding

Europe did play a role.[250] Aḥmad Bey certainly saw himself as a modernizer, and someone who needed to be able to deal with European powers on his own terms, and not simply as an underling of the Ottoman sultan. His anti-slavery moves were certainly encouraged by European consuls in Tunis, particularly the British consul Sir Thomas Reade, though there does not seem to have been any direct European pressure.

Egypt, on the other hand, was much more subject to European pressure, not least because of Egypt's increasing financial indebtedness to European powers. Egypt, like Tunisia, was also in a modernizing mode, and anxious to be as autonomous as possible vis-à-vis its Ottoman overlord. But it took many decades for slavery and the slave trade to come to an end. One of the resons for this was that the rulers of Egypt were themselves among the major slave owners. Another was that as from 1821 the major source of slaves, the Sudan, became an extension of Egypt, thus facilitating the trade in slaves to Egypt, and becoming itself a major utilizer of slave labor, especially in agriculture and the military. However, as the century progressed, Egypt's contacts with Europe, and especially with France and Britain, became ever closer. A new elite, educated in Europe, or in European schools in Egypt, came increasingly to feel that slavery was an outmoded approach to labor, and to be more and more sensitive to European opposition to slavery. The British Anti-Slavery Society put pressure on Egyptian rulers to put an end to slavery, and armed with knowledge about the horrors of slave capture in the Sudan and the role of Turco-Egyptian officials in encouraging the slave trade, they made efforts to have the trade suppressed, a move in which a number of European figures were eventually employed, especially during the reign of the Khedive Ismāʿīl (1863–1879). As early as 1842 Pasha Muḥammad ʿAlī closed the central slave market in Cairo, while in 1854 Pasha Muḥammad Saʿīd officially banned the slave trade. Neither of these moves had much effect. The attitude of Egyptians towards the idea of slavery changed only slowly. Khedive Ismāʿīl, despite the fact that he was a large slave owner, was more open to European pressure, as he needed European trade and technical aid, but his *approach was to try and cut off the source of supply rather than to actually ban the institution. However, it was not until 1877 that a convention for the abolition of the slave trade was signed between Egypt and Britain.*

(1) ABOLITION IN TUNISIA

Source: Ibn Abī Ḍiyāf, *Itḥāf ahl al-zamān bi-akhbār mulūk Tūnis wa-ʿahd al-amān* (Tunis, 1990), vol. 4, 98–99. Repr. in Munṣif al-Jazzār & ʿAbd al-Laṭīf ʿUbayd, *Wathāʾiq ḥawl al-riqq wa-ilghāʾihi min al-bilād al-Tūnisiyya* (Tunis: Maʿhad Būrqība, 1997), 39. The text is an address by Aḥmad Bey, ruler of Tunisia, to the Legislative Assembly, 1846.

It has been established by us without any doubt that the majority of the people of our province in this age are not good owners of those black slaves who have no power of their own, a quality inherent in their being owned according to the scholars, since the modality for it has not been established. The morning of faith dawned in their land long ago, and how can anyone own his brother in the lawful manner which the Lord of the Messengers recommended at the end of his time in this world and the beginning of his afterlife. Indeed, it is one of the principles of his path of law (*sharīʿa*) that one should seek out freedom and in cases of ill-treatment the slave should be liberated without the sanction of his owner. This being so, our investigation forced us, out of compassion for those who are underdogs in their worldly life, and for their owners in their afterlife, to forbid people from engaging in this lawful but disputed practice—this being the case—for fear they commit something which is ascertained and agreed by consensus to be forbidden, i.e. harming their brothers whom God placed under their control.

In so doing there are, in our view, political benefits, including the fact that the slaves will not seek refuge under the protection of officials who are not of our [Muslim] community. Thus we have appointed judicial officers at the *zāwiya* of Sīdī Maḥraz, the Bakrī *zāwiya*, and the *zāwiya* of Sīdī Manṣūr who will draw up an official document of freedom, without regard to the owner, for everyone who comes seeking refuge, and this document will be brought to us for signature. And—may God preserve you—if any slave fleeing his owner comes to you, or if any case concerning the ownership of a slave is communicated to you, direct the slave to us. Woe betide a slave owner who seizes such a slave, since your protection gives shelter to him who seeks it in order to free himself from an ownership which is most probably unlawful, and whose claimant thereto we shall not rule in favor of in this day and age. Avoiding something that is permitted for fear of committing something that is forbidden is [an act of] *sharīʿa*, especially if there is conjoined to it a matter that advantage decrees, in which case people must be made to carry it out. God guides to that which is most fitting, and gives the believers who perform acts of piety the good news that they shall have a great reward. Peace.

Written on 28 Muḥarram the Holy, the opening month of 1262 (Monday 26 January 1846).[251]

(2) EMANCIPATION: TUNISIA'S EXAMPLE TO AMERICA

Source: Extract of the reply of General Ḥusayn Pasha, mayor of Tunis, to a letter from the American Consul Amos Perry, asking about the results of emancipation in Tunisia, dated 31 October 1863. Text in Munṣif al-Jazzār & ʿAbd al-Laṭīf ʿUbayd, *Wathāʾiq ḥawl al-riqq wa-ilghāʾihi min al-bilād al-Tūnisiyya* (Tunis: Maʿhad Būrqība, 1997), 67–69, taken from Salīm Fāris al-Shidyāq (ed.), *Kanz al-raghāʾib fī muntakhabāt al-jawāʾib* (Istanbul, 1295/1878), vol. 6, 46–51.

As regards the effect of slavery and how people were affected by its abolition, the answer is that since ownership of human beings is neither obligatory nor necessary for sustaining life, abandoning it was not difficult, and the people of our kingdom were not grieved at its disappearance. Why would one who cares for luxury and good living regret freeing his slave when he is able to enslave free persons through money, in addition to which they have a religious belief that they will receive a reward from God in the Afterlife by freeing their slaves? Even if that was difficult at first for some people, because they considered the employment of slaves without wage to be easier and more profitable than employing others for a wage, or because they felt too mean to free them, preferring immediate over deferred gain, nevertheless such persons were immediately consoled since both theory and experience proved to them that free labor was more efficient than forced labor. Those who used to make use of slaves and were unable to employ free wage labor saw themselves going back to the natural and preferred way of doing things, which is for man to achieve the accomplishment of his essential goals by himself, and to reduce his dependence on his fellow human beings, since if one becomes used to employing others this can lead to inability to undertake even the least of essential tasks.

Man is more inclined by his very nature and his rational powers to cultivate goodness than he is to cultivate evil, since evil only arises through animal forces embedded within him; but inasmuch as he is a human being, he is more inclined towards goodness. If he finds a clever physician and is cured of the illness that has befallen him, then he restores him to the best state of health, hands are joined, cooperation increases, and paths to prosperity are multiplied. Following upon this, the secret of why countries in which there is general freedom and an absence of slavery are more prosperous will be apparent to you, as we indicated above.

The sole reason for this is that the end result of free labor is more profitable and more blessed than the end result of slave labor. I believe that universal freedom and an end to slavery have a bearing not only on the growth of prosperity but also on elevating human morality. Their bearing on the growth of prosperity is obvious, since there can be no prosperity without justice, and freedom is a product of justice. If it is lacking then there is oppression which heralds the collapse of prosperity and its disappearance through lack of freedom.

As for its influence on civilizing men, universal freedom distances men from inferior moral qualities such as arrogance, overbearing behavior and ill temper, etc., which slave owners generally cannot disengage from, since they have become accustomed to commanding and behaving in a superior way. You sometimes see them looking at people in the same way as they would look at their slaves, especially if they see a black man, whom they merely regard as they would regard dumb animals.

Once in the carnival days of 1856 I attended the Grand Opera in Paris accompanied by a young black man. All of a sudden I saw an American man pounce like a cat upon a mouse, trying to seize the young man's garment, spluttering from the rage of a double intoxication, "What's this black slave doing in the concert hall? What kind of a place is this, and when were slaves allowed to sit down with their masters?" The young black man was flabbergasted, since he did not understand what the man was saying, and had no idea why he was attacking him. I approached them and said to the man, "My dear sir, take it easy. We are in Paris, not Richmond." At this moment one of the ushers came up to them and informed the American that their law recognized no differences in skins, except their quality and the excellence of their tanning. In short it was not that poor black man's white handkerchief and yellow *fuwāntuwāt*[252] that saved him from the clutches of that man, but rather the whiteness of truth and the justice of freedom.

In sum, what is best suited to social order in the Tunisian state is the absence of slave ownership, and ignoring what some opponents of this might say to the effect that some slaves regretted leaving their masters' houses and sought to return to them under conditions of slavery, since "The eye may be unaware of the sun's light on account of ophthalmia, and the mouth may not recognize the taste of water because of sickness." At any rate this only occurred at the beginning of the process when slaves emerged, nervously reacting like frightened horses that had escaped from their tethers, before being prepared for the exigencies of earning a livelihood and for freedom. But now that they are ready, can you see the slightest inclination towards bondage? Let us leave aside this worthless objection and return to something more important, and say: "You, the American nation, are brothers of that nation of which ᶜAmr b. al-ᶜĀṣ, the Companion of our Prophet (may God bless him and grant him peace) said, 'They are the most mild-mannered of people in times of dissention, the quickest to recover after a disaster, the swiftest to attack again after a withdrawal, the kindest towards a helpless poor or orphaned person, and fifthly, the most resistant to the oppression of rulers.' "

You, I swear, are the most resistant of people to the oppression of rulers, since God blessed you with total freedom for yourselves and placed all of your political and civil affairs in your hands, whilst some others believe in civil rights to protect persons, honor and wealth, but do not experience them. What harm would it do you if you acted graciously towards your slaves in such a way as not to weaken your power, as a way of giving thanks to your Lord for the enormous blessings he bestowed upon you? You are too civilized and sophisticated to imitate those who with blinkered eyes repeat the mantra: "We found our fathers doing thus."[253] Know that human kindness and compassion call on you to exclude from your freedom those excesses that spoil it and harm it, and thereby to find joy on the lips of those poor slaves.

God loves the merciful among His servants, so "be merciful to those on earth, and He who is in heaven shall show mercy to you."[254] Finally, Mr Consul-General, we ask you to believe that we are greatly troubled by the wars occurring among your people, that are causing such grief to humanity, and to be assured of our great sympathy for those poor slaves.[255] We likewise ask you to believe in our most sincere friendship towards you.

Written by the mortal hand of him who is in need of his Most Exalted Lord, the Head of the City Council, at the end of Jumādā I, 1281 of the *hijra*, corresponding to 31 October 1863 of the Christian calendar.[256]

(3) A BRITISH APPEAL TO MUḤAMMAD ᶜALĪ PASHA TO END THE EGYPTIAN SLAVE TRADE

Source: Extract of R.R. Madden, *Egypt and Mohammed Ali, illustrative of the Condition of his Slaves and Subjects, &c. &c.* (London, 1841), 138–51. Madden had been charged by the General Anti-Slavery Convention of 1840 with the task of presenting an address, signed by Thomas Clarkson, President of the Anti-Slavery Society, to Muḥammad ᶜAlī Pasha, praising his good intentions and urging him to put an end to the slave trade. This address is published in Madden's book, pp. 138–51. The various chapters of the book (described as "Letters") were originally published in the newspaper *Morning Chronicle.* The extract of Letter XIV below was addressed to Muḥammad ᶜAlī.

Your Highness was pleased to inform me, that the great impediment to the suppression of this trade, or the restriction of slavery itself, was the sanction which the latter received from the law and religion of the land; and therefore, to effect any change, it would be necessary to go to Constantinople, and obtain the concurrence of the head of the religion and the law, in any measure that should be proposed for the abolition of slavery, or the trade in slaves.

The fact, I am perfectly aware, is not to be denied, that slavery, as it existed of old in the form of domestic servitude, is recognised by the law, but your Highness must be well aware that the barbarous wars which are made on the people of Africa, for the purpose of obtaining slaves; the perfidy that is practised in entrapping unwary natives; the violence that is employed in seizing on their defenceless women and children; the murders that are committed in the surprisal of their villages, and the surrounding of their habitations; the starving of their people into terms of submission, where they have resisted the marauders; the violation of their women; the capture of the young and the robust, the slaughter of the old and the infirm; the burning of their dwellings; the wasting of their lands—in short, that this savage warfare, and the atrocities that follow in its train, are nowhere prescribed or sanctioned by your law.

It would be a calumny to assert that the religion which is founded on that law is chargeable with the crimes that are committed by the wretches who follow this felonious trade. This trade, may it please your Highness, is at variance with every law human and divine, and the wickedness of it being unknown to the giver of your law, the system that has arisen from it, and exists only by its continuance, cannot be considered as that kind of servitude that was tolerated by him, and which had for its object the disposal of prisoners captured in wars, undertaken for an aim very different from

implores the state to take action

that of the slave-hunts of Sennar.

It cannot be denied, that it is in the power of your Highness, to prohibit the crime of stealing men on the part of your people, and the introduction of this species of plunder, into the countries over which you rule. A government without power to enforce its laws, or authority without the will to curb the violence of lawless men, or protect the weak and the defenceless from their hands, hardly deserves to be respected, and it is hardly to be desired that it should stand.

This evil has been permitted to exist too long for the character of Egyptian civilization. Lesser evils, whose removal was surrounded with greater difficulties, have been encountered and overcome by Mohammed Ali. One of the greatest calamities that the world has experienced during the last three centuries, is that modern barbarity of subsidizing savage nations, to wage wars with one another, for the purpose of making slaves. This recent custom of ravaging defenceless nations, for an object so unjust and wicked, as that of making human beings objects of sale and barter, no law can sanction, and no prince can be excused in the sight of God and man who tolerates it, on any plea of political or pecuniary advantage.

How then, may I ask your Highness, can it be said that such a trade is lawful, carried on as it is by means of wars that are not just or necessary, and that the state of the men thus stolen and sold into bondage is so sacred that it cannot be touched, nor even remotely affected, without going to Constantinople, and first asking permission of the Mufti to effect some change?

It would be in vain to tell the people of England that the slave-trade was to be tolerated in Egypt on the ground of its legality. That plea can only be admitted for its continuance by those who are utterly ignorant of Mohammedan law. It would not be believed that a prince who has the power to triumph over the deepest-rooted prejudices of his people—to carry his victorious armies into distant countries—to oppose successfully the greatest obstacles that can be thrown in the way of the accomplishment of his political designs, had not the means at his command of abolishing this trade, and putting an end to the evil practices that have grown out of it.

Amongst these, perhaps, the most barbarous of all is still tolerated, and even encouraged by your Highness—the cruel, sanguinary, and most atrocious practice of mutilating men for the purpose of enhancing their value in the market, and, to the disgrace of Egypt, this country still continues to be the only part of the Ottoman empire where it exists.

The civilization of Egypt, may it please your Highness, so long as this disgraceful crime is tolerated by your functionaries, and sanctioned by your Highness's purchase and employment of the stolen men thus mutilated, for the especial service of your private dwelling—it will be in vain to boast of.[257]

It will be said the only country where this barbarous custom exists is that which is under the rule of Mohammed Ali. This crime, that is attended with such peril to life, such frightful suffering, such degradation to its victims, is too disgraceful to be permitted in Stamboul; the infamy of it is unknown in Smyrna; in any other part of the dominions of the Sultan it would not be endured; it is only in Egypt that it is suffered, and only there that its profits are a source of revenue to the authorities of the place. Is Europe, indeed, to be told that the barbarous custom is not to be abolished while Mohammed Ali rules over the land! For nearly five and thirty years he has been its ruler, and he has suffered this evil to exist, and when he is told of the scandal its existence is to his government, is he to entrench the barbarity behind the protection of the law, and say, "You must go to Constantinople, because slavery has the sanction of the law?"

Is a custom like this, that slays its hundreds of human creatures every year; that degrades the miserable beings who survive its sufferings in the eyes of their fellow-men; that is sanguinary in its operation, and brutalizing in its influence on the perpetrators of it, to be considered not only a part, but a necessary consequence of that slavery that has the sanction of the law?

If the sanction that is accorded to slavery were to extend to such a crime as this, what a weapon would be placed in the hands of those who were hostile to that law, or whose opinions were regulated by another code!

It is not, please your Highness, from the experience of others I speak of this barbarous practice and its effects. In the year 1826, I was an eye-witness of them at the village of Zanwee-el-Deir, in the district of Siout.[258] The mortality of the unfortunate children who undergo the operation, by the admission of the wretches who live by the performance of it, was such, as could only be credited by persons who have visited the place, and heard the detail of its horrors from the murderous operators themselves.

In the course of fourteen years, I find that matters have undergone no change in this place. One of the most devoted of the servants of your Highness, Clot Bey, in his recent work on Egypt states, that the practice continues as heretofore; that not much above one-fourth part of the children who undergo this operation survive it; and that the number of eunuchs that are made every year is about 300. Some opinion may then be formed of the waste of life that takes place, of the hundreds it is necessary to kill to have the number that is here given of the survivors of it.

There may be some exaggeration in the account of the mortality given by Clot Bey, but it is still great enough to justify the use of the term "murderous," in speaking of this operation. The number of eunuchs made at this place is, however, under-rated by him; in the last year, the number amounted to four hundred. It is to be borne in mind that the persons on whom this cruelty is practised, are children from the age of six to twelve, and the price for which they are sold, varies from one hundred to two hundred dollars.

The operation is performed under circumstances most unfavourable to the safety of those who undergo it. It is performed by ignorant, brutal, and unfeeling men. It is one of a more serious nature than it is generally understood to be. The barbarous application of heated oil is the medication employed to prevent immediate death from hemorrhage; and the after treatment, the cruel practice of throwing the unfortunate child on his face in the hot sand, and piling it up about his loins, and then keeping him immoveably fixed in that position for thirty or forty hours, undergoing torments that cannot be described.

These things, may it please your Highness,
are done in Egypt!
They are done by Egyptians!
They are done on poor children!
And you are the ruler of the land!

What civilization has reached that land where such savage crimes are committed with impunity?—where they are encouraged by the highest officers of the state, who are compelled by their station to follow the example of your Highness, and to surround their doors with a retinue of mutilated men?

In conclusion, may it please your Highness, I would beg leave to recall the facts to which I have endeavored to direct your attention.

1. At the expiration of nearly fifteen years, I have visited Egypt for the second time, and I find slavery, and the trade in slaves, unchanged in their character, and unrestrained by any measure of your Highness adopted for their suppression.

2. I find the slave-markets glutted with negro women and children as heretofore.

3. I find the exportation of slaves from Alexandria for Turkey, on board European vessels, carried on openly at the present time.

4. I find the prices of slaves actually lowered by the increase of the numbers brought down to Alexandria and Cairo, and those slaves, children and women, selling from 600 piastres to 1,500 a head, or from six pounds sterling to fifteen pounds each.

5. I find the slave-hunts are carried on by your people, and even by your soldiers, as usual, and the only prohibition that has been issued is one given in the presence of certain European Consuls at Fezaglou,[259] that never has been carried into effect.

6. I find the same evils arising from this nefarious trade, and the same barbarous monoply in mutilated beings permitted as heretofore, and even encouraged by your authorities in Upper Egypt.

In the mean time, the spirit of reform is said to be moving over the land; we are told the enlightened views of your Highness are directed to the removal of all abuses. Those in the administration of the property of the mosques, which for ages had been protected even by the law itself, were got rid of by your Highness, without the trouble and inconvenience of going to Constantinople, and the sanction of the law itself was set aside to enable your Highness to turn these funds to an account more useful to the state.

But when the grand abuse of all is approached, and the outrages are pointed out that are committed on humanity, by the subjects of your Highness—when the barbarous traffic in the flesh and blood of human beings like ourselves is brought before you—when the question is not one of rents and revenue, of beans and cotton, but one of flesh and blood, of life and liberty, of duty and of justice; the advocate of the negro must be sent to Constantinople, to confer with the Mufti about the propriety of any change, because the veneration of your Highness for the law is such, as to extend even to the shadow of it, under which, slavery so tranquilly reposes in those countries that are subject to you.

Your Highness did not deem it necessary, when you recently established the national guard at Cairo, to send to the Mufti at Stamboul, (the head of the religion) to consult him on the investiture of the Sheik el Islem of El Masr (or the chief of the law at Cairo) with the military rank and dignity of a general, and yet the law and the religion had made this man their minister, and the exigency of the times made this minister your soldier. Here the law and the custom of ages were opposed to the change, but the wants of the state and the will of Mohammed Ali required that it should be made.

The same will I would fain see exerted in effecting another change, and one that would give the death-blow in Egypt to the crime of stealing men, and retaining these stolen men in slavery. I cannot allow myself to believe this will is wanting on the part of your Highness. Other matters, unfortunately considered of greater moment and more immediate political importance, have turned away the attention of your Highness from this subject, and afforded you but a single opportunity of manifesting a desire to repress the enormities of this traffic on the part of your military commanders at Fezaglou.

That lesson has been lost for want of repetition. It is not a sudden impulse of generosity, or a single effort of benevolence, that is sufficient to encounter and overcome an evil of such magnitude as that of slavery in any of its forms, but a series of energetic measures, wisely devised and resolutely directed to the abolition of it.

It is idle to pretend that because slaves are not purchased in Egypt for the purpose of employment in prædial labour, and because they are treated with a degree of humanity little known in Christian countries where slavery prevails, the suppression of the slave-trade is not to be desired.

At my recent interview with your Highness, in speaking on this subject, you observed that the negroes were in a wretched and distracted state in their own country; that they were perpetually at war with one another, but that in Egypt they were well fed and kindly treated, and were far better off than in their own country; and yet they died by hundreds in the barrack without any assignable cause after all.

Your highness adduced this fact as a proof of the great difficulty of civilizing the negroes; that after taking them from a state of savage warfare and making soldiers of them in Egypt (therefore civilizing them), they pined away, and they died by hundreds. The civilization, may it please your Highness, that is estimated by the advantage of converting an untutored savage into an Egyptian soldier, I do not understand.

As to the negroes being better fed and more humanely treated than in other countries, the injury that was done to them in tearing them from their country, surely must have been very great when so many hundreds of them perished, as you state, without any apparent cause.

The cause of this mortality, may it please your Highness, is very intelligible to persons who are well acquainted with the miseries which this traffic is productive of; to those who have some practical knowledge of the sufferings of the negro newly fallen into slavery—of the silent stupor—of the anguish which comes over his mind—of the ties of nature that are broken by his capture—of the throbbings of the heart for house and home, of the poor wretch who has been torn from the country (however barbarous it may be) which gave him birth—of the wearing down of his strength and spirits the farther he goes, and the more strongly that he feels, "he drags at each remove a lengthening chain."

To assign a cause for this mortality, it is necessary, may it please your Highness, to have seen how soon the strongest man sinks under the sense of slavery; how speedily his energies of mind and body are weighed down by it, and how sullenly and silently he pines away in that sickness of the heart which has no hope except in death.

No matter, however bland and lenient that slavery may be which separates a man from kith and kin—from the place where those nearest and dearest to him lived and died—where the "sheiks" and the chiefs of his tribes are buried, and (your Highness can well appreciate the force of that local attachment, amounting almost to a religious veneration for the spot) where, perhaps, the bones of his father and mother are likewise laid—you cannot compensate this man for the wrongs he has suffered, except by the restoration of that liberty of which he has been robbed.

• XV •

A Slave Narrative

The narrative below is translated from F.J.G. Mercadier, L'Esclave de Timimoun, *Paris: Edition France-Empire, 1971 (used by permission). Mercadier was commandant of Timimoun, the chief locality of the Saharan oasis of Gourara, from July 1944 to the end of 1947, a post he took up after serving as a* méhariste, *or camel corps commander, in the French Algerian Sahara. He says that he spoke Arabic and some Tamasheq. His book is derived from extensive discussions with Griga, a former slave, then in his late 90s, who worked in the oasis gardens of a certain Si Hamou ben Abdelkader, and died in 1945. Mercadier remarks that, despite Griga's advanced age, his memory was excellent, and Mercadier was often able to confirm some of what he was told from printed and archival sources. He calculated that Griga was born around 1847–48. At the time of his capture he is thought to have been about fourteen, and had already begun to make payments for a bride. The footnotes are by John Hunwick, specially written for this translation.*

Note: portions of this text have been earlier included in the book; see pp. 55, 105, 131.

* * * *

THE RAID

[p. 13] I was born of a Fulani woman who was the slave of a relative of the chief of Matankari.[260] When I was captured by the Tuareg I was about fourteen years old. I was good-looking then, with large bright eyes encircled by long lashes. People said I was so handsome that my mother must have slept with a Tuareg noble. But she was also very beautiful.

Matankari was an important regional market. Our huts had straw roofs, and around them waste matter thrown out from the market piled up, stinking terribly and attracting hordes of dogs. But we were not poor, you know; around the village and in the entire valley we had very good harvests of millet, tobacco, huge sweet onions, cassava, peanuts and indigo.

The day when I was captured there was a windstorm from the

south which stirred up eddies of sand, darkening the air. We were exhausted by this sandstorm mixed with red dust which penetrated everything. Nevertheless, it was necessary to go and fetch water. So, at sunset when the storm seemed to have died down, the women emerged and went from hut to hut calling each other to go together to the wells, accompanied by any young person capable of carrying a water pot. We went there as a group, above all to tell, or to listen to, the village gossip, and to see the girls.

So we went off all together, laughing and chattering, towards the water holes. It was almost night, and we began drawing water to fill our pots, whilst some sat awaiting their turn. Suddenly a party of Tuareg threw themselves on us, shouting, gesticulating and brandishing spears and swords. Though we were initially stunned, a rapid getaway ensued, everyone trying to escape as best he could. The Tuareg tried to encircle us. Turning round we saw our village burning. Panic-stricken we did not know where to head for. My friend Makoko tried to escape by slipping in between two Tuaregs, but one of them saw him and nailed him to the ground with a spear and Makoko shrieked in pain. Another, a eunuch of the chief, had his arm severed by a sword. The Tuareg surrounded us, herding us together with blows of spear shafts, the flat side of swords, and riding crops.

The attackers hurried us off northwards until we reached a depression where there were other Tuareg, some Arabs, and some camels. They counted us, and quickly tied our hands together with previously soaked ropes of goat hair. Altogether we were 43 women, 20 young men and fifteen children of both sexes. Four old women who were with us, and whom I did not include in the above number, quite simply had their throats cut. The eunuch who had been wounded in the arm with a sword was finished off with a dagger to the stomach. In this way they would not raise the alarm.

Without further ado we set off northwards, more or less in the direction of Forkas.[261] Those driving us went on foot and hit us with their riding crops to make us move faster. Others were mounted on riding camels, in front, behind, and on both sides. In this way they could watch over us and spot any enemy who might want to take their catch away.

Towards midday [the next day] the raiding party halted in an endless plain completely devoid of vegetation to let us breathe a bit. On the horizon in the north I thought I could make out a small line of dunes. The Arabs and Tuareg again gave us a little water, but it was not enough to quench our thirst, since we had walked almost a whole night and half a day without stopping.

[p. 19] Off again! The women dragged their feet painfully. Blows rained thick and fast on exposed backs; the slowness of our pace annoyed the raiders, who displayed some nervousness. Suddenly the convoy halted, and there was a dense swirl of dust. Koka, the Bornu woman, one of our neighbors in Matankari, had just collapsed. The woman she was attached to crouched passively awaiting the decision of the masters.

"Leave her to die," shouted an Arab called Ali (I knew his name because he appeared to be the leader of the Arabs, who called him Ali Laouar, because he was one-eyed).[262] The Tuareg were angry. They did not want to abandon her. She was young and represented a lot of money. Finally, after many shouts and curses, they hauled her up onto a camel and the march resumed.

[p. 24] The marauders no longer feared a surprise attack, even less a pursuit, and so, pleased at their most fruitful raid, they joked and laughed. The few Arabs in the group gathered round Ali Laouar who played a reed flute with six holes. He warmed up, then improvised some songs, and his friends beat out a rhythmic accompaniment with their hands. Then, since the marches were long and monotonous, they chatted, telling stories of their sexual prowess, or slandering their companions.

In particular they said that Elouter, the chief of the group, was feared for his cunning and cruelty. He belonged to the Kel Geres tribe.[263] An inveterate raider, he sowed terror from the Hoggar[264] to the borders of Lake Chad . . . . [p. 26] If my memory is correct, he had six Tuareg of his own tribe with him and as many Arabs. These Arabs were bandits born and bred, who had fled their land of birth and established themselves in the Agades region. There would have been four Chamba of Wargla,[265] and two Arabs of In Saleh,[266] belonging to the Ahl Azzi, who claimed to be of marabout origin. They made profit out of their prestige and their occult influence, since they were said to be versed in the magic arts. The Tuareg looked down greatly on the Chamba, but got on well enough with the Arabs of In Saleh.

The Arabs were already discussing how to divide up the loot. They had already set their heart on several of us. Nobody wanted adult Negroes who were difficult to sell, but everyone had their eyes on the women. The Chamba wanted above all the young Negro boys so as to castrate them and sell them as eunuchs in Ghadames, where the slave merchants, who came from Tripoli, and exported them to the Arab kingdoms, would pay very high prices for them.

* * * *

The author then tells of how they changed direction and headed south to meet up with another raiding party in the Dallol Bosso who had captured some seventeen persons in a raid on Gougoufema, a village close to Matankari. Among them was Griga's fiancée Mama, a beautiful Songhay girl from Menaka who had been captured by Tuareg and sold to the chief of Gougoufema. There, after much haggling and a sort of lottery, the totality of captives (95 minus four older women who were considered unprofitable and put to death), were divided up among the twelve Tuareg and ten Arabs who had conducted the raids.

* * * *

[p. 41] The Chamba were inclined towards castrating three of the children who had fallen to their lot. Naturally they chose the most robust and least exhausted of their share. It was important to operate immediately since only those who survived the operation would be taken away. To delay castration would mean giving food and water for several more days to creatures who might perhaps die. It was better that they should die right away. This would cost less.

Ali Laouar, crouched like a tailor close to his saddle, sharpened his knife—the knife which he otherwise used to shave his head—on a fine grained stone that he wore hanging from his neck together with a huge string of amulets. He spat on the stone to give it more bite. When he judged the knife to be sufficiently sharp he tested the cutting edge on the nail of his left thumb, whilst two of the Chamba brought one of the children and laid him down on the ground. One of the Arabs held down the arms of the boy with his knees, while he used his hands to press down the hips of the victim, who, in his fright, struggled, twisting, turning, and flexing his muscles. The other Arab took hold of the patient by the ankles and pulled his legs apart. The young Negro boy at first screamed, then wept, and finally moaned softly. Ali Laouar got up and crouched down beside the child. He uttered the ritual prayer: "In the name of God, the Beneficent, the Merciful," seized the testicles in his left hand, made them slightly taut, then cut. Inhuman screams of pain! We were all completely distraught, but unfortunately could do nothing. Ali Laouar wiped the blade of his knife on his patient's thigh, then stuck the blade into the ground. He dressed the wound with wood tar and powdered it with ground camel dung to stop the bleeding. The child screamed! Two Arabs raised him up, each one taking an arm, and forced him to take a few steps, to relax his muscles so they said. Then they let him fall down beside their baggage, and went on to the next child, who tried to bite them and twisted about like a snake.

Do you think anyone could forget that? Even in my tomb I shall see once again the frightful spectacle of those tortured children.

Unmoved in the face of this inhuman suffering, the Chamba calculated for each one of the boys operated on the chances of his survival and the fabulous price that the merchants of Ghadames who export Negroes to the kingdoms of the east would pay for him.

When, after several hours, the bleeding of one of the emasculated boys had not stopped, his wound was cauterized with a red-hot iron. Hideous new screams! The smell of burnt flesh! He nevertheless died in the night.

In the morning the Chamba and Ahl Azzi prepared to depart northwards. From Anderamboukane,[267] where they would take on water, they would reach In Gall,[268] then Agades. The Kel Geres, on their way to sell their loot either at Gao or at Timbuktu, would pass quite close to a number of villages, where we could, if the opportunity presented itself, seek refuge and raise the alarm. So they prepared strong bonds to tie us together.

* * * *

Not long after the above events, the caravan was ambushed by a group of Tuareg belonging to the Taitoq branch of the Kel Ahnet. A massacre ensued and the Taitoq became the new owners of the slaves. They were acting in the interest of El Hadj Abdelkader ben Bajouda, chief of the oasis of Tidikelt,[269] who needed twenty female slaves to send to the ᶜAlawī sultan of Morocco, Muḥammad IV, whom he wanted to persuade to protect them against the French advance. The caravan at last arrived in the vicinity of In Saleh, the chief locality of Tidikelt in south-central Algeria, though at that time (c. 1862–63) it had not yet been conquered by the French.

* * * *

SLAVE MARKETS

[p. 118] That year the Pasha of Timi[270] had demanded from the town of In Saleh the value of 5,000 francs in gold *mithqāls*[271] for his lord the Sultan of Fez, and for himself the "diffa"[272] and three young negroes.

As a priority, El Hadj Abdelkader chose the slaves destined for the Pasha. He set aside three young negroes who would, no doubt, become handsome young men, but who cost less.

Then it was the turn of Mohamed Bouafs, representative of the villages of Igosten, Hassi El Hadjar and Sahela. He also had to provide three slaves. Grumbling, he purchased three nearly adult and very ordinary-looking girls. After much haggling he paid 150 francs apiece. He immediately handed them over to El Hadj Abdelkader and went off.

Next Si Abdelkader ben Kouider of Timimoun made his selection. He needed a few Negro males to look after his garden and several girls for his house. In addition he had been charged by the assembly of elders of Timimoun to select twenty beautiful female slaves to offer to the Sultan. This man became very important in the eyes of Gueradji, who immediately charged Metouki with presenting the people one by one.[273] I was accepted right away for 200 francs. The Zenata[274] bought another male negro and two children, and then came the women slaves. According to the use for which they were intended, these latter had no [fixed] price. Young women, well formed, with firm and ample breasts, plump and rounded buttocks, light complexions, and attractive faces, who in theory were destined to share the bed of certain aged owners, were sometimes worth up to 600 francs, according to the law of supply and demand.

Si Abdelkader carefully examined their teeth, fingered their breasts, buttocks and thighs, and made them exhale to be sure that their breath was not bad, which would be an unpardonable fault in a concubine!

He chose Mama and a Songhay girl for his personal use and then twenty females destined for the Sultan. He then bartered corn, tea and sugar for some other males to be resold on the market of Timimoun. During this time the Ghadames merchants haggled over eunuchs and negro boys. The former were bought at 500 francs a piece.

Some local buyers then presented themselves. Everything was sold by the time of the evening prayer. The Tuareg had done excellent business.

[p. 122] At dawn the next day our convoy set out, urged on by five Arabs armed with clubs and long guns. However, Si Abdelkader, who still had some business to finish, would join us in a few hours.

We walked in a herd like sheep. We were able to talk freely to one another in our own language, but laggards or refractory individuals sometimes received blows.

I walked by Mama. A negro woman, despairing because her son had been sold to the merchants of Ghadames, let out long howls from time to time. At a halting place the Arabs put her in irons, since she had tried to escape several times when they were not paying attention, and they did not wish to tire themselves running after her.

Twice a day the bachamar,[275] that is the leader of the caravan, gave out dates of inferior quality called "acheuf," which the Zenata keep for the domestic animals. When he found a bit of wood he would give out some crushed barley to make pancakes which we cooked under the cinders.

After eight days' walk on the blackish and arid plateau of Tadmaït, the caravan stopped in the evening at a terraced cliff that overlooks the town of Timimoun.

WITH MY MASTER

[p. 127] Barka, the head of Si Abdelkader's slaves, took us to his master, who possessed numerous servants and large gardens. The master's wife, through daily contact with negro house-girls, had learned a few Sudanic phrases,[276] and had established a veritable hierarchy within the house.

This included Barka, the head of the slaves, who had been freed by Si Abdelkader's father shortly before his death. Once liberated, he had refused to leave his master's house. Every day he received orders concerning tasks, discipline and possible punishments. In addition he distributed clothes and food. Next in order was the head serving woman of the house, freed as the result of a vow. She too had refused to leave her mistress, and was in charge of household tasks, for the general upkeep of the house and of the children. In addition she kept a very discreet eye on the master's concubines to prevent them from going out, since they could have contracted one of those very common and difficult to cure illnesses. . .

Barka told me that all the Negroes had become Muslims, but they had not become so by force. Seeing everyone frequenting the mosques and praying in the streets or in public places when the muezzin called to prayer, their primitive imagination was struck by the religion of Muḥammad, by its externalization as well as the profound faith that saturated a milieu where, in all acts of life, even the most insignificant, the name of God was invoked.

Little by little, he told me, at first in the spirit of imitation, and then, emulating the elders, the slave would call upon God, aspiring to that paradise peopled by houris and flowing with wine and honey. One day they presented themselves to their masters and recited the profession of faith: "There is no god but God and Muḥammad is the prophet of God!" They were circumcized and considered to be Muslims, though their masters, in keeping with their temperament, made them understand that paradise was reserved uniquely for Whites!

He also taught me that in addition to the domestic hierarchy which existed in all great families, there was also a village organization. The slaves had their chief called "Corat El Abid"—the Chief of the Slaves[277]—who carried out the orders of the Assembly of Elders at the time of important happenings such as repairing a public mosque, the collapse of a foggara,[278] or an attack on the village by a group of bandits. "Neighborhood chiefs," assistants to the "Corat El Abid" settled various matters affecting the Negroes: quarrels, marriages, etc.

The "Corat El Abid" also organized the meetings and festivals of slaves, mainly that of "Sidna Boulal," modelled on Muslim celebrations.[279] According to tradition, the Prophet Muḥammad—peace be upon him—had a slave called Belal (become Boulal in Gurara) who was of exemplary conduct and faithfulness to his master throughout his life.[280] It was natural that he should become the "patron saint" of slaves.

Thus Barka taught me what it was appropriate to know immediately so as to avoid committing any faux pas.

Si Abdelkader had the unsold slaves taken to one of his houses and put Barka's assistant, Bekas, who was as yet not freed, in charge of them. As a new slave of the household, I was designated to assist Bekas, the aforementioned Negro.

Through the latter I learned, that the following evening Si Abdelkader had received a visit from the "dellal"—the auctioneer,[281] who played the role of go-between. Masters entrusted him with servants they wanted to get rid of. Others, who for personal reasons did not wish to purchase slaves in public, would come to him, such as old morally depraved Zenata, who preferred to examine a young man or woman at their homes beyond the reach of indiscreet looks, taking their time, in the silence and darkness of their provision store where the accumulated items would excite the lust of the captives. First hunger, and then the whip would allow many concessions . . .

The go-between had come to Si Abdelkader on behalf of Pasha Simou[282] who wanted to treat himself to one or two concubines. He wanted them to be young, fleshy, well-built and intelligent. Si Abdelkader, attentive to this senior sharifian public servant, sent him a choice of two Hausa and two Shuwa girls.[283] The Pasha bought two of them for 350 francs apiece and gave the town crier 2.5 francs as a tip.

The following day Si Abdelkader sold a Negro to Dahmani, who took him for three days to try him out. Finally, one of the Awlād Sīdī al-Shaykh bought the rest from him as a single lot. He would resell them in Figuig and Oujda.[284]

* * * *

[p. 131] Heaven knows, I can't say I was unhappy living with Si Abdelkader. I was properly fed; I worked—obviously—but one has to work anywhere doesn't one? I would see Mama from time to time, and always cherished a crazy hope.

Soon I was initiated by Barka into the horticultural tasks. I now knew the various types of palm, and learned how to pollinate female trees. O.K., I'll tell you about this because it was very tough. First of all you had to climb up the palm tree, but then when you got to the branches you had to seek out the most open pathway between the palm leaves, slip in there slowly with infinite precaution so as to avoid being pricked by the enormous spikes that bristle along their underside, and reach the heart of the tree. I then powdered the clusters of female flowers with pollen, and sometimes left there a small branch of male flowers.

When I had finished I climbed down, with legs, arms, the whole body scratched to the point of bleeding by the thousands of spikes, and then I went on to the next tree.

You know, pollinating palm trees is an art, but even more, it is a ritual. If there is the least moment of inattention, the smallest wrong movement, one or more spikes, a dozen or so centimeters long, very hard and fluted, sharp and wounding, will penetrate deeply into a limb or the abdomen and cause wounds that are difficult to heal.

[p. 133] I told you how slaves became Muslims, and that they did not do so by force, but you should also know that those who did not become Muslims within a few months were prey to all kinds of annoyances, and that such harrassment came more from their fellow slaves than from their masters. Nevertheless, all of us, deep in our hearts, clung to our ancestral customs, though most of the Negroes, to make themselves look better, aped their masters and exaggerated everything. In our meetings they discussed an Islam into which they added the taboos, the wise sayings, and the customs of our fathers. In the end, knowing nothing, because they did not know how to read Arabic, they were inspired by a primitive faith, unrestrained as regards whatever appeared to them as mysterious and occult was concerned. The reputation enjoyed by makers of amulets and Arab magicians hypnotized them; little by little they became fanatics, burning to take their turn at becoming venerated, even holy persons. They would have liked to acquire that power of miracle-makers which God, or one of His immunerable holymen [*marabouts*], would perhaps some day bestow on them. In the end, through contact with them, I became like them. But everything that I did was done so as to have Mama for myself. Hence I tried to learn everything in order to be able to master destiny.

If I now knew auspicious moments for sowing, I knew how to conjure the evil eye on the gardens by a camel bone attached to a tree, or even with a clay cooking pot covered with designs representing stylized eyes, placed back to front on a garden wall.

I admired the Muslims who, through their incantations, were

able to separate out the sun from the moon when the stars were trying to eat one another up.[285] I wore amulets—I still have some, since they work—because I saw men miraculously cured of convulsions of devilish origin, by mysterious signs traced on parchment with an ink made of cumin, rose essence and gum arabic, compounded in a secret process whilst calling on certain holymen.

I acquired a taste for all such things, and during conversations with old Negroes I had learned what sorcerers did to make the moon come down into a calabash full of water with the object of making love philters or death potions. You know, everything I am telling you is true!

When I was not working at pollinating palm trees or repairing irrigation channels, I would bring to my master's house the vegetables needed for the day. Thus, almost every morning, I saw Mama who worked in the kitchen. How beautiful and well dressed she could be! But I did not succeed in seeing her alone to talk to her every day. Often we we did no more than exchange commonplace formalities. She was certainly one of our master's concubines, but he was getting on in years and could not have been able to satisfy her, for every time Mama saw me I could read in her eyes a desire to be with me.

* * * *

[p. 139] That year the owners decided to refurbish the Amraïer foggara. Seven kilometers [4 miles] long, it was made up of 300 wells interconnected by an underground tunnel that brought water drained from the sandstone of the plateau down to the town's gardens. Its rate of flow had considerably diminished through obstruction of its canals, due no doubt to collapses. The owners of the foggara, who did not own enough slaves to carry out the necessary repairs with rapidity, asked for a "touiza," or work party, from the various quarters of the town.

Two days later at dawn, the drum went up and down the streets summoning to work the Negroes who had been detailed the night before. Everyone—men with short-handed hoes, women and children with palm-frond baskets—gathered together at the place where the foggara emerged, where the Zenata elders discussed the best way to accomplish this task.

They organized teams of ten Negroes, each of which had to clean out, cleanse, and rehabilitate ten wells. I and ten other Negroes under Barka's command were alloted to the wells of the plateau, which were more than 80 cubits [120 feet] deep.

We quickly made a hoist with the help of three palm trunks and attached to it a pulley carved out of acacia wood. I went down into the first well, without a rope, putting my hands and feet in the rough crevices of the sides of the well to stop myself falling. After a descent that was long and painful, since I was hit on the head by falling stones, I reached the water and bent myself down in the narrow tunnel that joined the two wells, whilst another slave followed me, preceded by a shower of stones. The Blacks who remained on the surface sent us down a basket on a rope, in which were a pick, a hoe, an oil lamp and a flint. As soon as the lamp was lit, work began. It was cold and humid. I cleaned out the canal, filled the basket with soil and gravel and passed it to my comrade, who fastened the rope. Once it had gone up to the top, the receptacle was emptied and sent down again.

You know, it often happens during this mole-like work that a lump of clay gets loose, obstructs the passage and entombs or crushes the workers. Then there is an incredible, superhuman effort, in a narrow, dark, and humid tunnel, to create a passage through this stopper of sticky, clayey paste, behind which the water rises inexorably.

Exhausted, my comrade and I went back up to the suface with the help of the rope, whilst our place was taken by two other slaves.

Suddenly, farther down around the one hundredth well, we hear cries. Everyone runs, gathers together, and discusses. It seems to me that someone is calling for help. We run there. The slaves explain that while descending the well, Moumen, the slave of Abdelali, had slipped and fallen forty cubits [60 feet]. Two men had just gone down to try and bring him up. Si Abdelkader and Abdelali, having been immediately informed, show up.

By using two ropes placed under his armpits, Moumen is hauled to the surface. He breathes with difficulty. He is laid out on the ground. Si Abdelkader bends over him, prods him, then slowly, then straightens up, shaking his head.

"He will die," he said, "His thighs and his ribs are broken. Take him to the village, and the rest of you, instead of looking and doing nothing, get back to work!"

"It's a loss for me," said Abdelali, by way of funeral oration, "I bought him last year for two hundred francs!"

Moumen died the next day at daybreak, just as the drum was calling his brothers to work.

* * * *

After some six or seven years as a slave, Griga was given his freedom, as was his former fiancée Mama. Their freedom was occasioned by El Hadj Abdelkader's wife discovering her husband's attachment to Mama and threatening to disgrace him by walking out on him and letting the story be known.

* * * *

I AM FREED!

[p. 169] Yes, we have been manumitted, but we cannot leave Timimoun despite being free. You, you think everything is possible because you are not a poor Negro. If we had wished to return to Matankari it would have been necessary for us to be able to hire two camels, one for Mama and one for myself. It would have been necessary for us to join many different caravans that knew the desert routes: first of all Arab caravans going from Timimoun to In Salah, then Tuareg caravans going from In Salah to Gao or Agades. We had no money to pay for the hire except by offering to work.

And supposing we had this unfortunate idea, remind yourself that Arabs and Tuareg take part in the slave trade and that neither would have failed to strip us of the few things we possessed, and then to sell us either to some nomads or to slave caravans making their way to Morocco or Tripoli. You know that these merchants have no heart, and there would have been a very good chance that we would have been sold separately.

Having been freed at Timimoun, we were obliged to stay there for our own security, since a freed Negro is only free in his own village. To leave it would have been too dangerous for us. Si Abdelkader had given us the usage of a garden and it was therefore in our interest to stay, the more so because we knew other Negroes and had made friends. Here, at least, we were safe.

During the period of Mama's purification called for by the religion, she continued to stay with our master.[286] I benefitted by her absence to erect a fine hut with walls of adobe and a door. Then, as the elders had suggested, I asked the help of their slaves to help me prepare our garden.

On the said day, when the turtledoves were warbling high up in the palm trees, greeting the rising sun, there were ten of us Negroes in line. We sang as we hoed. It fell to me to sing the first phrase, which the others then took up in chorus. The end of every phrase was punctuated with ten strikes of the hoe which made the soil fly back behind us. We call this way of working a "touiza," that is, a work party.

The soil, quickly turned over, was then leveled into successive terraces according to the slope of the land. But the garden had no irrigation tank. This tank is called a "majen."

Some donkeys borrowed from our masters brought loads of red clay which was immediately set out to dry. In the highest part of the garden, closest to the channel that brings water from the foggara, the soil is built into a rectangle of three cubits [4 ft. 6 in.] wide and six cubits [9 ft.] long. We spread the clay paste over the rectangle to make it waterproof, then we did the edges to hold the water.

Two by two, in rhythm, the one resting his hands on the shoulders of his counterpart, we tamp down the clay. Then the tank is filled with water which remains there all night.

Next day I return to the garden, empty the tank and heap more clay in with the aid of a paddle made from the lower, and in fact largest, end of a palm branch. Then I prepare a hole to let the water out, and so that the planting soil should not be carried away I make this hole in a slab of sandstone which I dress with clay. Whilst the tank fills again, I begin to trace out the squares which I shall sow, making a small wall of earth around each, so that every one will receive the same amount of water.

Through my master I ask some elders for permission to take the content of their cesspools to manure my garden.

In principle, the removal of this "fertilizer" is to be calculated in cash against a certain quantity of corn, barley, or dates. It is something rare and precious in the oases!

I share the fertilizer out by hand to every bed, then irrigate in such a way as to impregnate the soil. Then I dig small not very deep holes in which I put a sprinkle of fertilizer and a dozen corn seeds, which I cover over very carefully, since these wretched birds only wait for me to leave to swoop down on the sown squares.

As soon as a camel caravan arrives in the market, I run to gather up the dung in a basket. Many women and children do the same, but they sell their harvest of dung to the landowners.

Every day I look at the beds, repair the edges, and watch for the appearance of the first shoots. I am filled with wonder: this crop will be mine! This is *my* corn shooting up. All along the ditches I have sowed sweet melon and watermelon seeds, and now here they are growing, their shoots already creeping along. I also have some peanuts. And all that is mine!

But in my elation I have quite simply forgotten that I only have the right to one fifth of the crop!

Despite being a freedman, and hence at liberty, I was heavily dependent on my master. I owed him four-fifths of the crop, and now I had to cater for myself and for Mama. It was also necessary for us to buy some items for the winter, since nights are cold in Gurara!

I want you to understand this well: I, a freed man, was a good deal less fortunate than the slaves, who were fed, clothed and lodged by their master! My fate had not changed in any sense, except on a scrap of paper. I was a sharecropper of the owner of the garden, I was exploited by the so-called Muslim scholars doing business in amulets, who tried to force my hand to buy some, so that by means of occult powers or unknown holymen I could change my scarcely enviable fate. Under constraint and pressure I therefore bought some, so as not to be badly thought of.

In short, for us it is almost misery. We are not free: freedom, inasmuch as it consists of having responsibilities, facing up alone to the pitfalls of life, deciding alone what would be for us good or bad, has never been able to change the color of the skin, or the structure of the environment in which one lives.

To get our food, Mama and I worked like animals. Our crop was at the mercy of sandstorms, locusts, or even the regularity of the working of the foggara.

I am as much a slave as the least of slaves, because I am in debt. I owe my master, as an obligation, no matter the circumstances, the agreed share of the crops. Now our future means little to him, you understand? For example, he gave me ten azguens[287] of corn seed. The yield, if you will, was about ten to one, giving in theory a crop of one hundred azguens out of which I owed him four-fifths, that is eighty azguens, leaving me twenty!

When the year is bad, we have to borrow from more fortunate freedmen in order to live, and even from Arab or Mzabi merchants.[288] But this loan has to be repaid at a hundred percent interest!

If there is no way around this, the owner may take back his garden. And then? Well, there's nothing left for you but to lay down and die, and for your wife, if she is still attractive, to prostitute herself!

Afterwards, when the French arrived, they forbade trade in slaves. They allowed owners to buy slaves coming from the Sudan,[289] but they forbade them to resell them to Morocco or the Arab kingdoms of the east. This was a tough blow for the slave traffickers who found themselves thus doomed to ruination. There was yet something better: any Negro who wanted his freedom could present himself to the French Bureau, and he immediately became free!

That was fine, but what sort of fate awaited a slave who had become free? Leaving aside the French who could give a slave work from time to time, no property owner would consent to employ him any longer, no one would wish to rent him a garden or a hovel in the village. It was impossible for him to marry; the other Blacks, being servile towards their masters, would refuse him their daughters!

Hence, only slaves belonging to very harsh and brutal masters went to the Bureau to gain their freedom. But I have to tell you that they disappeared very quickly, and never did anyone hear of them again. Their masters, not wanting to lose their money, had them very discreetly watched, then snatched them up and handed them over to the nomads who were conducting a traffic in slaves towards Morocco across the Great Erg.[290] Resistance was useless. The slave, first given a good thrashing, then chained up to keep him quiet, was kept on a minimal diet and little water, then taken off to the Erg. The Erg is huge and its lofty dunes make walking difficult. If the French came to inquire about the disappearance of this Negro in the course of their inspections, it was easy for the established authorities to say that this Negro was mentally unstable, that he had left the village and had been found dead of thirst by the nomads of the Erg. Who would go out to check the truth of what the elders had vouched for? The other slaves were well aware of the fate that was in store for their unfortunate fellow man, but they kept quiet so as not to suffer the same fate!

There were a thousand more ways of deceiving the French so as to trade in Negroes.

You know that the Qurʾān prescribes that Muslims should make the pilgrimage to the Holy Places of Islam at least once in their lifetime; the elders or the rich landowners, in order to get to Mecca and Medina, formed a group every year to make up a caravan that would take them to Arabia via Ghadames, Tripoli and Cairo. As was right and proper, these caravans had an escort and guides and moved quite slowly. Each pilgrim took with him some Blacks to serve him en route. The Blacks washed the laundry, prepared food, loaded camels, etc. They were by preference chosen from among the young ones who were only too happy to go with their master to Mecca . . . but he would sell them during the journey if he had need of money. Some of these Blacks were even offered for service in the Holy Places, as a result of some vow.

When the caravan returned to Timimoun the families would come to ask after their children, and their absence did not fail to worry them. Then their master, putting on a sad face, would declare that their young son had unfortunately died in the Ḥijāz, following an epidemic, or rather he had strayed during a night march in the deserts of Tripolitania and had not rejoined the caravan, which had, nevertheless, waited almost a whole day for him! He would add, assuming a compassionate and formal stance, that that was the equivalent for the young Black to having made the pilgrimage, and that he was doubtless now in God's paradise like a good Muslim. You understand?

Yet others, at the supposed request of a religious figure, the head of an important Moroccan *zāwiya*,[291] sent to Morocco young Blacks who would very rapidly become literate and good Muslims, and would perhaps later become members of the Sultan's personal guard . . . In actual fact they were sold and never returned.

Finally: others still were sent to Morocco, to the house of some local elders under the pretext of serving an old uncle, or an old sister who had become disabled.

But, all things considered, and despite these tricks, the ban which the French placed on selling slaves was a good thing, since owners began to behave more humanely towards their slaves, so as not to lose them, which would have been the equivalent of total ruin for them.

* * * *

[p. 179] You see, I have become very old. I have seen and learnt many things in my life. My head is still in the sun, but my feet are already in the tomb. After Mama's death I returned to my master.[292] In his household I worked as I had done before being set free.

I hardly sleep any more and have a lot of time to think. Pardon me for what I am about to say to you, but if I were not a poor Negro, I would be your grandfather. In truth, therefore, I tell you: each one of God's creatures on earth aspires to liberty and tries to act, depending on its circumstances, as if it had that freedom. But in fact, each action we take, no matter how insignificant, is ordered in advance. In other words, everyone has his destiny fixed and cannot change it.

Have you noticed that where the *merkeba*[293] grows, there are many snakes? Have you wondered why? Well, it is because the seeds of the *merkeba* attract mice and jereboas, and these are the preferred prey of the snakes.

The bird which appears to be free is not. You see it flying around the sky, and you hear it singing in the palms. Well, it is not free either. It is always in danger when in the air and on the ground. In the air because of birds of prey, and on the ground because of children and hunters.

And you, are you free? I don't think so. You are in charge of everything in Gurara, and many of your colleagues envy you your position. Your lot is not a pleasant one because you have to think about everyone and for everyone. You, too, have to give an account to your bosses. They come here to judge your work. If you displease them they will send you off and bring in another. They also answer to other, more important, bosses. So, whether you like it or not, you obey someone.

Certainly, you eat better than I do, and you are better dressed than me. You give orders to elders who respect you and heap praises on you, but it is often hypocrisy on their part. In fact, you are alone in facing up to your responsibilities.

I repeat: man's liberty is a illusion. As for equality, it's better not to talk about it. None of this has ever existed and it never will.[294] Man, no matter who he is, can never do entirely what he pleases: he is constantly subject to powers greater than himself, whether they be laws of society or laws of God. Whoever attempts to escape them is always cut back, either by his peers or by God. Men envy those among them who succeed, since they wish for equality. Men are the enemies of any man who wants to try changing what already exists, since they want to have the liberty to to do what gives them a personal advantage. You know, man is always an unsatisfied creature.

When all is said and done, man is superior to the donkey only because he possesses the ability to think, but he suffers the same beatings, and is always in the service of someone or something else.

Only death creates perfect equality among God's creation, from worm to man. Rich or poor, none can escape it. Death also gives liberty to the spirit, which returns to its Creator, and leaves to the earth what returns to the earth: the cocoon of his soul.

My friend Griga was a wise man.

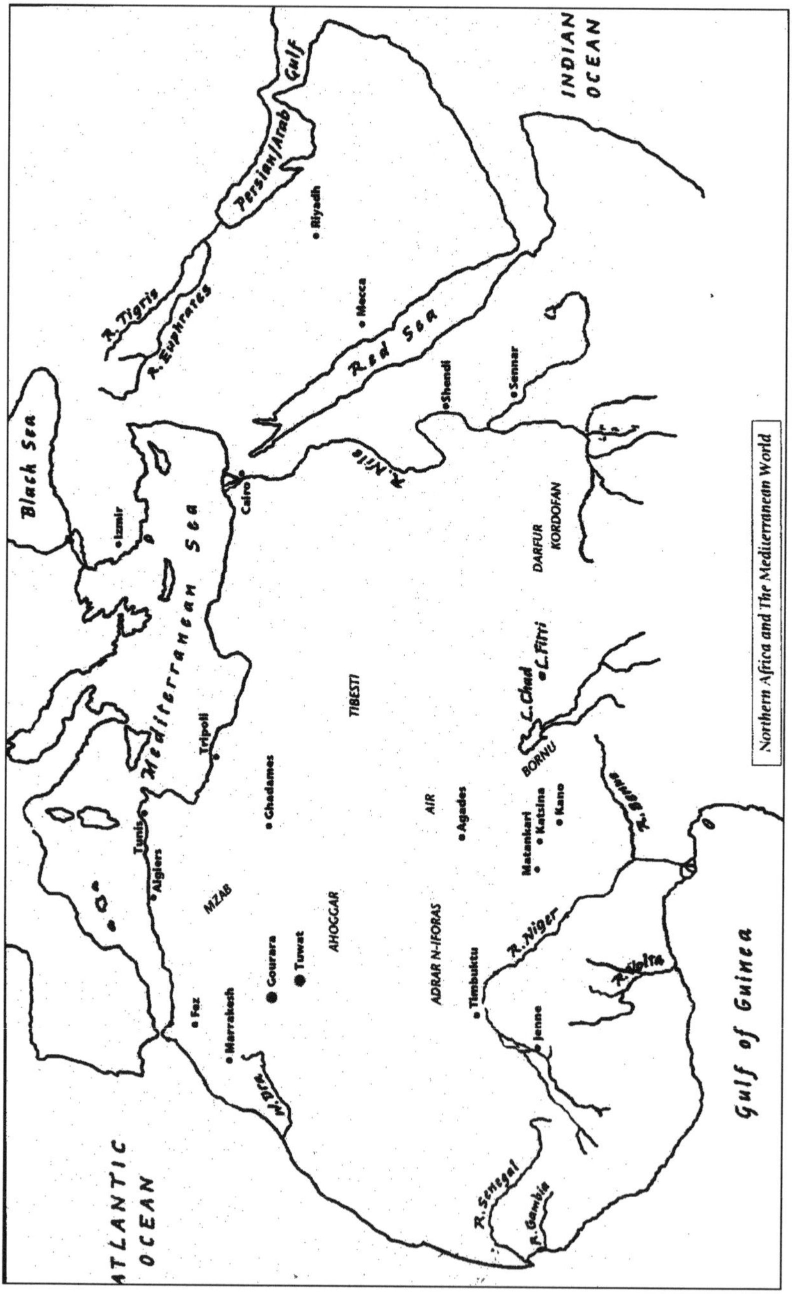

Northern Africa and The Mediterranean World

◆ Notes ◆

Notes to "The Same But Different"

1. Bernard Lewis, *Race and Slavery in the Middle East* (New York: Oxford University Press, 1990), vi.
2. See Khair El-Din Haseeb (ed.), *The Arabs and Africa* (London: Croom Helm, 1985), 55.
3. See Y.F. Hasan, "The historical roots of Afro-Arab relations," in Haseeb, op. cit., 33.
4. Mohammed Ennaji, *Soldats, domestiques et concubines; l'esclavage au Maroc au XIXe siècle* (Casablanca: Editions EDDIF, 1994). An English translation is now available: *Serving the Master: Slavery and Society in Nineteenth-century Morocco* (Basingstoke: Macmillan, 1999).
5. L. Blin, "Les noirs dans l'Algérie contemporaine," *Politique Africaine* 30 (juin 1988): 22–31.
6. Muḥammad al-Hādī al-Juwaylī, *Mujtamaᶜāt li'l-dhākira, mujtamaᶜāt li'l-nisyān* (Tunis, 1994).
7. New York: Simon & Schuster Macmillan, 1997 (4 vols.).
8. New York: Oxford University Press, 1984.
9. Saadi Simawe of Grinnell College, Iowa, is currently engaged in a study of the images of blacks in Arabic literature, and kindly allowed me to read a draft of a paper of his on blacks in *Alf layla wa-layla* ("The Thousand and One Nights," commonly called *The Arabian Nights*). This monument of oral literature clearly reflects popular late medieval Arab images of black Africans, and portrays them as very inferior and highly libidinous beings.
10. See, for example, my "Islamic law and polemics over slavery in North and West Africa, 16th–19th century," in Shaun Marmon (ed.), *Slavery in the Islamic Middle East* (Princeton: Markus Wiener, 1999), 43–68.
11. Centre de Documentation et de Recherche Historique Ahmad Baba, Timbuktu, MS no. 3851(v).
12. A. Adu Boahen, *Britain, the Sahara and the Western Sudan 1788–1861* (Oxford: Clarendon Press, 1964), 158.
13. See Hanns Vischer, *Across the Sahara* (London: Edward Arnold, 1910), 148. See also John Wright, "The Wadai-Benghazi slave route," in Elizabeth Savage (ed.), *The Human Commodity: Perspectives on the trans-Saharan slave trade* (London: Frank Cass, 1992), 174–84.
14. See William John Sersen, "Stereotypes and attitudes towards slaves in Arabic proverbs," in John Ralph Willis (ed.), *Slaves and Slavery in Muslim*

Africa, vol. 1, *Islam and the Ideology of Slavery* (London: Frank Cass, 1985), 92–105. As recently as 1988 I heard the term *ᶜabīd* used in Nigeria by Lebanese to refer to Nigerians in general.

15. On Graeco-Roman stereotypes, see Frank M. Snowden, Jr., *Blacks in Antiquity* (Cambridge: The Bellknap Press of Harvard University Press, 1970), ch. 8.
16. See Akbar Muhammad, "The image of Africans in Arabic literature: some unpublished manuscripts," in Willis, *Slaves and Slavery in Muslim Africa*, vol. 1, 47–74.
17. Ibn Khaldūn, *The Muqaddimah,* trans. Franz Rosenthal (2nd edn., Princeton University Press, 1967), vol. 1, 174–76.
18. "Sūdān" is shorthand for *bilād al-sūdān*—the land of the blacks.
19. Aḥmad b. Khālid al-Nāṣirī, *Kitāb al-istiqsāʾ li-akhbār duwal al-maghrib al-aqṣā* (Casablanca, 1955), vol. 5, 131.
20. Vischer, op. cit., 82.
21. See Richard Hill, *A Black Corps d'Elite: An Egyptian Sudanese Conscript Battalion with the French Army in Mexico, 1863–67, and Its Survivors in Subsequent African History* (East Lansing, 1995).
22. See G. Makris & Ahmad al-Safi, "The Tumbura spirit possession cult of the Sudan past and present," in I.M. Lewis et al. (ed.), *Women's Medicine: The Zar-Bori Cult in Africa and Beyond* (Edinburgh, 1991), 118–36; Sophie Ferchiou, "The possession cults of Tunisia: a religious system functioning as a system of reference and a social field for performing actions," in I.M. Lewis, Ahmed al-Safi & Sayyid Hurreiz (eds.), *Women's Medicine: the zar-bori cult in Africa and beyond* (Edinburgh, 1991), 209–18.
23. See J.D. Andrews, "La fontaine des Génies," Alger, 1903.

Notes to “The Silence of the Slaves”

1. Ehud Toledano, *Slavery and Abolition in the Ottoman Middle East* (Seattle, Wash.: University of Washington Press, 1997), 113–16.
2. Ibid., 113.
3. See above, p. 13.
4. Urs Peter Ruf, *Ending Slavery: Hierarchy, Dependency and Gender in Central Mauritania* (Bielefeld, 1999).
5. Mohammed Ennaji (trans. Seth Graebner), *Serving the Master: Slavery and Society in Nineteenth-Century Morocco* (New York: St. Martin’s Press, 1999), 28.
6. Gustav Nachtigal, *Sahara and Sudan*, trans. Allan B. Fisher & Humphrey J. Fisher (London: C. Hurst & Co., 1974), vol. 1, 7.
7. Nachtigal, *Sahara and Sudan.* Translators’ Introduction, p. x.
8. Snouck Hurgronje, *Mecca in the Latter Part of the 19th Century* (Leiden: E.J. Brill, 1970), 11.
9. Nachtigal, op. cit., 209.
10. Hurgronje, op. cit., 16.
11. Ibid., p. 17.
12. Ibid., p. 19.
13. Mary Louise Pratt, *Imperial Eyes: Travel Writing and Transculturation* (New York: Routledge, 1992), p. 53.
14. The Earl of Cromer, *Modern Egypt* (London: MacMillan Co., 1909), vol. 2, 496.
15. “Sa^{c}īd wa-Bakhīta,” *al-Ustādh* (Sept. 13, 1892), reprinted in^{c}Abd Allāh al-Nadīm, *al-^{c}A$^{\supset}$dād al-Kāmila li-majallat al-Ustādh*, vol. 1 (Cairo: al-Hay$^{\supset}$a al-^{c}āmma li’l-kitāb, 1994), 91.
16. Ibid., 93.
17. Ibid., 92.
18. Ibid., 93.
19. Interview with Mary John Malou, American Research Center in Egypt, August 10, 1997.

Notes to the Documents

Abbreviations used in the notes:

EI (2) *Encyclopaedia of Islam*, new edn. Leiden: E.J. Brill, 1960– (in progress).

GAL Carl Brockelmann, *Geschichte der arabischen Literatur*, 2nd edn., 2 vols. Leiden: E.J. Brill, 1943–49; Suppl. [*GAL S*], 3 vols., 1937–42.

* * * *

1. Literally "a small slave woman," but here a personal name.
2. Qurʾān, 51:56.
3. The word *ʿabd* may be used both in the religious sense of the individual Muslim as the "slave" of God (*cf.* the common name ʿAbd Allāh), and in the sense of "slave" as property of another human being.
4. Saʿd al-Dīn Masʿūd b. ʿUmar al-Taftāzānī (d. 792/1390), *al-Talwīḥ bi-kashf ḥaqāʾiq al-Tanqīḥ*. See *GAL S,* vol. 2, 300.
5. Muḥammad/Aḥmad b. Ṣadr al-Sharīʿa ʿAbd Allāh al-Maḥbūbī. See ʿUmar Riḍā Kaḥḥāla, *Muʿjam al-muʾallifīn* (Damascus, 1957–61), vol. 1, 308.
6. Text: *safar*, read *safah.*
7. Like youth, madness and sickness, slavery is a only a temporary condition, not one that is part of a person's nature. Slavery can be "cured" by manumission, and the freed slave is legally on a par with the free Muslim who was never enslaved.
8. I.e. the Prophet Muḥammad.
9. I.e. the slave is not a complete human being and does not enjoy the privileges of the complete, free, human being.
10. A frequent designation of a slave is "a talking animal" (*ḥayawān nāṭiq*).
11. Qurʾān, 21:92.
12. Qurʾān, 49:13.
13. Qurʾān, 17:82.
14. Al-Ḥasan al-Baṣrī (Abū Saʿīd b. Abī'l-Ḥasan Yasār), d. 728, was a celebrated preacher resident in Basra (modern Iraq), whose sayings became an important source of religious guidance; see *EI* (2), vol. 3, 247.
15. This legal ruling was sometimes exploited by slaves in the Sahara who wished to change their masters. The slave would cut the ear of a camel belonging to the person whose slave he preferred to be; in compensation, his current owner would hand the slave over to the person whose camel he injured. A late-19th-century jurist of Arawan, to the north of Timbuktu, issued

a ruling abolishing this practice; see MS 1689, Centre de Documentation et Recherche Ahmad Baba, Timbuktu.

16. This refers to the "authorized" (*maʾdhūn*) slave, who has been given permission by his owner to undertake business transactions. In such a case he is not to be sold or handed over to another in payment of his debt.
17. This because they come under his personal guarantee (*dhimma*), and not his physical body (*nafs*).
18. Aṣbagh b. al-Faraj b. Saʿīd (d. 839), pupil of a pupil of Mālik.
19. ʿAbd al-Malik b. ʿAbd al-ʿAzīz, Ibn al-Mājishūn (d. between 827 and 830), a Persian pupil of Mālik.
20. Ash'hab b. ʿAbd al-ʿAzīz al-ʿĀmirī (d. 819), a pupil of Mālik.
21. Abū Ḥanīfa (d. 767), founder of the Ḥanafī law school. The Ẓāhiryya was a school of legal interpretation that based its rulings on the literal or surface meaning of texts of the Qurʾān and Ḥadīth, and rejected the use of deduction, analogy, etc.
22. ʿAbd Allāh b. Wahb al-Fihrī (d. 812), a pupil of Mālik.
23. Muḥammad b. Idrīs al-Shāfiʿi (d. 820), founder of the Shāfiʿī law school, which is the predominant school in East Africa.
24. For a free married person the punishment is 100 lashes; for a slave only 50.
25. Abū Bakr was the first temporal successor (*khalīfa*) of the Prophet Muḥammad, ʿUmar the second, ʿUthmān the third, and ʿAlī the fourth.
26. *Mudabbar* literally means "having been placed after," i.e. freedom has been placed after the owner's death.
27. Literally "flute playing."
28. Probably corresponding to Put.
29. I.e. in India.
30. The Qurān, or Goran, are the Tubu, who live in, and to the west of, the Tibesti mountains in present-day Chad. They were one of the earliest African peoples to see some of their number taken off in slavery to the Middle East.
31. I.e. the ancient Egyptians.
32. The brothers being Shem and Japheth. Shem is considered to be the ultimate ancestor of the Arabs, and Japheth of the Europeans.
33. *Azhār al-ʿurūsh fī akhbār al-ḥubūsh* ["Flowers of the Thrones, comprising information about the Abyssinians"] is al-Suyūṭī's abridgement and reworking of his own *Rafʿ shaʾn al-ḥubshān* ["Raising the Status of the Abyssinians"].
34. A well-known Companion of the Prophet, d. 32/653; see J.-C. Vadet, art. "Ibn Masʿūd," *EI* (2), vol. 3, 873–75.
35. The term *sūdān* literally means "black people," as opposed to *bīḍān*—"white people," a term which includes the Arabs and has more to do with culture than color of skin. The Abyssinians (or Ethiopians) are later distinguished from the rest of black Africans and called Ḥabash. In West Africa

the Fulani were also often classified separately as neither *sūdān* nor *bīḍān.*

36. Abū Ja^{c}far Muḥammad b. Jarīr al-Ṭabarī, d. 310/922, author of a large *tafsīr* and a world history, *Ta$^{\supset}$rīkh al-rusul wa'l-mulūk.*
37. I.e. al-Ḥākim al-Naysābūrī, d. 405/1015. His principal work of *ḥadīth* is the *Kitāb al-mustadrak.*
38. ^{c}Abd al-Raḥmān b. ^{c}Alī, known as Ibn al-Jawzī, d. 597/1200, a Ḥanbalī jurist of Baghdād and a prolific author. Among his writings is *Tanwīr al-ghabash fī faḍl al-sūdān wa'l-Ḥabash* ["Lightening the Darkness, concerning the Virtues of the Sūdān and the Abyssinians"]; see Akbar Muhammad, "The Image of Africans in Arabic Literature," in *Slaves and Slavery in Muslim Africa*, ed. J.R. Willis (London: Frank Cass, 1985), vol. 1, 47–74; Elizabeth Hodgkin, "A Discussion of Ibn al-Jawzī's *Tanwīr al-ghabash fī faḍl al-Sūdān wa'l-Ḥabash"* (M.A. thesis, University of Birmingham, 1978); Imran Hamza Alawiye, "Ibn al-Jawzī's Apologia on behalf of the Black People and their Status in Islam: A Critical Edition and Translation of *Kitāb Tanwīr al-Ghabash fī Faḍl al-Sūdān wa'l-Ḥabash*" (Ph.D. thesis, University of London, 1985).
39. See Saud H. al-Khathlan, "A Critical Edition of *Raf^{c} sha$^{\supset}$n al-ḥubshān* by Jalāl al-Dīn al-Suyūṭī" (Ph.D. diss., St Andrews University, 1983), Arabic text, p. 6, where al-Suyūṭī quotes a *ḥadīth* on the authority of Abū Hurayra in which the Prophet defines the descendants of Shem as the Arabs, the Persians and the Byzantines, the descendents of Japheth as the Turks, the Slavs and "Gog and Magog," and the descendants of Ham as the Copts, the Berbers and the *sūdān.* See also Abū 'l-Fidā$^{\supset}$ Ismā^{c}īl b. Kathīr, *Qiṣaṣ al-anbiyā$^{\supset}$* (Beirut, 1408/1987), 86–87.
40. Jalāl al-Dīn ^{c}Abd al-Raḥmān al-Suyūṭī, Egyptian polymath, d. 1505.
41. Abū Mūsā al-Ash^{c}arī, a Companion of the Prophet.
42. See Abū Ja^{c}far Muḥammad b. Jarīr al-Ṭabari, *Ta$^{\supset}$rīkh al-rusul wa'l-mulūk/ Annales auctore Abu Djafar Muḥammad Ibn Djarir al-Ṭabarī*, ed. M. J. De Goeje et al. (Leiden, 1879–1901), vol. 1, 212.
43. I.e. not all unbelievers are black.
44. Earlier Aḥmad Bābā had quoted the *ḥadīth*: "Look after the *sūdān*, for among them are three of the lords of Paradise, Luqmān the Sage, the Najāshī [i.e. the Ethiopian ruler who sheltered some early Muslim refugees from Mecca], and Bilāl the muezzin."
45. I.e. the Prophet Muḥammad.
46. I.e. West Africa.
47. See *Mi^{c}rāj al-ṣu^{c}ūd: The Replies of Aḥmad Bābā on Slavery*, annotated and trans. John Hunwick and Fatima Harrak (Rabat: Institute of African Studies, University Mohammed V Souissi, 2000).
48. By "Nīl" is to be understood the Niger-Senegal river system. Pre-modern Arab geographers posited the existence of a "Nīl of the Sūdān" which

flowed out of a lake in Central Africa westwards to reach the Atlantic where the mouth of the R. Senegal now is. Its basis in reality is a conflation of the rivers Komadugu Yobe in Bornu, the Middle Niger and the Senegal River.

49. Qurʾān, 7:23.
50. In fact, she goes on to do this, but limitations of space prevent us from including any of them in this volume.
51. The Mograbini are presumably the "Maghārba," "a millitary miscellany which included men from the Barbary Coast and blacks from Central Africa"; see Richard Hill, *Egypt in the Sudan, 1820–1881* (London: Oxford University Press, 1959), 9. There were some 4,000 Maghārba in the original Egyptian expeditionary force to the Sudan in 1820–21.
52. I.e. Baqqāra—cattle nomads.
53. Nubia here refers to the Nuba mountains in southern Kordofan.
54. *Shayba*—a forked branch of wood affixed to the slaves' necks to keep each pair attached to one another.
55. El Obeid [al-Ubayyiḍ] in SW Kordofan.
56. Matankari is a town in south-eastern Niger, close to the Nigerian border. It is about 125 miles east of the present capital, Niamey.
57. I.e. Iforas, or Adṛaṛ-n-Iforas, an upland region to the northeast of Gao.
58. His Arabic name, properly *al-aᶜwar*, means "one-eyed."
59. ᶜUmar Dallāji, emir of Katsina, 1806–35.
60. I.e. *sarki*, the Hausa equivalent of the Arabic *amīr* [emir].
61. I.e. *wakīl*—"agent."
62. Arabic: *khabīr*—"caravan leader."
63. A cubit (Fr. *coudée*) is the length from the elbow to the fingertip, i.e. about 18 inches or half a meter.
64. A reference to the siege of the Tijānī center of ᶜAyn Māḍī in southern Algeria by the Amīr ᶜAbd al-Qādir (leader of armed resistance to the French) in 1838–39. This comparison by the narrator is evidently an afterthought, since it is clear that the events described at Katsina took place before 1835, the date of the death of the *amīr* (serki) ᶜUmar [Dallāji].
65. The narrator appears to use the term "Makhzen" (Arabic: *makhzan*) to mean royal army. Below, his term "Mekhazenia" appears to mean the location where this army was quartered, while later the term is used to mean units of this army.
66. Lit. "sergeant" from Arabic *shāwīsh/jāwīsh* from Turkish *çāvūs,* but probably used here simply with the meaning of "guards."
67. I.e. giraffe—*jamal al-khalā,* lit. "camel of the wilderness," though there is a word for giraffe in Arabic—*zarāfa.*
68. Muḥammad Bello was, from 1817 to 1837, the ruler (*amīr al-muʾminīn*) of the Islamic state founded by his father ᶜUthmān b. Muḥammad Fodiye (d. 1817): Katsina was a subordinate emirate within that larger state.

69. The narrator evidently did not understand perfectly what was being said. *Moutanin* [mutanen] in Hausa means "men of" and the announcement was doubtless addressed to "mutanen Kashna"—"men of Katsina."
70. I.e. Zamfara, a Hausa-speaking region to the southwest of Katsina.
71. Zinder is a Hausa city-state to the northeast of Katsina.
72. In Saharan Arabic *kuḥlān* (sing. *akḥal*) is the equivalent of *sūdān*— "blacks" with a pejorative connotation.
73. I.e. companies, from the Arabic *qawm*—"people."
74. A resin containing benzoic acid used as incense. The French word "benjoin" is derived from the Arabic *lubān jāwī*—"Javanese frankincense."
75. Perhaps the Arabic word *sunbul,* which is used to designate (with some defining epithets) a number of plants. The most probable one in this context is lavender.
76. Arabic: *shāshiya*—"skull cap," hence any close-fitting head covering for men, worn either alone or with a turban wound round it. In Egypt and the Nilotic Sudan it is called *ṭāqiya.*
77. I.e. Hausaland.
78. I.e. *wada*ᶜ—"cowries."
79. I.e. Baḥr al-Nīl—the river Nile. Arab geographers had traditionally called the Niger *Nīl al-sūdān*—"the Nile of the Blacks," and believed it eventually connected up to the hydrographical system of which the Egyptian Nile forms the main branch. In fact, cowries originated in the Indian Ocean (especially in the Maldives) but were being imported into West Africa by British merchants from the beginning of the 19th century. In 1833 the exploratory trading mission of Laird and Oldfield had reached as far up the Niger as Rabba, near modern Jebba, though local traders were probably bringing cowries up the Niger obtained from trade with European vessels on the coast before that. Slave raiding was rife at Rabba, too:

    The army of Rabba is composed of liberated slaves, whose freedom is granted to them on consideration of their taking up arms. In the winter or wet season they follow their ordinary occupations; and in the summer or dry season, when the Quorra [i.e. Kwara—the Niger] is low, they assemble from all parts of the kingdom of Houssa, Soccatoo, Kano, etc. They travel very quickly, taking the unsuspecting inhabitants by surprise. They seldom fail in capturing hundreds of prisoners, as well as cattle, horses, etc. The slaves are disposed of to the Arabs; and some are sold at towns on the banks of the Niger, and eventually reach the sea-side, where they are shipped on board Spanish slavers. The Fellatah army of Rabbah is commanded by several Bornuese. (Macgregor Laird and R.A.K. Oldfield, *Narrative of an Expedition into the Interior of Africa by the River Niger* [London, 1837], vol. 2, 87–88.)
80. Presumably wooden bowls.

81. This term is untranslatable. It is indicative of a medical condition in which the hair becomes entangled and stuck together.
82. From the description that follows it is clear that he is referring to guinea-worm.
83. Since the slaves are going to be "islamized" before being sold to Muslims in North Africa, they must be circumcized. Young boys can be operated on easily with little risk of complications. Not only may adults suffer considerably more, but Islamic morals forbid one adult to set his eyes upon the genitals of another, which, to all intents and purposes, precludes circumcision.
84. Islamic law prohibits eating the flesh of an animal that has died of natural causes. All mammals or birds have to be ritually slaughtered and their blood allowed to drain out before they can be considered lawful for Muslims to eat.
85. Wasting of the body usually associated with tuberculosis.
86. It is not clear who is being referred to by this term.
87. It is not clear who is meant by "Jewish Negroes" as there is no historical record of any indigenous Jews in Hausaland. It is possible there is a semantic and functional confusion with "Dyula," the name given to Manding merchants who operated widely in Hausaland.
88. The point of such examinations was no doubt to ensure that none of the prohibited categories of person was being carried off into slavery and that no freeborn Muslim was being enslaved. It may also have been so as to ensure appropriate taxes were paid (the French "fraude" meaning not only "cheating, fraud" but also "tax evasion").
89. The district of Ningi at the edge of the hilly region of the Bauchi plateau, to the southeast of Kano, was a regular zone of slave raiding for the Emir of Kano.
90. Presumably an Arabic term—*al-ᶜanaqiyya*—derived from the word *ᶜanaq*—"neck."
91. I.e. *khalīfa*—"deputy," i.e. emir subordinate to Sokoto.
92. Modern Hausa: *famfami,* glossed by R.C. Abraham, *Dictionary of the Hausa Language* (London, 1946), as "a wooden trumpet blown for a chief."
93. Modern Hausa: *molo,* glossed by Abraham as "a three-stringed guitarre."
94. Modern Hausa: *goge,* a one-stringed bowed lute.
95. This is evidently Arabic: *ṭās* is a shallow drinking vessel, hence here perhaps meaning a bowl that can be beaten like a drum.
96. Modern Hausa: *ganga,* a type of drum.
97. North African dialectal usage: *gnāwiyya,* meaning "language of the blacks." The term "gnāwa" (related to Berber *igginaw*—"black" [cf. "Guinea"]) is used in Morocco to designate members of a quasi-religious confraternity chiefly composed of former slaves. In Katsina the language used to address the sultan would have been Hausa. Daumas gives a translated text of the song (p. 214), but it is omitted here.

98. "Touba" is evidently a rendering of the Arabic *thawb,* pronounced *tōb* in several dialects and meaning a large cloth. Noufia is "Nufi," i.e. Nupe, a kingdom and, since the Sokoto *jihād*, an emirate, bordering the R. Niger with its capital at Bida.
99. Perhaps a printing error for "barka," given above as the "name" of the slave market.
100. Evidently a misprint for "mekhazenia."
101. Arabic: *umm al-walad* (sic). In Islamic law a slave woman who bears her master's child acquires the status of *umm walad.* For the legal situation of the latter, see pp. 29–31 above.
102. Abū Hurayra, a celebrated Companion of the Prophet and narrator of many *ḥadīth*s.
103. See above, p. 8, *ḥadīth* no. 728.
104. See note 54 above.
105. Arabic: *dukhn*—"pearl millet."
106. I.e. al-Ubayyiḍ, usually written as El Obeid.
107. See note 66 above.
108. A *douro* was a Spanish silver dollar, a coin used as currency in several parts of Africa; see Lars Sundström, *The Exchange Economy of Pre-Colonial Tropical Africa* (London: C. Hurst & Company, 1965), 97.
109. The conventional distance of a league is three miles.
110. *Aṣīda* is a porridge of sorghum or other grain to which is added clarified butter or honey.
111. Arabic: *qaṣ*^{c}*a,* pl. *qiṣa*^{c}.
112. Arabic: *mihrās.*
113. Tassaoua (or Tasāwa) is a town about 50 miles due north of Katsina.
114. In a legal sense the child would only be a Muslim if his father were a Muslim, but perhaps the local practice was to extend this since the slave-woman's owner was a Muslim.
115. I.e. the representative of Muḥammad Bello, Commander of the Faithful and ruler of the Sokoto Caliphate, 1817–37.
116. Damergou is an area to the north-northeast of Tassaoua. Here and below it is made to sound like a town, but the reference may be to Tanout, the principal town of the region.
117. I.e. Ṭarāblus—Tripoli in Libya.
118. Hausa: *turawa*, pl. of *bature*, meaning a light-skinned person, nowadays applied to Europeans, but in the above context evidently referring to Arabs/Berbers.
119. I.e. the *shahāda*—profession of faith ["There is no deity save Allāh; Muḥammad is the messenger of Allāh."].
120. This appears to be a form of the ubiquitous word, apparently borrowed from some African language, gris-gris or gree-gree (in earlier English sometimes

"gregory").

121. Pouring dust or sand over the head while prostrating is a customary sign of respect to a superior in several Sahelian cultures (e.g. Mande, Songhay, Hausa).
122. Arabic: *al-kiyāfa*—"tracking."
123. A curved single-edged sword of Turkish manufacture.
124. Perhaps jasmine (Arabic: *sīs*).
125. Islamic law does not, in fact, allow a man to sell a concubine who has borne a child of his; see above, p. 30.
126. Bagirmi was a kingdom just to the southeast of Lake Chad, whose rulers converted to Islam in the 16th century.
127. Nachtigal, op. cit., 133, describes Lamino (or al-Amīn) as "the most powerful of all the dignitaries of Kuka," while a footnote to the Fishers' translation indicates that he was close to a status akin to that of vizier to the ruler of Bornu, Shaykh Muḥammad al-Amīn.
128. Shendi, a town on the Nile, some 150 miles north of Khartoum.
129. Kobbe, or Kobbei, a commercial center in Dār Fūr, in the west of the Sudan, to the northwest of Al-Fāshir, the capital. It was the terminus of the "Forty Days Route" (*darb al-arba*ᶜ*īn*), leading from Upper Egypt to Dār Fūr.
130. I.e. *dhurra*, sorghum, and *dukhn*, bulrush/pearl millet. The term *durra/dhurra* is also applied to maize, but usually with the epithet *shāmī*, "Syrian."
131. Scars of smallpox indicate that the individual had contracted the disease and recovered from it. He was thus immunized against any further attack. The risk for a non-immunized slave was that he might contract the disease and die from it.
132. The Bishārīn are an Arabic-speaking Beja group from the eastern Sudan.
133. I.e. the Swahili of the Mozambique coast.
134. El Obeid [Arabic al-Ubayyiḍ], a major commercial center in southwestern Kordofan.
135. The ᶜAbabda are Arabized Beja nomads, whose territory ranges through Upper Egypt and the northern Sudan, bordering Nubia.
136. Generally spelled Isna, a town on the Nile, between Luxor and Aswan.
137. I.e. Asyūṭ, a town on the Nile in central Egypt.
138. I.e. *Wikālat al-jallāba*—see T. Walz, "The Wikâla al-ǧallâba," *Annales Islamologiques*, 13 (1977), 217–45.
139. Al-Azhar, a mosque and college in Cairo, founded in 972 CE.
140. Smyrna, or Izmir, is a port on the western coast of Turkey.
141. This and other transliterations follow the northern Sudanese pronunciation of Arabic.
142. In the country of Sennaar the slave is not called Abd but Raghig [JLB].
143. Arabic: *sūg al-ghanam guddāmak*—"drive the sheep/goats forward."

144. I.e. Amhara, the predominant ethnic group of the central highlands of Ethiopia.
145. I.e. the Banda. See note 147 below.
146. Borgho, or Borgu/Borku, lies to the northeast of L. Chad.
147. According to Ahmad Alawad Sikainga, in the nineteenth century, "Within the western Bahr al-Ghazal [southwestern Sudan], the term Fertit was applied by Muslim groups such as the Feroge to non-Muslim groups such as the Kreich and Banda." See his *The Western Bahr al-Ghazal under British Rule, 1898–1956* (Athens, Ohio, 1991), xvi, n. 5.
148. I.e. *ᶜulamāᵓ*—"learned men."
149. Souakin, or Sawākin, was a major port on the Red Sea coast, a little south of present-day Port Sudan; see A. Hofheinz, art. "Sawākin," *EI*(2), vol. 9, 187–89.
150. The figures Burckhardt gives show that about 96–98% survive the operation. Tournès (see p. 101 above) estimates that only 40% survived, whilst Madden, citing Clot Bey (see p. 191 above), puts the survival figure at only 15%.
151. In the original text this passage is in Latin. I am grateful to John Swanson for providing the above translation.
152. The "Grand Signor" was presumably the Ottoman sultan.
153. During the wars of the Sherif of Mekka with Saoud, the chief of the Wahabi, the Arab tribe of Kahtan was particularly obnoxious to the Sherif as being zealous proselytes of the Wahabi faith. He once took forty of them prisoners, and telling them that he had already killed individuals enough of their tribe, he ordered the whole to be mutilated and sent to their homes. As they were all grown up men, two only survived the operation; these rejoined their families, and became afterwards most desperate enemies of the Sherif Ghaleb; one of them killed the cousin of Ghaleb with his own hand, in battle; the other was killed in endeavouring, on another occasion, to pierce through the ranks of Ghaleb's cavalry, in order to revenge himself personally upon the Sherif. The Sherif was much blamed for his cruelty, such an action being very contrary to the generally compassionate dispositions of the Arabs; I mention it to show that the ancient practice of treating prisoners in this manner, as represented in the paintings on several of the temples of Upper Egypt, particularly at Medinet Habou, is not quite forgotten: but the above is the only instance of the kind I ever heard of. [JLB]
154. I.e, *mukhayyaṭ*—"sewn up."
155. *It is* [i.e. was] *my duty to examine the black girl who had undergone this operation. Her labia [majora] had been thoroughly opened up* [detecta, lit. uncovered] *and sewn together by me with a needle and thread, with a narrow aperture remaining into her urethra. In Esne, Siout* [see notes 136, 137] *and Cairo there are barbers that remove the* [or 'an'] *obstacle with a razor,*

but the wound seldom proves fatal. [JLB]. This passage was in Latin in the original; I am grateful to Grant Parker for the translation.—JH

156. See W.G. Browne, *Travels in Africa, Egypt and Syria from the Year 1792 to 1798* (London, 1799), 347–49.

157. Excisio clitoridis. The custom is very ancient. Strabo (p. 284 [17.2.5]) says —*"This is one of the most keenly observed practices of the Egyptians, namely to rear every child born* [i.e. not practise exposure], *to circumcise the males, and practise clitorodectomy on the females. This custom also occurs among the Jews, who are themselves Egyptian.*" [JLB] The italicized passage is in Greek in the original text. I am indebted to Grant Parker for tracking down the source and providing the translation.—JH

Its effect in rendering them *Mukhaeyt* has not been noticed by the ancients. *After the excision of the clitoris, the very walls of the vagina join together, leaving a small hole. When it is time for wedlock, the membrane which closes the vagina, is cut, with the assistance of the husband himself, in the presence of many bridesmaids. Sometimes it happens that the operation cannot be effected without the assistance of an experienced woman, who makes a deep cut in the vagina with a knife. On the next day the husband spends most of his time with his wife: from which the Arabic saying originated* "laylat al-dukhla mithl laylet al-futūḥ," *i.e. the night of entry is like the night of opening. Thanks to this custom, it happens that the husband is never deceived, and it is for this reason that in Upper Egypt unmarried girls reject lustful men, saying:* "tabusnī wa-lā takhriqnī" *("embrace me but don't penetrate me"). But the degree of reluctance with which the girls observe this abstinence becomes clear after their marriage, when they indulge in as much sexual pleasure as possible.* [JLB] This italicized passage is in Latin in the original text. I am grateful to John Swanson for the translation.

158. *Abūya*—"my father."

159. *Kurbāj*—"hippototamus-hide whip."

160. Rif is the name given to Egypt throughout those countries; it means properly a low ground abounding in water. [JLB]

161. A curious proof of this happened while I was in Upper Egypt; a great man who had bought two girls at Siout from the Darfour caravan, soon afterwards made a party with some friends to spend an afternoon in the cool caves in the mountain behind Siout, and ordered the two girls to attend him. When they entered the caves, they immediately conceived it to be the place destined for their immolation; and when the knives were produced to cut the meat that had been brought for dinner, one of them ran off, and endeavoured to escape, while the other threw herself on the ground, imploring the company to spare her. It required a considerable time to convince them that their fears were ill-founded. [JLB]

162. The *kūfiyya* is a male headdress consisting of a folded kerchief held down

to the skull by cloth-based cords.

163. Shubra is a small town a few miles north of Cairo, and now a suburb of the city.
164. *Shibbūk*—a very long-stemmed Turkish smoking pipe (*çibuk*), a term anglicized as "chibouk."
165. *Giaour*—a derogatory Turkish word (*giaur*) for a non-Muslim, especially a Christian.
166. The Chamba are a semi-nomadic Arab group based in and around the Mzab region of Algeria, and a small number of them formed part of the gang that kidnapped Griga and other slaves in this narrative.
167. El Hedjra is glossed by Burckhardt as "the Prophet Muhammad's tomb." A map of Medina and a key to locations can be found in Burckhardt's *Travels in Arabia*, 320–21.
168. The *bayt Allāh*—"house of God," the Ka^{c}ba.
169. In Italy in the nineteenth century, many of the operatic sopranos were *castrati*—castrated males.
170. For a portrait of such a figure (there called Kislar Agha), see N.M. Penzer, *The Ḥarēm* (London, 1936), 130, a reproduction of a picture from W. Miller, *The Costume of Turkey* (London, 1802).
171. The reference is to the Ottoman sultan Salīm III, who reigned 1789–1807.
172. I.e. Mouradgea D'Ohsson, *Tableau de l'empire ottomane* (Paris, 1788–1824).
173. Yanbū^{c} on the Read Sea coast of Arabia.
174. Arabic: *sa^{c}ādatkum*—"Your Excellency."
175. Lane notes: "Unless there be a eunuch, the saḳḳà is generally the chief of the servants."
176. Arabic: *mamlūk*—"possessed one."
177. Lane: A Muslim cannot take as a concubine a slave who is an idolatress.
178. The Galla are a people living to the south of the central highlands of Ethiopia.
179. Lane notes: "The white female slave is called 'Gáriyeh Beyḍà;' the Abyssinian, 'Gáriyeh Ḥabasheeyeh;' and the black, 'Gáriyeh Sódà.'
180. Lane notes: "The Gellábs generally convey their slaves partly over the desert and partly down the river." The term "gellāb" (*jallāb*) literally means "importer," and is used for long-distance traders in the Nile valley, especially for slave-traders.
181. Burckhardt made a similar observation about the greater value of slaves who had already suffered smallpox and recovered, meaning they would be immune to future attacks; see p. 89 above.
182. Earlier in the book reference had been made to the son of the Indian merchant and his African concubine who was once addressed as if he were the slave of his father.

183. Hurgronje notes: "Among these slave women the story of the curse of Adam as the origin of slavery is current in various forms. Very wide-spread is the naive tale that Adam and Eve were going about naked in Paradise when of all the girls present only the Abyssinian girls and some negresses laughed at them and therefore they were turned into a slave race."
184. I.e. "suitable, or desirable, things."
185. *Bint* ᶜ*amm* literally means "cousin," i.e. the daughter of a father's brother, the socially preferred marriage partner in many Arab societies.
186. The general rule was that a period should be allowed for ascertaining absence of pregnancy (*istibrā*ᵓ) following a change of ownership of a female slave. This was normally until the completion of a menstrual cycle.
187. The various law schools have different opinions on the definition of the waiting period (ᶜ*idda*) after divorce; it is either the passing of three menstruations, or the passing of three periods of purity between menstruation.
188. It is one of the ironies of Islamic law that whereas a free wife may be repudiated by the husband at any time and for any reason, the slave concubine who has borne her master's child may not be disposed of either by sale or by gift.
189. The child of a free man is always legally free, no matter the status of its mother.
190. In Arabia the virtue of a Black concubine was thought to be that her skin was cool.
191. Legally, she becomes free only upon her master's death.
192. Stambul is, of course, Istanbul, the seat of the sultans of the Ottoman Empire. Sultan-Mehemet [Meḥemmed] is a quarter of Istanbul, named after one of the sultans. Tophane is correctly Topkhāne, "suburb" of Istanbul on the other side of the Golden Horn. For a map of the city, see *EI* (2), vol. 4, between pp. 232 and 233.
193. Wadi Safra is situated about 150 miles north of Jiddah, and flows into the Red Sea.
194. If their "fathers" were Takrūrīs, they had presumably been brought from West Africa. The term "Takrūrīs" is commonly used in Arabia and some other parts of the Middle East to describe West African Muslims. The use of slaves as "traveler's checks" for pilgrims was not uncommon; see, for example, p. 216–17 above.
195. I.e. the system of justice within the jurisdiction of the Sharīf of Mecca.
196. To "enlarge" is here used in the archaic sense of "to set free."
197. I.e. the Moroccan kingdom ruled by Mūlāy Ismāᶜīl, 1672–1727.
198. Ruler of Morocco, 1578–1603.
199. G. Deverdun describes al-Ḥawz as "the region of Marrakesh, the Haouz, a wide embanked plain drained by the *wādī* Tansift with its tributaries, and by the *wādī* Tassawt," while *al-dīr* is the foothills of the Atlas. See *EI* (2),

vol. 3, 300–301, art. "Ḥawz."

200. The *ḥarāṭīn* (sing. *ḥarṭānī*) were essentially freed black slaves, who nevertheless remained as clients to their former owners. Even today there are many *ḥarāṭīn* in Mauritania, whose social situation differs little from actual slaves.

201. The Plain of Mashra^c al-Ramla lies to the north of Wādī Sebou, north of Salé. The term "maḥalla" is used in Morocco to mean a military force.

202. The Gharb is a coastal region of northern Morocco between *wādī* Lukkus and *wādī* Sebū. See R. Le Tourneau, art. "Gharb," *EI* (2), vol. 2, 1008–9. The territory of the Banū Ḥassan lies to the north of the *wādī* Bū Ragrag.

203. Habaṭ is the extreme northwestern area of Morocco, leading up to Tangier and Ceuta.

204. Tāmasnā is a coastal strip straddling the *wādī* Umm al-Rabīᶜ. Dukkāla is the name of a tribal confederation that inhabits a region between the *wādī* Umm al-Rabīᶜ, the *wādī* Tansift and the Atlantic coast. See Deverdun, op. cit., and his art. "Dukkāla" in *EI* (2), ii, 623.

205. The *zāwiya* of Dilāʾ was a Ṣūfī center in the Atlas that became a forum of political power in the mid-17th century, following the decline of the Saᶜdian dynasty.

206. The most esteemed corpus of Prophetic *ḥadīth.*

207. By "first rank" here is presumably meant the lowest, or entry rank.

208. Visitation *(ziyāra)* of a saint's tomb is undertaken to offer prayers for blessing or to ask for the saint's intercession or material aid.

209. *Fitna* means strife, tumult, discord, temptation. Here the implication is that the place contained something which was discordant with true Islamic faith and which could perhaps undermine the faith.

210. The sense of "play" here appears to be "perform a ritual," probably with the aid of musical instruments.

211. I.e. *bilād al-sūdān*—"the land of the Blacks."

212. Ar.: *yaktaffū aydīhim min warāʾihim.* The translation of this phrase is uncertain, but the verb *yaktaffū* is no doubt similar in meaning to the verbal form *yastakiffū*, which means to place the hands in an upturned position as in begging.

213. The religiously correct way to slaughter any creature is to cut the arteries on the side of the throat to let the blood flow out, while invoking God's name with the phrase: *bi'smi 'llāh* ("in the name of God").

214. Ar.: *maṭāmīr* (sing. *maṭmūra)*—"mattamore" or underground storage place, usually for grain.

215. I.e. they never perform these acts as part of the Islamic worship sequence.

216. Ingestion of blood is forbidden *(ḥarām)* in Islam; hence during slaughter, even for everyday purposes, the animal's throat is slit and the blood drained from the animal's body.

217. I.e. it is to be considered like meat that has not been ritually slaughtered.
218. "Majūs" was a term originally used for "Magians" or followers of the religion of Zoroaster in Iran, but was later applied much more widely to include followers of Berber religions and even pre-Christian Europeans (such as the Vikings). In Islamic law (contrary to what our author says here) *majūs* were treated like Jews and Christians, i.e. allowed to retain their religion and pay special taxes. Hence the term was applied to "unbelievers" whom various Muslim communities wished, for social or economic reasons, to tolerate. In West Africa it was applied by Muslim Hausa to non-Muslims of the same language and culture living in rural areas. In Hausa such persons are called "Maguzawa," plural of Ba-Majūsī. It is not clear that our author was aware of this particular usage.
219. Arabic: *al-dajjāl.* The *dajjāl* will appear at the end of time when upheaval (*fitna*) reigns on earth. The Mahdī (a Muslim "messiah") will appear and, aided by Jesus who will descend from heaven again, will fight and destroy the Anti-Christ and his allies and usher in an era of justice and harmony before the Day of Judgment.
220. The author uses the word "Sudan" in its Arabic sense—"the land of the Blacks," i.e. West Africa.
221. I.e. Zazzau, or Zaria, a city just over 100 miles south of Kano. Katsina, a major trans-Saharan trading entrepot, lies about 100 miles northwest of Kano, while Borno is the name of both an area and a large state to the east of Kano and around L. Chad.
222. All names of peoples living in the area of the Middle Niger. The Tombo are more usually known nowadays as the Dogon and the Gurma as the Gurmanche.
223. On the rituals of the seven fountains of Algiers, see J.-D. Andrews, *Les fontaines des génies (Seba Aioun): croyances soudanaises d'Alger* (Alger: A. Jourdan, 1903).
224. Classical Ar.: *jadhb,* i.e. [mystical] "attraction" or "possession."
225. In a note the author tells us that the year was 1369 A.H.=1950 A.D.
226. The term *dardaba* in Arabic primarily means fleeing out of fear, but the same root is associated with terminology for a drum. Hence the ceremony is one in which there is much drumming as the spirits flee to take their retreat for the month of Ramaḍān.
227. This seems to be a way of deceiving malevolent spirits. A similar practice occurs in Turkey. In the town of Gaziantep a woman who has lost a child at an early age goes to the cereal market with her most recently born child and concludes a fictive sale with the first black she sees. In return for handing over a certain quantity of cereals, she "buys" from the black her own child. Henceforth her child will be known as "the black." See P.N. Boratov, "Les Noirs dans le folklore turc et le folklore des noirs de Turquie," *Journal de*

la société des africanistes, 26 (1956), 8–9.

228. The *godia* in Hausa *bori* terminology is the "mare" which the spirit rides, and by extension the female cult-adept. See F.E. Bessemer, *Horses, Musicians and Gods: The Hausa Cult of Possession-Trance* (Zaria: Ahmadu Bello University Press, 1983), 158.
229. Najd, an upland area of east central Arabia.
230. The Arabs of ancient Arabia saw themselves as divided into two major stocks: the descendants of Qaḥṭān, and the descendants of Ismāʿīl (Ishmael son of Abraham). These divisions reflect the cultural cleavage between South Arabians and central and northern Arabians; see Philip Hitti, *History of the Arabs*, 6th edn. (London: Macmillan, 1956), 32.
231. I.e. Riyāḍ, now the capital of Saudi Arabia.
232. On the various paths to freedom from slavery, see Section III above, "Slavery and the Law."
233. "Burmoosed," i.e. wearing a *burnus*—a cloak with an attached hood.
234. I. e, *barrakān*—a robe, normally white.
235. The author may have in mind the so-called "Sokoto Caliphate," which was established in the early 19th century and integrated the several independent Hausa states into a single Islamic empire.
236. The reference is to Maradi (in southern Niger), which was where the ruler of the Hausa state of Katsina re-established himself after defeat by forces loyal to the Fulani jihādist Shaykh ʿUthmān dan Fodio in 1806.
237. By the term "Central Sudan" the author probably means the Sahelian lands lying between the Niger Bend and Lake Chad, or beyond it to the borders of what is now the Republic of the Sudan. The term "Sudan" is the Arabic *sūdān*—"[land of] the Blacks"
238. Hausa is remotely related to Arabic, since both languages belong to the Afro-Asiatic family—Hausa belonging to the Chadic branch, and Arabic to the Semitic. In the nineteenth century Hausa was beginning to be written in the Arabic script. Because of the activities of long-distance Hausa merchants, their language was widely understood in the Sahelian regions and north of the forest zones of West Africa.
239. Rābiḥ ibn Faḍl Allāh, a man perhaps of slave origins, was a commander in the forces of the 19th-century Sudanese slave raider and merchant Zubayr Raḥma al-Manṣūr, who conquered Dār Fūr, the most westerly region of the Sudan (and certainly *not* a Hausa state) and then lost control of it to the Turco-Egyptian state of the Sudan in the 1870s. Later Rābiḥ established himself independently and moved farther west, in the 1890s conquering Bornu, a state just to the west of Lake Chad, bordering on the Hausa-speaking territories. He died in battle with the French in 1900.
240. The term *garfla* is evidently a rendering of the Arabic word *qāfila*—"caravan."

241. Adamawa was one of the emirates of the Sokoto Caliphate, situated across the northern reaches of the river Benue, in an area that is now the borderland between Nigeria and the Cameroon. Its ruler was not a "king," but an emir.
242. "Filahni" may be a rendering of "Fulani," the name of the ruling ethnic group in Adamawa.
243. *Dawa*, in fact, means "guinea corn" (*sorghum vulgare*). Bread, as such, did not exist in this region in the nineteenth century.
244. It was a common practice to make whips from rhinoceros hide.
245. Cowries are small shells originating in the Maldive Islands in the Indian Ocean. They were used as "small change" throughout much of West Africa.
246. "Bashaw" is another way of writing "Pasha," a Turkish term meaning "governor." The term was not, however, used in the lands of the Sokoto Caliphate, where Sālam's experiences took place. The term for such an office there was *amīr*, or "emir." The emirs were all local rulers subject to the ultimate authority of the Sultan of Sokoto, known as *amīr al-muʾminīn*—"Commander of the Faithful."
247. Kano is still one of the major cities of Nigeria, situated in the far north, not far from the border with the Republic of Niger. It was founded approximately a thousand years ago, and from the sixteenth century it was a major entrepot for trans-Saharan commerce. It fell into the hands of the British colonial authorities in 1903.
248. Kola, or Cola, nuts are the seeds of the tree *Cola nitida* or *Cola accuminata*, which grow in the forest zones of West Africa. The kola nut contains caffeine and theobromine, which ward off weariness and stimulate activity.
249. Ouaragla, or Ouargla/Wargla, is approximately 250 miles northwest of Ghadames, in the Mzab valley of Algeria.
250. *The Tunisia of Aḥmad Bey 1837–1855* (Princeton: Princeton University Press, 1974), 321–25.
251. Ibn Abī Ḍiyāf notes that Aḥmad Bey ordered that when slaves were freed it should be recorded that patronage belonged to their owners; he did not assign their patronage to the Treasury. The personal link between master and slave was thus retained.
252. *Fuwāntuwāt* is not an Arabic word, but is likely a transcription of a French term, given an Arabic plural. One possibility is that the French word is "pointu," perhaps referring to fashionable pointed shoes. The description seems designed to show that the black man was dressed like a smart Frenchman, and that it was not this, but a sense of humanity and justice, that prompted the intervention to save him from the clutches of a racist American.
253. Qurʾān, 43:22. The verse continues: "And we follow in their footsteps."
254. These are the words of the celebrated "*ḥadīth* of mercy."

255. The reference here is to the U.S. Civil War, already underway when the letter was written, and which was closely linked to the issue of the emancipation of slaves.
256. Ehud Toledano, who refers to this letter in his *The Ottoman Slave Trade and its Suppression* (Princeton, 1982), 277, remarks that he has not been able to trace the original of this letter in U.S. archives, but admits that he can adduce no reason why the text should be a forgery. In any case, it appears in an Ottoman source some fourteen years later and is thus indicative of changing attitudes towards slavery.
257. The reference here is, of course, to the castration of youths and their employment as eunuch guardians of the harems of the ruler of Egypt. On this practice, see above, pp. 99ff.
258. Zāwiyat al-Dayr? = Dair al-Jandala, a monastery near Abu Tig in Upper Egypt near Assyūṭ. See J.L. Burckhardt, *Travels in Nubia* (London, 1822), 294.
259. Fezaglou (or Fazoglu) was a town on the Blue Nile, close to the border of the Sudan with Ethiopia.
260. Matankari is a town in southeastern Niger, close to the Nigerian border. It is about 125 miles east of the capital, Niamey.
261. Ifoghas, or Adrar-n-Ifoghas, an upland region to the northeast of Gao.
262. His Arabic name, properly *al-aᶜwar*, means "one-eyed."
263. The Kel Geres are a Tuareg federation nomadizing in southern Niger.
264. The Hoggar, or Ahoggar, is a mountainous region in south-western Algeria.
265. The Chamba, or Chaamba, are an Arab group based in and around the Mzab region of Algeria. Some are settled, other branches are nomadic with a reputation for banditry; see Lloyd Cabot Briggs, *Tribes of the Sahara* (Cambridge, Mass.: Harvard University Press—London: Oxford University Press, 1960), 190ff.
266. In Saleh (ᶜAyn Ṣāliḥ) is the chief locality of the Tidikelt oasis region of central Algeria.
267. Anderamboukane lies at about 16° 25' N—3° 01' W.
268. In Gall is about 75 miles southwest of Agades.
269. El Hadj Abdelkader ben Bajouda was the host of the German traveler Gerhard Rohlfs, who visited In Saleh in 1864 (he calls him Abd-el-Kader-Ould-Bou-Gouda); see V.A. Malte-Brun, *Résumé historique et géographique de l'exploration de Gérhard Rohlfs au Touât et à In-Çâlah d'après le journal de ce voyageur* (Paris, 1866), 127. Rohlfs gives an interesting description of In Salah.
270. Timmi consists of some twenty villages in the northern reaches of the oasis of Tuwāt.
271. A *mithqāl* was a weight of approximately 4.25 grams.
272. A present consisting of food items such as sheep, corn, etc. [Note of

Mercadier]. The "diffa" is probably the Arabic word *ḍiyāfa*, meaning "hospitality."

273. Gueradji was the chief of the Taitoq and a good friend of El Hadj Abdelkader ben Bajouda. Metouki was his trusted Bambara freedman. Mercadier was acquainted with the latter's son.
274. I.e. Si Abdelkader ben Kouider. The Zenata are a sub-division of the Berbers of North Africa.
275. This sounds like an Arabo-Turkish term: *bash-āmir*, which would mean "chief commander," though I have not found the word in any dictionary.
276. I.e. phrases in one or other language of black Africa. This would seem to imply that they obtained their domestic slaves again and again from the same area.
277. Perhaps *ghurrat al-^{c}abīd*. The word *ghurra(t)* may be used to mean "chief" or "first among equals."
278. A *foggara* is a subterranean irrigation tunnel connecting a series of wells leading to the oasis; see A. Lô, "Les foggara de Tidikelt," *Travaux de l'Institut Saharien*, 10 (1953), 139–79, and 11 (1954), 49–77.
279. The *dīwāns* of Sīdī Bilāl were an important element in the religious and social lives of slaves and freedmen in Algeria; see above, p. 163, "The Black Diwans of Algeria."
280. Bilāl b. Rabāḥ was a freedman of Abū Bakr, and an early convert to Islam, who attached himself to the Prophet and became the first muezzin in Islam. He is generally accepted to have been of "Ethiopian" descent; see *EI* (2), vol. 1, 1215.
281. Arabic: *dallāl*—"broker," especially one who deals in slaves.
282. Pasha Simou would have been the Moroccan governor of Gurara, hence he is later described as a "sharifian" public servant, the ruling dynasty of Morocco being the ^{c}Alawī *shurafāʾ*.
283. Shuwa is a name applied to various groups of Arabic-speaking nomads in the western Lake Chad region. They are generally considered to be Muslims, though in the early 17th century, there was some contention over this, and whether or not they could be enslaved; see John Hunwick & Fatima Harrak, *Mi^{c}rāj al-ṣu^{c}ūd: Aḥmad Bābā's Replies on Slavery* (Rabat, 2000), 47.
284. Figuig is an oasis in eastern Morocco, on the present-day border with Algeria; Oujda is a town in eastern Morocco, close to the Mediterranean coast, on the present-day border with Algeria.
285. The allusion here is to a solar eclipse.
286. When a slave woman passes from the sexual custody of one man to another, through sale, gift, or manumission and marriage (as is the case here), she must observe a waiting period—a process called *istibrāʾ*—"declaring free [of pregnancy]." She must be kept in a secure location until she menstru-

ates so there can be no dispute over paternity.

287. An *azguens* is close to one kilogram, i.e. around 2 pounds.
288. Mzabis are persons originating in the Wādī Mzāb (the Wargla-Gardaia region) who are Berber ethnically and belong to the Ibāḍī sect. They travel all over Algeria to conduct trade, often absenting themselves for years.
289. I.e. *bilād al-sūdān*—"the land of the Blacks," here West Africa.
290. The great area of sand dunes northwest of Gurara.
291. A *zāwiya* is a religious retreat connected to a Ṣūfī order.
292. Mama died around 1922, as did her son by Griga, during an epidemic of spino-cerebral meningitis. Her grandson Mohamed survived and served in the Second World War. Presumably by this time Si Abdelkader was dead and his estate was run by his son Hamou, whom Mercadier met in the 1940s.
293. A common Saharan grass (*Aristida pungens*) whose seeds are edible.
294. In commenting first on liberty and then equality, Griga is making fun of the French national slogan: Liberty, Equality, Fraternity.

◆ Bibliography ◆

Abū 'l-Ḥasan al-Mālikī. *Kifāyat al-ṭālib al-rabbānī li-Risālat Ibn Abī Zayd al-Qayrawānī*. Cairo, 1938 [with the *Ḥāshiya* of ᶜAlī al-Ṣaᶜīdī al-ᶜAdawī].

Aḥmad Shafīq Bek. *al-Riqq fī'l-Islām*. Cairo, 1309/1892.

Alawiye, Imran Hamza. "Ibn al-Jawzī's Apologia on Behalf of the Black People and Their Status in Islam: A Critical Edition and Translation of *Kitāb Tanwīr al-Ghabash fī Faḍl al-Sūdān wa'l-Ḥabash*." Ph.D. thesis, University of London, 1985.

Bessemer, F.E. *Horses, Musicians and Gods: The Hausa Cult of Possession-Trance*. Zaria: Ahmadu Bello University Press, 1983.

Boratov, P.N. "Les Noirs dans le folklore turc et le folklore des noirs de Turquie." *Journal de la société des africanistes*, 26 (1956), 7–23.

Boratov, Pertev N. "The Negro in Turkish Folklore." *American Folklore*, 64 (1951), 83–88.

Bousquet, G-H. *Abrégé de la loi musulmane selon le rite de l'imâm Mâlek*. Alger, 1956.

Bridgman, Frederick Arthur. *Winters in Algeria*. New York: Harper Brothers, 1890.

Briggs, Lloyd Cabot. *Tribes of the Sahara*. Cambridge, Mass.: Harvard University Press; London: Oxford University Press, 1960.

Brown, L.C. *The Tunisia of Aḥmad Bey 1837–1855*. Princeton University Press, 1974.

Browne, W.G. *Travels in Africa, Egypt and Syria from the Year 1792 to 1798*. London, 1799.

Burckhardt, John Lewis. *Travels in Nubia*. London, 2nd edn., 1822.

———. *Travels in Arabia*. (London: Henry Colburn, 1829, repr. 1968).

Cromer, Earl of. [Evelyn Baring.] *Modern Egypt*. New York: MacMillan, 1909.

Croutier, Alev Lytle. *Harem: The World behind the Veil*. New York: Abbeville Press, 1989.

Daumas, Eugène. *Le Grand Désert. Itinéraire d'une caravane du Sahara au pays des nègres, royaume de Haoussa*. 4th edn., Paris, 1860.

Dermenghem, E. *Le culte des saints dans l'Islam maghrébin*. Paris, 1954.

al-Dimashqi Shams al-Dīn Muḥammad b. Abī Ṭālib. *Nukhbat al-dahr fī ᶜajāʾib al-barr wa 'l-baḥr,* ed. A Mehren. Leipzig, 1923.

Ennaji, Mohammed. *Soldats, Domestiques et Concubines. L'Esclavage au Maroc au XIXe siècle.* Casablance: Editions EDDIF, 1994. Trans. Seth Graebner, *Serving the Master: Slavery and Society in 19th century Morocco.* New York: St. Martin's Press, 1999.

Fisher, Alan. "Studies in Ottoman Slavery and Slave Trade, II: Manumission." *Journal of Turkish Studies*, 4 (1980), 49–56.

Furlong, Charles Wellington. *The Gateway to the Sahara.* New York, 1909.

al-Ghazālī, Abū Ḥāmid. *Iḥyāʾ ᶜulūm al-dīn.* Beirut: Dār al-Maᶜrifa, n.d.

Hanoum, Leïla. *Le harem impériale au xixe siècle.* N.p. [Brussels]: Editions Complexe, 1991.

Hill, Richard. *Egypt in the Sudan, 1820–1881.* London: Oxford University Press, 1959.

Hull , E. M. *Camping in the Sahara.* New York, 1927.

Hunwick, J.O. "Islamic Law and Polemics over Race and Slavery in North and West Africa (16th–19th centuries)." In Shaun Marmon (ed.), *Slavery in the Islamic Middle East.* Princeton: Markus Wiener, 1999, 43–48.

——— and Fatima Harrak. *Miᶜrāj al-ṣuᶜūd: Aḥmad Bābā's Replies on Slavery.* Rabat: Institut des Etudes Africaines [Université Mohamed V], 2000.

Hurgronje, C. Snouck. *Mekka in the Latter Part of the 19th Century.* Leiden, 1931.

Ibn Abī Ḍiyāf. *Ithḥāf ahl al-zamān bi-akhbār mulūk Tūnis wa-ᶜahd al-amān.* Tunis, 1990.

Ibn Abī Zayd al-Qayrawānī. *Al-Risāla. La Risâla ou Epître sur les éléments du dogme et de la loi de l'Islam selon le rite mâlikite.* Texte arabe et traduction française . . . par Léon Bercher. Alger: Éditions Jules Carbonel, 1949.

Ibn Buṭlān. *Risāla fī shirāʾ al-raqīq wa-taqlīb al-ᶜabīd*, ed. ᶜAbd al-Salām Muḥammad Hārūn in *Nawādir al-makhṭūṭāt*, vol. 4. Cairo, 1954, 333–89.

Ibn Khaldūn. *Al-Muqaddima.* Cairo: al-Maktaba al-Tijāriyya, n.d.

Ibn Juzayy (d. 1340). *Qawānīn al-aḥkām al-sharᶜīyya wa-masāʾil al-furūᶜ al-fiqhiyya.* Beirut, 1974.

al-Jārimī, Muḥammad al-Sanūsī b. Ibrāhīm. *Tanbīh ahl al-ṭughyān ᶜalā ḥurriyy-at al-sūdān*, MS. no. 1575, Centre Ahmad Baba, Timbuktu.

al-Jazzār, Munṣif, & ᶜAbd al-Laṭīf ᶜUbayd. *Wathāʾiq ḥawl al-riqq wa-ilghāʾihi min al-bilād al-Tūnisiyya*. Tunis: Maᶜhad Būrqība, 1997.

Khalīl b. Isḥāq al-Jundī. *Al-Mukhtaṣar*. Paris, 1900.

al-Khathlan, Saud H. "A Critical Edition of *Rafᶜ shaʾn al-ḥubshān* by Jalāl al-Dīn al-Suyūṭī." Ph.D. diss., St Andrews University, 1983.

Koubbel, LE., and Matveev, V.V., *Arabskiye Istochniki*. 3 vols. Moscow-Leningrad, 1960–85.

Lane, Edward William. *Manners and Customs of the Modern Egyptians*, 5th edn. London, 1860.

Lawrence, T.E. *The Seven Pillars of Wisdom*. New York, 1936.

Lenz, Oskar. *Timbouctou, Voyage au Maroc, au Sahara, et au Soudan*. 2 vols. Paris: Librairie Hachette, 1886.

Madden, R. R. *Egypt and Mohammed Ali, illustrative of the Condition of his Slaves and Subjects, &c. &c.* London, 1841.

Mercadier, F.J.G. *L'Esclave de Timimoun*. Paris, 1971.

Meyers, A.R. "Slave Soldiers and State Politics in Early ᶜAlawī Morocco, 1668–1727." *IJAHS*, 16 (1983), 39–48.

Millingen, Frederick. "Slavery in Turkey." *J. Anthropological Society of London* (1870), 85–96.

Muhammad, Akbar. "The Image of Africans in Arabic Literature." In J.R. Willis (ed.), *Slaves and Slavery in Muslim Africa*. London, 1985, vol. 2, 47–74.

Penzer, N.M. *The Ḥarēm*. London, 1936.

Nachtigal, Gustav. *Sahara and Sudan*, vol. 2, *Kawar, Bornu, Kanem, Borku, Ennedi*. Trans. Allan G. Fisher and Humphrey J. Fisher. London: C. Hurst & Company, 1980.

al-Nāṣirī, Aḥmad b. Khālid. *Kitāb al-istiqṣāʾ li-akhbār duwal al-maghrib al-aqṣā*, Casablanca, 1954–56.

Palgrave, William Gifford. *Personal Narrative of a Year's Journey through Central and Eastern Arabia (1862–3)*, 5th edn. London, 1869.

Sersen, William John. "Stereotypes and Attitudes towards Slaves in Arabic Proverbs." In Willis, *Slaves and Slavery in Muslim Africa,* vol. 2, 92–108.

Shaarawi, Huda. *Harem Years: the Memoirs of an Egyptian Feminist*. Translated and introduced by Margot Badran. London: Virago Press, 1986.

Temimi, Abdeljelil. *Etudes d'histoire Arabo-Africaine*. Zaghouan, 1994 [Publications de CERMODI].

Tharaud, Jérôme & Jean. *Fez ou les bourgeois de l'Islam*. Paris: Librairie Plon, 1930.

Toledano, Ehud. *The Ottoman Slave Trade and its Suppression*. Princeton, 1982.

Tournès, G. *Les Eunuques en Egypte*. Genève, 1869.

Walz, T. "Black Slavery in Egypt during the Nineteenth Century as Reflected in the Maḥkama Archives of Cairo." In Willis, *Slaves and Slavery in Muslim Africa*, vol. 2, 137–60.

Walz, T. "The wikālat al-ǧallāba." *Annales Islamologiques*, 13 (1977), 217–45.

Willis, J.R. (ed.). *Slaves and Slavery in Muslim Africa*. 2 vols. London, 1985.